Urban Sociology:
Critical Essays

Urban Sociology: Critical Essays

edited by
C. G. Pickvance

Tavistock Publications

First published 1976
by Methuen & Co Ltd
11 New Fetter Lane London EC4P 4EE

Selection, editorial matter, translation and introduction
©C. G. Pickvance 1976

Typeset by Preface Limited, Salisbury, Wilts.
Printed in Great Britain by Whitstable Litho,
Whitstable, Kent.

ISBN 0 422 76110 9

First published as a Social Science Paperback in 1976
by Tavistock Publications Ltd
ISBN 0 422 76100 1

Contents

Preface

This book owes its origin to the awakening of my interest in urban
sociology, while a postgraduate at Manchester University, by Clyde
Mitchell and Valdo Pons. For sustenance of this interest since then I
would like to thank Manuel Castells, Clyde Mitchell, Ray Pahl and
Bryan Roberts, as well as many others at Manchester and elsewhere.

I would like to thank my wife, Roselyne, for her help and
forbearance in resolving thorny problems of translation on numerous
occasions, and Pradeep Bandyopadhyay for some similar help, and for
helpful criticism while writing the Introduction. Both are of course
absolved from responsibility for any errors remaining in the
Introduction or translations.

Finally, I am very grateful to Edith Gillett and Marilyn Dunn of
the Faculty of Economics and Social Studies, Manchester University,
for their assistance in preparing the typescript.

C.G.P.
Manchester, December 1974

Translator's Note

The translations in chapters 2 to 7 are complete: no excisions have
been made in either text or footnotes.

Full publication details of references quoted have been added,
where absent, and English editions cited wherever possible.

All explanatory footnotes and other changes introduced by the
translator have been indicated by square brackets.

A small number of errors in the original articles have been
corrected thanks to the cooperation of their authors.

C.G.P.

Introduction

1

Historical materialist approaches to urban sociology

The aim of this book is to make available to English-speaking readers a sample of recent French-language writings on urban sociology by authors adopting a historical materialist, or Marxist, viewpoint. These writings are not only generally inaccessible to many English-speaking readers but, more important, represent a quite new theoretical perspective in urban sociology.

It is this common theoretical viewpoint which distinguishes the writings collected in this book rather than the fact that they all originally appeared in French — a fact which conceals the varied nationalities of their authors (French (Lojkine); French-Canadian (Lamarche) and Spanish (Castells, Olives)) and the existence of non-Marxist French urban sociology. Nevertheless it is no coincidence that this new perspective in urban sociology should have taken root on the Continent where the Marxist political and intellectual tradition is much stronger than that in the 'Anglo-Saxon' countries.

While it is beyond the scope of this Introduction to provide an adequate definition of historical materialism, its origins and principal variants, we may describe it briefly as the theoretical corpus based on Marx's fundamental theses that the material economic base of society determines the superstructure of social, legal and political institutions, rather than vice versa, and that each historical society is characterized by struggles between the opposing social classes arising from the particular processes of production within it. Within this general position however the contributions in this book (which reflect their authors' views up to ten years ago) vary in the emphasis they give, for example, to economic trends and to political organization. Thus chapter 4 places more emphasis on the former, chapters 6 and 7 on the latter, while chapter 5 places equal emphasis on both.

Interest in the application of historical materialism in the field of 'urban sociology' developed during the 1960s, and was given an extra impetus by the 'events' of May 1968 in France, and their repercussions. Institutionally, this interest was helped by the French government's provision of finance for urban research in universities or

1

independent research institutions[1] following its interpretation of the
'events' as in part due to urban malfunctioning. That this finance has
helped develop a new and critical approach not only within urban
sociology but also in the form of political action regarding urban
issues is a curious paradox. In 1970 there was sufficient support for a
new journal to be founded devoted to a critical study of the urban
field (and embracing architecture and planning).[2] And in 1973 an
important series of monographs started to appear in which the first
book-length products of historical materialist work in urban sociology
became available.[3] Thus all the signs are present for one to be able to
assert with confidence that an important new theoretical current has
appeared in the field of urban sociology, and one which English-
speaking readers cannot afford to ignore.

The articles selected for inclusion in the present volume were
deliberately chosen to complement the monographs mentioned above,
which, one hopes, will eventually be translated into English. The first
two articles (chapters 2 and 3), by Castells, provide an assessment
from an historical materialist standpoint of the theoretical significance
of previous work in urban sociology. The next three articles outline
historical materialist modes of analysis in three fields: (i) land,
housing and property (chapter 4, by Lamarche), (ii) urban
development (chapter 5, by Lojkine) and (iii) urban social movements
(chapter 6, by Castells). The sixth article, on protest against urban
renewal (chapter 7, by Olives), indicates how Castells's theoretical
approach to urban social movements might be applied, and the final
article (chapter 8) has been added to provide a more detailed
assessment of certain aspects of the recent studies of urban protest
(including that of Olives) which follow Castells's approach.

The remaining sections of this Introduction will be devoted to
clarifying and discussing the main arguments advanced in chapters 2
to 7. In the next section we discuss Castells's argument regarding the
theoretical status of urban sociology, in section III we discuss
Lamarche and Lojkine's theses on the role of the city in the capitalist
mode of production, and in section IV we discuss Castells's theoretical

[1] One of the most important of which is the Centre de Sociologie Urbaine (118
rue de la Tombe-Issoire, Paris 14).
[2] *Espaces et Sociétés*, published quarterly by Editions Anthropos, 12 avenue du
Maine, Paris 15.
[3] The series 'La recherche urbaine', published by Mouton, Paris. At the time of
writing (December 1974), eight titles have appeared covering topics such as
urban renewal, property development, public-housing development, urban
policy, the development of a new urban-industrial complex (Dunkirk), etc.

framework for the study of urban social movements and the studies which adopt it.

II The scientific status of urban sociology

To anyone who puts the question, 'What is urban sociology?', the answer may be given, 'What urban sociologists do'. However fashionable such an answer is, it essentially sets aside the original question of the theoretical specificity of the field of urban sociology as irrelevant. The fact that researchers are employed to resolve 'urban' problems and are labelled 'urban sociologists' does not suffice to establish the scientificity of urban sociology.

At first sight chapter 2 ('Is there an urban sociology?') and chapter 3 ('Theory and ideology in urban sociology') might be read as reviews of the Anglo-Saxon literature on the subject (besides containing a useful summary of recent French literature – in chapter 2). To make such a reading would be basically to misunderstand their author's purpose.

The import of the two essays is rather an insistence that the question of the scientific status of urban sociology cannot be set aside as irrelevant, and that its precise status must be determined, since if it is not scientific the field must be reformulated or else denounced.

Since it is likely that the terms in which Castells's examination of the status of urban sociology is couched will strike many readers as unfamiliar, a brief introduction will be supplied here.[4]

These terms in fact derive from the Althusserian reading of Marx. For Althusser, Marx constituted a science, historical materialism, in a field, political economy, where until that time bourgeois or ideological conceptions had held sway. Similarly, Castells's aim is to found a science in the theoretical space occupied by urban sociolo. To do this it is necessary to separate 'ideological' aspects of the knowledge produced in this field from those which have some 'scientific' relevance. For Castells, like Althusser, the term science, by definition, refers to historical materialism, the science of social formations.[5] Hence the opposition in the title of chapter 3 between 'theory' and 'ideology'.

[4] For a considerably extended discussion of Castells's critique of urban sociology, see my article, On a materialist critique of urban sociology, *Sociological Review* 22 (1974) 203–20.
[5] In my view the use of the term science to describe historical materialism is at best premature and at worst unjustified (in that it excludes the possibility that approaches developed to explain objects of study ignored by historical materialism may prove complementary).

Castells formulates the question of the scientificity of urban sociology in the following terms:

Does urban sociology have a theoretical object?
If so, is that theoretical object 'urban'?
If not, does urban sociology nevertheless have a real object which could be described as 'urban'?

This formulation of the question is based on the thesis that if a science has neither a theoretical object nor a real object to which it applies theoretical concepts, then it does not merit the name 'science': it is an 'ideology'. In the particular case of urban sociology, it would be necessary to show that it has either an *urban* theoretical object, or is applied to an *urban* real object. The term theoretical (or scientific) object belongs to the opposed pair: theoretical object-real object. These terms in turn belong to the Althusserian conception of knowledge. Whereas in the conventional ('empiricist') conception of knowledge, theoretical objects, or concepts, are produced as a result of abstraction from reality (real objects), Althusser dismisses abstraction as an 'empiricist' process which has no place in his 'materialist' epistemology. Since the precise relation between theoretical object and real object is the matter of some debate,[6] let us simply say that the real object refers to some aspect of reality, ready-wrapped in preconceptions which are usually 'ideological', which the science seeks knowledge of in the form of a theoretical object. (Theoretical knowledge is seen as arising not from the action of a subject (thinker) on the real object, but by the action of theoretical concepts on the real object.)

Castells examines the question of the scientificity of urban sociology in four stages:

(1) Has urban sociology had an urban *theoretical* object in the past?
(2) Could it have an urban *theoretical* object in the future?
(3) Does urban sociology have an *urban* real object?
(4) If it has neither urban theoretical objects nor urban real objects, can the (non-urban) theoretical and real objects it has sought to understand be retrieved and made the basis for a 'scientific' urban sociology?[7]

---

[6] N. M. Geras, Althusser's Marxism: an account and assessment, *New Left Review* 71 (1972) 57–86; C. G. Pickvance, Althusser's 'Empiricist' Conception of knowledge: a comment on Mr Hindess's review article, *Economy and Society* 2 (1973) 506–10.

[7] Stage (1) of the argument is discussed in chapters 2 and 3, stage (2) in chapter 2, and stages (3) and (4) in chapter 3.

(1) Firstly, Castells argues that research in urban sociology is fragmented 'into several branches each with a quite different scientific object' (p. 35), e.g. urbanization, social disorganization, community power. According to Robert Park's research programme, urban sociology was to study every social phenomenon occurring in the urban context ('a non-specific theoretical object'). In fact the research carried out was much more limited in scope, e.g. it focussed on the process of acculturation of immigrant groups (or their resistance to acculturation) to American society ('a different and non-explicit scientific object'). A second major field within urban sociology was the study of spatial organization, e.g. urbanization. Castells argues that the object of this field, space, is a real object or 'material element', and not a theoretical object. A third field, the 'ecological complex' approach developed by Duncan, is argued to be no less than a general theory of social structure, and not an urban theoretical object.

In brief, while urban sociology in the past has had theoretical objects (if not always explicit) it has not had an *urban* theoretical object. So it cannot justify a claim to be a science based on the specificity of its theoretical object.

(2) In view of this conclusion, is there any prospect that urban sociology will have an urban theoretical object in the future?

Castells rephrases this question in the following, rather unfamiliar, form, viz. what is the likelihood that a 'social unit' will coincide with a 'spatial unit'? A 'social unit' may be defined within any one of the three approaches distinguished by Touraine:[8] within a functionalist approach the 'social unit' is a social system; within a historical approach, a 'system of action'; and within a semiological approach, a 'system of signs'. In the first case, when a social system exists within a given spatial unit, or area, the term 'community' is usually used to describe the result. (As, for example, in Coing's study of urban renewal, discussed by Castells.) But Castells argues that communities are on the whole only 'vague recollections', and in any case not exclusive to urban areas. (We shall return to the latter point below – p. 8.) Hence the search for communities is a somewhat 'precarious' base on which to found an urban sociology.

In the second case, when a 'system of action' coincides with a spatial unit, the term 'urban institution' is usually used. By 'system of action' Touraine means the system of means which underlies the

---

[8] Alain Touraine, *Sociologie de l'action* (Seuil, Paris, 1965). See also the translations of his work in A. Giddens (ed.), *Positivism and Sociology* (Heinemann, London, 1973).

process of transformation of society. Thus, in Weber's description of
the medieval city in *The City*, the political-administrative system had
a large degree of autonomy and did have such a shaping role in
society. While referring approvingly to the Belgian economist Rémy's
conception of the city as source of innovation and exchange (hence,
of change) and at the same time as means of controlling change,
Castells doubts whether autonomous urban institutions are likely to
be found in societies today.[9] Hence this second possibility seems an
unlikely basis for an urban theoretical object on which to found urban
sociology. (The third case, where a system of signs coincides with a
spatial unit, i.e. an urban sociology based on a semiological approach,
is not discussed by Castells.)

Thus while the two cases discussed suggest that urban theoretical
objects may have existed in the past, they also suggest that the
prospects of a 'scientific' urban sociology based on an urban
theoretical object in the future are remote.

(3) The third stage in the argument is to inquire whether urban
sociology has an urban real object (in the same way that industrial
sociology is the application of sociological theory to a specific real
object, the firm), or whether it covers a motley collection of
non-urban real objects.

We have already noted that a major theme within urban sociology
has been the study of space (as in studies of 'spatial structure',
'urbanization', etc.). Now Castells describes space as a 'material
element' whose relationships with other aspects of society certainly
constitute an important field of study, but which itself is a real object.

At this point the question arises whether space is an *urban* real
object or not. In order to answer this question we must examine the
definition of urban a little more closely. In stage (1) of the
argument – where it was denied that *urban* theoretical objects had
existed in the past – no definition of urban was offered! And in
stage (2) we accepted Castells's rephrasing of the question as to the
future prospects of an urban theoretical object in terms of whether a
spatial unit coincided with a social unit.

Clearly urban has a number of referents: it may refer to a spatial
form (city as opposed to country), to a cultural pattern ('urbanism' as
opposed to 'ruralism', as ways of life) or to a structural form (e.g. the
city as a source of 'control' in an urban hierarchy). And often

[9] Due to the quite different role of cities today. On this, see M. Freitag, De la
ville-société à la ville-milieu, *Sociologie et Sociétés* 3 (1971) 25–57, with its
pertinent comments on Sjoberg's *The Pre-Industrial City*.

definitions will link one or more of these aspects: thus, in Wirth's
theory of urbanism, the urban 'way of life' is seen as a characteristic
tendency produced by the city. Now whereas in feudal society city
and country as spatial forms were also opposed as cultural patterns
and structural forms, as Pirenne and Weber showed, in most
industrialized societies the spatial and cultural distinction between
urban and rural is increasingly difficult to make. As Pahl, for example,
showed in *Urbs in Rure*,[10] the 'urbanized fringe' with its 'commuter
villages' cannot be meaningfully regarded as either urban or rural in a
spatial sense. And any distinction between urban and rural cultural
patterns is increasingly difficult to make.

Castells concludes from this that in highly urbanized societies the
spatial and cultural distinctions between urban and rural are
unfounded and that the persistence of the contrast in sociological
usage is due to (a) the identification of urban in the cultural sense
with industrial modern (Western . . .) and (b) the causal analysis of the
'industrial, modern . . . way of life' as a product of the city as a spatial
form. Against the latter two arguments he asserts that urbanism is the
'cultural expression of capitalist industrialization, the emergence of
the market economy and the process of rationalization of modern
society' (p. 38).[11] In other words, the term urban is ideological in its
function in that it implies a false explanation of the nature and causes
of cultural patterns.

If, then, urban lacks any specific referent in the spatial or cultural
senses, one possibility would be to reformulate the field of urban
sociology as the sociology of 'modern' society as numerous writers
such as Martindale, Manheim, Glass and others have advocated.
Castells hesitates before this possibility (p. 74), since even he admits
that this would be to deny that in the past urban sociology has in fact
specialized in two narrower fields: relationships to space and
'collective consumption'.[12] Whether these are adequate grounds for
rejecting the above reformulation is a matter of debate.

Let us now return to the main issue in stage (3) in the argument —
the question of the existence of urban real objects — Castells's answer
is categorical: 'there is no field of reality which can be termed
"urban" ' (p. 74). But is such a blunt answer really justified?

[10] R. E. Pahl, *Urbs in Rure*, L.S.E. Geographical Paper No. 2 (London School of
Economics, London, 1965).
[11] See also Pickvance *op. cit.*, 212, for a qualification of this assertion.
[12] As we shall see in stage (4) of the argument, his own reformulation of 'urban
sociology' is based on these two fields.

In stage (2) of the argument we saw that Castells redefined the question of an urban theoretical object as one of the coincidence or not of a social unit and a spatial unit. He then went on to note that when the social unit was a social system (i.e. as in the functionalist approach), the term 'community' was usually used to describe this coincidence. But one of his reasons for rejecting 'community' as an urban theoretical object was that communities were not limited to urban areas (or 'urban sub-cultures'). This argument is inconsistent with his denial that the distinction between urban and rural spatial forms is useful, since it implies an urban-rural contrast. I would rather deduce a different conclusion: given that the latter distinction is not useful, then it seems correct to assert that 'community', as defined, *remains* a valid theoretical object. And, moreover, it must be an *urban* theoretical object in the sense of being a product of modern, capitalist, industrial. . . society. In brief, a sociology of community — seen as a product of capitalism — has a valid claim to a share in the succession to the estate of urban sociology: urban sociology need not be identified with a sociology of modern society, with sociology *tout court*.

One could go a step further. It was argued earlier that spatial, cultural and structural aspects of the urban-rural distinction could be distinguished, but only established that the first two of these aspects were no longer useful. Does this imply that a distinction between urban and rural as *structural* forms is still useful? My answer is yes. One of the sources of differentiation between settlements is the particular functions they perform in the economic system as a whole. Some will house headquarters of corporations with branches spread throughout the country; others will house only the subordinate branches. This will have repercussions in the fields of stratification, housing, politics, etc. which must not be neglected.

In brief, if one accepts the notion of a social formation in which capitalist and industrial forms are predominant and are the source of cultural patterns, it still remains to study (a) how the economic base is spatially structured, and how this is a source of differentiation between settlements, and (b) how particular social systems operate in given settlements (i.e. a sociology of community).

In other words, I would modify Castells's statement that urban real objects do not exist, and suggest that the former fields of study represent two such.

(4) The final stage in Castells's argument concerning the scientific status of urban sociology is to suggest that certain (non-urban) real

objects studied previously can be retrieved and made the basis of a new theoretical field. (In my view, the same can be argued for some of the (non-urban) *theoretical* objects too.)

The two fields of reality he chooses for this purpose are: relationships to space and collective consumption (e.g. housing, transport facilities). In my view, some 'relationships to space' are *urban* real objects.)

These he proposes may be analysed from within any one of the three perspectives mentioned earlier: functionalist, historical and semiological, and at either the level of structures or that of actors.[13] This he says

constitutes a new theoretical field. This field is not that of a new urban sociology, but is simply a redefinition of the real problems tackled and discoveries made within the ideological field described as urban sociology. (p. 77)

His denial that the label urban sociology can be applied to this new field follows from the argument that it is meaningless to talk of urban theoretical or real objects.

It is important to bear in mind that Castells's subsequent work derives from the choice of only *one* of the three theoretical approaches, namely the historical approach. No doubt this choice follows from a commitment to historical materialism as the science of social formations. It implies focussing on 'the study of *transformations* of the relationships between society and space' (p. 76, my emphasis), rather than the functional integration (as in the 'ecological complex' approach) or semantic field of a spatial unit. One of the interesting areas for further development lies in the use of all three approaches: as I argue in section V of this Introduction, adoption of a historical materialist approach need not exclude certain other approaches.

The fact that Castells has chosen two real objects which have been the focus of work in urban sociology in the past for his further development of the subject should not preclude others from retrieving other real or theoretical objects and submitting them to further theoretical elaboration.

To sum up, it can be seen that chapters 2 and 3 are far more than 'reviews of the literature'. They are reviews with a definite purpose: namely, to establish the 'scientific' status of urban sociology. Castells argues that such a status is currently lacking, and makes proposals for

---

[13] For a discussion of the latter distinction, see p. 23.

a revised approach which would merit the label scientific. The last
sections of chapter 3 in which he outlines this new approach will be
discussed in section IV of this Introduction when we focus attention
on chapter 6, his proposals for the study of urban social movements.

III The shaping of urban space: the roles of property development, collective means of consumption and urban planning

Whereas Castells's arguments in chapters 2 and 3 regarding the
scientific status of urban sociology are made from a historical
materialist standpoint, they do not indicate the nature of the
alternative, historical materialist, analyses of the objects concerned.
Examples of such analyses will be found in chapters 4 to 7.

In the present section we are concerned with the processes which
shape 'urban space', i.e. which determine the social forms contained in
the units conventionally defined as cities or urban areas. Lamarche's
analysis (chapter 4) does not depend on any notion of urban: he is
concerned with the relations to space of the capitalist economic
system — though in fact his main concern is with those elements of
the latter which relate to the 'city' rather than to the region. Lojkine
however, in his analysis (chapter 5), does use the term city, or to be
more precise he defines the capitalist city as a particular form of
concentration of means of production, circulation and *collective*
consumption (defined below). And when he refers to urbanization or
urban development it is to the emergence of such concentrations,
which for him have a necessary function in capitalist social
formations. Thus Lojkine works with a historical materialist
conceptualization of the city, which denies that the city is something
apart from the social formation. (For an alternative conceptualization
see chapter 6, and p. 25 below.)

Chapters 4 and 5 emphasize two factors shaping urban space,
property development and collective means of consumption.

The planning role of property development

The central argument of chapter 4 is that while certain problems exist
which are specific to the city, such as insalubrious housing, high rents
and expropriation, these are not the product of a 'specifically urban
logic' (p. 86) or a 'specifically urban structure . . . independent of the
social structure as a whole' (p. 117), but are 'local consequences of
capital accumulation' (p. 86). In short, 'the urban question is first and
foremost the product of the capitalist mode of production, which
requires a spatial organization which facilitates the circulation of
capital, commodities, information, etc.' (p. 86).

Lamarche makes the connexion between space and the capitalist mode of production with the help of the concept of circulation. Let us see what place this concept has in Marx's economic theory.

For Marx, *production* under capitalist conditions involves the capitalist in transforming his capital (in its money-form, M) into commodities (C) in the form of labour power, raw materials and instruments of production, in order to produce a finished product which is then sold, so that his capital has now increased (M'). This metamorphosis (M-C-M') permits capital accumulation to take place. *Circulation* refers to the various transactions in which money is exchanged for labour power, raw materials, etc., prior to the production process, and for the product at the end of the production process (i.e. the realization of the product in its money-form). The spheres of production and circulation are thus logically distinct.

Furthermore, the spheres of production and circulation are opposed in that the former involves productive activity while the latter involves unproductive activity.[14] This follows from the labour theory of value according to which the value of the product leaving the production process derives from the labour crystallized in it. However, the production process is characterized by 'relations of production' which give it a contradictory character: namely, that while the value contained in the product results from the labour of the worker, the worker is paid (in wages) less than that value, the difference being appropriated in the form of surplus-value by the capitalist. The exploitative nature of capitalist production Marx saw as the eventual source of its overthrow.

Only capital engaged in the production sphere is capable of being expanded through productive labour. Thus, from the capitalist's point of view, capital engaged in circulation is capital lost to the process of accumulation. Hence the search by capitalists for ways of reducing the amount of capital engaged in circulation at any one time (i.e. ways of reducing circulation costs or circulation time).

This search results in a division of labour in which different fractions of capital emerge, each with a particular function. Industrial capital is that part engaged in production; commercial capital is that part involved in supplying commodities to and realizing the products of the production process (exchanging commodities and money); and financial capital that part used to concentrate money-capital not engaged in industrial or commercial operations. Commercial capital

[14] For a detailed discussion of the distinction between productive and unproductive labour, see I. Gough, Marx's theory of productive and unproductive labour, *New Left Review* 76 (1972) 47–72.

thus ensures (except in inflationary periods) that as little money-capital as possible is tied up in commodities (so that, for example, a finished product can be returned as soon as possible to its money form), while financial capital also speeds up the circulation of capital by reducing as far as possible the amount that need be kept in liquid form, e.g. as working capital.

By definition, the activities of financial and commercial capital (apart from transport and storage)[15] are unproductive, so the profits accruing to them cannot derive from the value of the labour involved. In fact, Marx argued, the profits of commercial capital derive from the purchase of commodities below their value for resale at their value. Industrial capital is willing to forego the share of surplus value from which these profits derive because of the increased productivity resulting from hiving off commerce to a specialized capital (thus enabling its own capital to return to production faster). In other words, the division of labour between specialized capitals increases the overall efficiency of use of capital. (The profits of financial capital likewise derive from the savings in circulation costs produced, and not from value produced by its own activity.)

Having outlined the role of circulation, and the two specialized capitals devoted to circulation, we can now proceed to examine the link advanced by Lamarche between space and the capitalist mode of production.[16]

The distance between economic agents and the spatial organization of their activities is a source of circulation costs (p. 90). In other words, space gives rise to certain costs of circulation. Lamarche thus argues that a fraction of capital may be conceived, operating in the circulation sphere, whose particular function is to plan and equip space in order to increase the efficiency of commercial, financial and administrative activities, by reducing their 'indirect costs'. This fraction he calls 'property capital', and illustrates by referring to the activities of property developers (who generally plan and let, but do not build, developments). Property capital has a 'planning' role, as we shall see, in the way it selects sites, and an 'equipping' role in the types of building it develops on them.

---

[15] Transport and storage are seen as productive in that they are required to make commodities available for consumption – see p. 129, fn. 17. In fact not all transport and storage has this role.

[16] So far we have mainly referred to the economic level of the capitalist mode of production. Clearly the exploitative nature of capitalist relations of production requires a complex legal, political and cultural apparatus to legitimize and reproduce it.

Property capital is not engaged in the production sphere (construction) but in the circulation sphere, where 'it plays the same role at the level of property as does commercial capital at the level of movable goods' (p. 93).[17] Lamarche rejects the argument that the profits of property capital can be treated simply as those of commercial capital, i.e. as a portion of the surplus value produced in the building industry, on the grounds that monopolies are not sufficiently developed nor technology sufficiently advanced for the building industry by itself to justify a capital specializing in selling its product, and that even if this were the case rents would have to reflect construction costs, whereas in fact they vary considerably, e.g. according to a building's location.

Hence he advances a more complex picture of property capital: rather than *buying and selling buildings*, it is involved, he suggests, in the *buying and letting of floor space* (i.e. part of buildings, usually). Its profits are thus explicable in terms of the difference between construction costs and *'rents' obtainable*,[18] not between price paid and value (construction cost).

This leads to the important question of the determination of 'rents'. Following Alquier and Lojkine's extension of Marx's writings on rents — which mainly applied to agricultural land — to urban land,[19] Lamarche argues that 'rents' depend not only on construction costs and the cost of capital immobilized in a building, but also on differential rents I and II. *Differential rent I* is a function of the advantages offered by the location of a building and is termed differential because these advantages are differentially distributed over space. These advantages (excluding 'natural' advantages) are the result of (1) investment by other private developers, e.g. a shopping centre, or office block, or (2) public investment, e.g. in schools, hospitals and collective facilities. Thus while a particular private developer has not brought about any of these advantages he is able to charge a higher 'rent' because of the access his building gives to them. The crucial role of public investment for property capital can be seen here: the profitability of the latter is directly dependent on the extent of the former. As public investment spreads geographically (as in the extension of railway lines into rural areas around cities), so the

[17] The term property capital (*capital immobilier*) as used by Lamarche does not refer to land.
[18] For the distinction made here between 'rent' (*loyer*) and rent (*rente*), see p . 86, fn. 1b.
[19] See below p. 100, fn. 14.

opportunities for private investment increase (e.g. in housing development).

   Differential rent II is a function of advantages *within* the property, e.g. the presence of a bank and a stockbroking firm would be advantageous to a merchant located in the same building. Here the property developer merely provides a physical structure. The increased profits which enable him to obtain higher 'rents' derive from the combination of tenant firms which are located there. The more property capital extends its control over urban space the more it is able to create the conditions of its own profitability.

   Four conclusions can be drawn about the type of activity developers will engage in. Property capital will (1) concentrate its developments in areas with good situational advantages, (2) order high-rise buildings in such areas (to multiply the mass of differential rent I extracted), (3) favour developments where tenants have complementary functions (and for which differential rent II can be extracted), and (4) favour large developments (for the last reason and to internalize more situational advantages in the form of differential rent I).

   Characteristically, property capital favours buildings for administrative, commercial and financial activities, e.g. office-blocks and shopping-centres (or frequently complexes including both). Buildings for these types of use are most likely to display the four characteristics stated above. In particular, these three uses are the main ones with complementary functions. Lamarche argues that in view of the profitability of, and scope for investment in these types of developments, housing will take a second place. Certainly, *luxury* residential developments will be built — but since the ability to pay for accessibility is restricted to a wealthy élite, this type of development is not broad enough to be the basis of profitability of development, potentially profitable only in so far as it is part of office or shopping complexes.

   Crucially, property capital is in the business of *letting* floor space. In other words, by retaining *ownership* it reserves the right to increase 'rents' as external and internal factors increase the tenants' willingness to pay higher amounts, thereby exacting a large share of the excess profits created for firms established there. In the same way, the urban land-owner anticipates the future profitability of land use (as a result of the developer's activity) and increases the selling price of his land accordingly. The right of ownership of land gives the land-owner the right to withhold land from the market (until its potential profitability has increased sufficiently), and it is this and not simply anticipated profitability which explains the land-owner's profits. 'The anticipated profits made possible by the right to withhold land, appear in the form of *absolute rent*' (p. 108). Absolute rent corresponds to 'the portion of differential rents (rent I mainly) attributable to the land-owner's action in withholding land' (p. 108). (The distinction between absolute and differential rents is thus an analytical one.)

Finally, Lamarche interprets three indices of 'the housing question' in terms of his theoretical analysis. The expropriation of workers of their homes in areas undergoing urban renewal is due to the priorities of property capital which give office, commercial and luxury residential developments preference over (unprofitable or less profitable) middle- and low-income housing. Insalubrious housing conditions result from speculation by land-owners on future developments: as surrounding areas are developed, the properties they own become less valuable than the land they stand on, maintenance declines and excess 'rents' may even be charged until large-scale redevelopment takes place. Thirdly, the shortage of housing at 'reasonable' 'rents', i.e. at 'rents' which do not include an element of situation rent, is due to increased public investment (creating situational advantages throughout an urban area), and the increased investment by property capital which follows it, appropriating rents for the latter advantages and creating still further advantages.

For Lamarche, then, it is property capital which plans and equips space, profiting from public investment, and feeding off other private investment. Hence, for him, planning can only be 'real' if it fits in with the plans of property capital.[20] It follows that any analysis of intervention by planning instances is meaningless unless the planning role of property development is first understood.

Lamarche's procedure is to start from Marxist economic theory — particularly as regards the circulation sphere — and deduce what form the activities of property capital will take, in planning and equipping space. His analysis has the advantages — and disadvantages — of any economic model. Essentially it is concerned with *tendencies* which

[20] Or as a recent report on the relations between poor housing conditions and property development in London concludes: 'The history of planning shows that private ownership of land and private initiative in, and profit from, its development, set forces in play which will always break through the obstacles of any planning measures, which start from an acceptance of their legitimacy and permanence.' *The Recurrent Crisis of London* (Counter Information Services, London, n.d. 1973) 51.

will appear in reality to a greater or lesser degree according to how far
the initial assumptions are met. Thus, for example, his evaluation of
the scope of planning by local authorities may be based on either
(1) the ineffectiveness of such planning in Montreal and/or (2) the
exclusion of the political sphere from his economic analysis. If the
former is true, this may be a reflection of the lack of development of
working-class organizations (a conjuctural effect) in Montreal rather
than a necessary feature of State intervention in the capitalist mode of
production.

More generally, Lamarche's analysis does not dwell on the
contradictions within the development of property capital, or
between the development of the latter and the development of
industrial capital. As an example of the former, the demand for
office-blocks and shopping-centres gives rise to increasing congestion
and places some limit on the density of such developments within a
city centre (i.e. so that certain differential and absolute rents cannot
be realized). Similarly, it seems unlikely that the extension of
property development activity can be considered as independent of
industrial activity. In financial terms we know that property and
industrial capital are alternative placements — which would suggest
some general interdependence between them. In spatial terms too
there may be a contradiction between their respective development:
thus, certain otherwise profitable locations will not be used for
property development because of the presence nearby of industrial
plant; and even with careful zoning of industry some border areas will
exist where this is the case. The degree to which contradictions appear
either within the property capital field or between this field and
industrial capital depends of course on the extent to which ownership
of property capital is (a) concentrated, and (b) overlaps with
ownership of industrial capital — a subject discussed by Lojkine in
chapter 5 (p. 136).

Considerations such as these, then, will affect the ease with which
Lamarche's analysis can be applied to concrete situations.

Collective means of consumption

In our brief discussion of Marxist economics above we stated that
capital was expanded by being engaged in the production process,
without indicating how this happened. In order to prepare the way for
discussion of chapter 5, it is first necessary to explain how capital
accumulation takes place, and in what way it is a contradictory
process.

Capital accumulation results from the production of surplus-value, i.e. from the fact that the wage paid to the worker is less than the value of the labour he imparts to the product. Thus surplus-value (s) depends on labour or 'variable capital' (v) and not on constant capital (c), e.g. machines. The rate at which surplus-value is produced (and capital accumulation made possible) is therefore given by s/v.

Now the time spent by the worker in the production process can be divided into 'necessary labour' (that required to produce value equivalent to his wage) and 'surplus labour' (that required to produce surplus value), and the rate of surplus-value (s/v) can thus be expressed as surplus labour/necessary labour. It follows that the rate at which surplus-value is produced will depend on the total working time of the worker, and the proportion of necessary to surplus labour.[21] This rate will therefore be higher the longer the working day, the lower the level of the real wage, or the higher the productivity of labour. These are of course the three fronts on which capital directs its fight to raise the rate of accumulation.

While the first and second of these fronts are not unimportant at the current time (particularly as regards real wages in a period of inflation), the third one is the major source of expansion. And the most usual way of increasing labour productivity (value produced per unit of labour power) is by the greater use of machinery. But mechanization has a contradictory effect. This can be seen in the following way. Total value produced is equivalent to the value of constant capital (c) and that contributed by labour power which divides into wages or 'variable capital' (v) and surplus-value (s). As more machines are employed, the ratio of constant capital to constant capital plus variable capital (c/c + v) increases, i.e. the 'organic composition of capital' increases.

But since, as we saw earlier, only labour is creative of surplus-value, the increased use of machines does not alter the *amount* of *surplus-value* (s) produced. Hence the rate of profit, which can be expressed as s/c + v (if the share of surplus-value paid in the form of rent is ignored), actually *declines* as more machinery is added. This is the 'falling *tendency* of the rate of profit'.[22] Thus, expanded

---

[21] In total, the mass of surplus-value will depend also on the number of workers employed.
[22] The above presentation is highly schematic. For example, it assumes that all capital is used up during the production period. Thus no distinction is made between constant capital as a stock concept which enters the calculation of the profit rate, s/c + v, and capital as a flow concept (i.e. the raw materials used up and depreciation costs incurred in the production process) which contributes to

capitalist production is doubly contradictory: on the one hand it places workers and capitalists in a contradictory relationship of exploitation, and, on the other hand, the attempt to increase labour productivity by the increased use of machinery strengthens the tendency of the rate of profit to fall (making further investment less profitable). An important theme in the Marxist understanding of capitalist economics concerns the attempts to counter this tendency (which is after all a tendency).[23]

We observed that the rate of capital accumulation depended on the amount of capital put to work in the production sphere and, earlier, that this in turn depended on the speed of rotation of capital. It is Lojkine's contention (chapter 5) that the capitalist city can be seen as a spatial form which, by reducing indirect costs or production, and costs of circulation and consumption, speeds up the rotation of capital. And it achieves this by concentrating not only means of production and circulation (e.g. factories, banks, shops) — which is true even of cities in non-capitalist social formations — but also 'collective means of consumption'.

Lojkine's thesis centres on the role of collective means of consumption in 'developed capitalist formations' so it is important to define them clearly. Whereas *individual means of consumption* (e.g. food or clothing) are (1) commodities, separate from their means of production, (2) consumed individually and (3) destroyed in the process of consumption, collective means of consumption (e.g. schools, hospitals) produce (1) services (or 'useful effects') (e.g. lessons, medical care) — not commodities — which are inseparable from their means of production, (2) which are consumed collectively, and (3) which are not destroyed in the act of consumption.

Collective means of consumption are 'material supports of the activities devoted to the extended reproduction of labour power' (p. 121). The latter phrase perhaps requires clarification. For a social

---

total value ($c + v + s$). More generally, the validity of the falling tendency of the rate of profit is currently the object of considerable debate. This centres on the fact that while the rate of profit is expressed in price terms, the analysis from which its tendency to fall is derived is expressed in value terms. The problem of moving from value accounting to price accounting is known as the 'trans-formation problem'. A distinct problem is that even *within* the value accounting procedure confusions exist between physical quantity and value, e.g. an increase in the physical quantity of machines in use does not necessarily imply an increase in their value and hence in the organic composition of capital. See, on this whole debate, G. Hodgson, The theory of the falling rate of profit, *New Left Review* 84 (1974) 55—82, and the references contained therein.
[23] For a discussion of this topic see, for example, P. M. Sweezy, *The Theory of Capitalist Development* (Modern Readers, New York, 1968 (1942)) chapter 6.

formation to be reproduced, its economic system, political and legal apparatus, cultural patterns and ideologies must be reproduced. In the case of the economic system not only must the 'relations of production' be reproduced (e.g. by ensuring that the legitimacy of private appropriation is not successfully challenged by social movements) but also the technical requirements — continued supplies of means of production and labour power — must be assured. In the case of the former, the capital goods industry provides for future productive capacity. The reproduction of labour power means not just the presence of a labour force (a demographic or physiological question, i.e. 'simple' reproduction) but of a labour force which is adequately housed, fed, clothed, educated, cared for, etc., to provide the work capacity (and acceptance of existing relations of production) required to perpetuate the productive system.[24]

Lojkine's thesis is that the development of collective means of consumption and their concentration in agglomerations side by side with means of production and circulation is increasingly a factor producing higher labour productivity (and hence capital accumulation). The emergence of such concentrations — in which consumption is 'socialized' — can thus be seen as a 'general condition of production' (additional to communications systems and transport networks, identified by Marx), i.e. a contextual condition promoting the expansion of individual capitalist firms.

As in the case of the greater use of machinery to increase productivity, Lojkine argues that the provision of collective means of consumption also has the effect of increasing the organic composition of capital, and hence strengthening the tendency of the rate of profit to fall. The argument is as follows: the extended reproduction of capital involves not only direct costs of production and indirect costs of production (circulation costs) but also — a factor neglected by Marx — *consumption costs*, and these costs are financed by a deduction from surplus-value, which he calls *'expenses capital'* (and whose function in the consumption sphere parallels that of commercial and financial capital in the circulation sphere). Since expenses capital is not productively utilized, but does increase the mass of accumulated social capital, it increases the organic composition of capital.[25] Thus, like the employment of machinery, the setting aside of an expenses capital to finance collective means of

[24] The precise dividing line between simple and extended reproduction may be drawn elsewhere, see chapter 6 (p. 157).
[25] It is not clear to me whether this argument is correct, i.e. why unproductive capital should increase the organic composition of capital.

production in order to increase productivity strengthens the tendency of the rate of profit to fall.

To say that the provision of collective means of consumption articulated to means of production and circulation, i.e. the 'rational, *socialized*, planning of urban development' (p. 128), is *necessary* to capitalist accumulation, is not to say that it will be forthcoming. Lojkine identifies three obstacles to this process.

The first is *financial*. We have seen that the services or useful effects provided by collective means of consumption are quite different from those of commodities. Usually they cannot be sold. Thus the capital invested in providing collective means of consumption is generally devalorized,[26] i.e. is expected to yield a rate of profit below the average (and which may even be nil).[27] We are thus in the presence of a contradiction: while these facilities are required by capitalist development their financing is not profitable to capitalist agents. The possibility of a partial resolution of this contradiction will be discussed below.

The second obstacle to the 'rational, socialized, planning of urban development' pertains to the anarchic *competition* between capitalist firms. In brief, firms prefer location which are well-equipped in 'urban infrastructure', i.e. collective means of consumption, communications facilities and transport networks. The result is that cities and regions which are well equipped in this respect tend to become increasingly congested, while those which are poorly equipped decline. Space thus becomes increasingly differentiated.

The third obstacle relates to the *private ownership of land*. Marx

[26] Lojkine points out that there is not a difference in kind between expenses capital (devalorized) and capital engaged in productive activity (remunerated at the average rate of profit). For example, capital engaged in the transport industry (a productive activity, though in the circulation sphere — see fn. 15 above) has such a high organic composition that the rate of profit is very low, i.e. is highly devalorized. The difference between such capital and expenses capital is simply one of degree of devalorization. (This argument rests on a shift from value accounting to price accounting procedures, see fn. 22 above.) The notion of devalorized capital forms a central part of the theory of state monopoly capitalism developed from Marx's *Capital* by the French Communist Party. See *Le Capitalisme Monopoliste d'Etat: Traité Marxiste d'Economie Politique*, 2 vols (Editions Sociales, Paris, 1971), and Paul Boccara, *Le Capitalisme Monopoliste d'Etat, sa Crise, et son Issue* (Editions Sociales, Paris, 1974).

[27] The low (or nil) rate of profit derives from the nature of the 'product' (a useful effect) and not from the fact that collective means of consumption are unproductive. As we saw earlier in our discussion of property capital, surplus-value may be *appropriated* (though not produced) in the circulation sphere.

stressed the role of land as an instrument of production (e.g. in agriculture) and as a passive support of means of production, circulation and consumption (e.g. factories, shops, housing). Lojkine argues that a third function is increasingly important – the capacity of land for '*concentration*, i.e. for *socially combining* the means of production and means of reproduction of a social formation' (p. 135) – and that the private ownership of land is more and more an obstacle to the performance of this function. (Ownership he sees as concentrated to a growing extent among large international financial groups, rather than scattered among a large *petite bourgeoisie*.) The private ownership of land by big monopolies is reflected in social segregation within the city, where the city-centre is increasingly reserved for the headquarters of these monopolies.

In view of the existence of these three *obstacles* to the provision of collective means of consumption, the fact that educational and health facilities, subsidized housing, etc., exist at all requires explanation.

Lojkine argues that it is through State intervention that such provision exists, and this has important implications for an analysis of the capitalist State.

The fact that it is unprofitable, generally speaking, to provide collective means of consumption, and yet they are necessary to raise productivity, is partly resolved by the State's undertaking the financing of such provision. Thus the State steps in on behalf of capitalist agents who, individually, find such provision unprofitable. And this economic function of the State is not something restricted to early stages of capitalism, as some have argued, but is 'a constant and growing necessity for the extended reproduction of the capitalist mode of production' (p. 140). Thus, in addition to its functions of reproducing the political, legal and ideological conditions of capitalist production, the State has a crucial economic role.

But since, for Marx, the State is the 'condensed reflection of the class struggle', the provision of collective facilities must be seen as resulting from working-class pressure and not from 'independent' action by the State.

In addition to financing the provision of collective means of consumption, the State (as a result of worker pressure) in developed capitalist formations has resolved certain immediate 'problems' (e.g. unsanitary housing conditions) by the control of land-use (urban planning), and, to a limited extent (e.g. by 'municipalization'), weakened the effects of monopolistic private ownership of land.

Despite these immediate 'successes', argues Lojkine, the

contradiction between the imperatives of capitalist accumulation and
the imperatives of 'socialized consumption' is not resolved, but
widened, and extended into the urban sphere by State intervention.

Lojkine is very much aware of the contradictory nature of
capitalist development and the important role of State intervention in
regulating it. In both respects his analysis differs from that of
Lamarche. This may be partly because Lojkine's focus on interest is
the consumption sphere of the economic system, whereas Lamarche's
focus is on the circulation sphere. But it is also likely that they hold
different conceptions of the State, for example, as regards the
closeness between the policies of the State and the interests of the
various fractions of the capitalist class, and whether the State ever
subordinates the short-term interests of the capitalist class to its
long-term survival.

IV Urban social movements
So far we have presented the capitalist mode of production and its
development as containing contradictions but without indicating how
the expressions of these contradictions within the political sphere
might be analysed. In this section we therefore turn to a discussion of
Castells's theoretical framework for the analysis of urban social
movements (chapter 6), and Olives's application of it to movements in
the field of urban renewal (in chapter 7). This discussion is extended
in chapter 8.

The theoretical framework advanced by Castells in chapter 6 is
intended to apply to the 'new theoretical field', outlined by him in
chapter 3, which is to take the place of urban sociology. While the
framework applies to both aspects of this new field, urban planning
(level of structures) and urban social movements (level of practices),
we shall mainly focus on the latter.

Our discussion of chapter 6 will be somewhat more extended than
that concerning chapters 2–5 because of its difficulty. The reasons for
this difficulty are two-fold: firstly, because it attempts to put into
practice the oft-stated declaration that the city cannot be analyzed
except as part of society, and, secondly, because it adopts a
particular – structuralist – framework for carrying out this analysis –
a framework which, by definition, is somewhat more abstract than
many of its rivals.[28]

[28] For a definition of 'structuralist', as used here see, p. 198, fn. 1. For an illustration
of the main rival approach to this problem, functionalism, see Scott Greer's *The
Emerging City* (Free Press, New York, 1962) and R. L. Warren's *The Community
in America* (Rand McNally, Chicago, 1963). See also Castells's discussion of
human ecology as a general theory of social structure in chapter 3 (pp. 71–73).

Castells's theoretical framework has two starting-points: a conception of society (or 'social structure') and a conception of urban system.

In his conception of *society*, Castells follows Althusser. He sees a society (or social formation) as comprising several modes of production, one of which is dominant. In turn, a mode of production consists of a combination of several 'systems', e.g. economic (base), political-legal and ideological (superstructure). Each system comprises a number of elements which are combined in various relations. Thus, in the *capitalist* mode of production, the economic system consists of three elements: labour power, means of production and 'non-worker' (i.e. capitalist), linked by two relationships, ownership[29] and real appropriation, which are 'homologous', i.e. the capitalist not only *owns* labour power and means of production but also *controls* the 'technical' process by which they are combined together.

Analysis of a social formation may start at either of two levels: structures or practices. The former level relates to the fundamental (structural) elements of a system, how they are combined into systems, and how the systems are themselves related. Practices, on the other hand, refer to the level of 'actors' or 'support-agents'. Actors, however, are not conceived as subjects (and practices as their behaviour), but as supports of the 'places' or positions defined by the structural elements and their inter-relations: hence the term 'support-agent'.[30] For example, the relation of exploitation between labour power and 'non-worker' is supported by the agents occupying these two positions. The central question is whether structures and practices are merely different ways of abstracting from the same phenomenon, or whether practices, in combination, can produce effects which are relatively autonomous. As Castells argues,[31] support-agents are grouped into social classes, and class relations can thus be seen as the social expression of the way in which the elements, systems, etc., of a given social formation are combined.

A social formation is not a functionally integrated, harmonious

[29] This refers to *de facto* as opposed to *de jure* ownership, the latter being a phenomenon belonging to the political-legal system. The former concept is necessary to mark the distinction between, for example, the 'public ownership' of a company (legally defined) and the (*de facto*) private ownership of means of production, etc. Other translators sometimes use the term 'property relation' where I have used 'ownership relation'. For a fuller dicussion of this distinction, see N. Poulantzas, On Social Classes, *New Left Review* 78 (1973) 27–54, esp. 28–9.
[30] This term indicates the analytical level to which priority is given, namely, the structural level of fundamental elements, relations, etc.
[31] M. Castells, *La Question Urbaine* (Maspero, Paris, 1972) 307.

whole, as in the structural-functionalist conception, but is essentially characterized by contradictions (between its component modes of production, systems, elements, etc.). Castells's decision to focus on the analysis of transformations of social formations (rather than on synchronic functioning or semantics — see p. 76) leads him to give priority to the analysis of politics ('the system of power relations'), since 'it is politics which structures the totality of the field and determines how it is transformed'.[32] The analysis of politics refers to the analysis of class struggle, and especially 'political class struggle', i.e. that over control of the State apparatus. The distinction between the two levels of analysis, 'structures' and 'practices', refers to that between 'analysis of changes in the configuration of the system' and analysis of the 'processes by which it is transformed' (p. 149), or, in the case of urban politics, between urban planning and urban social movements.

Turning now to Castells's conception of *urban system*, we find it has two sources.

The first derives from the conception of social structure outlined above. Thus, the economic system (with its component spheres: production, circulation (or exchange), and consumption), the political-legal system and the ideological system are spatially structured, have spatial expressions. Castells thus uses

> the term *spatial structure* (or 'urban system' to conform to
> tradition) to describe the particular way in which the basic
> elements of the social structure are spatially articulated. (p. 78)[33]

Thus the term 'urban system' refers to the relation between elements in the spheres of production (e.g. factories), exchange (e.g. transport facilities) and consumption (e.g. housing), as well as in the political system (the 'management element' in the urban system whose function is to regulate relations between the first three, e.g. urban planning agencies).[34] However, certain aspects of any element or system will be excluded from any given urban system: hence Castells's distinction between determinations of (1) the latter elements and systems ('*general social structure*') and (2) (those present in) the

---

[32] *Ibid.*, 306.
[33] Castells's reasons for identifying spatial structure and urban system will be discussed immediately below.
[34] The ideological system is not discussed in great detail as an element in the urban system in chapter 6. A fuller discussion is provided in Castells, *op. cit.* (p. 273 *et seq.*, p. 302, etc.), where it is referred to as the 'urban symbolic'.

urban system. Finally, just as support-agents or actors occupy the
'places' of elements, relations, etc., constituting the social structure, as
indicated above, so a *system of urban actors* can be defined in terms
of their occupation of 'places' in the elements of the urban system.

The second source of Castells's conception of urban system refers
to the basis of delimitation of the spatial unit concerned. Here he is
following up his argument in chapter 3 that problems relating to
collective consumption (i.e. to the reproduction of labour power)
were one (non-urban) focus of research in urban sociology in the
past which deserved a fresh start. He argues that the area
conventionally referred to as a city or agglomeration is in the last
analysis 'a residential unit of labour power' (p. 148) or 'unit of
collective consumption' (*ibid.*) — defined by the limits of commuting,
or as a labour market area. It cannot be delimited as a unit in relation
to the ideological or political systems (except in the case of the
medieval city, which does not concern us here), or in relation to the
production sphere in the economic system.[35] Castells likens the role
of the city or agglomeration in the consumption sphere to the role of
the firm in the production sphere.

In other words, the term urban system has a double specification: it
refers (1) to the articulation of elements of the social structure
within (2) a unit of collective consumption. This is why Castells
makes the transition from spatial structure to urban system.

In addition to social structure and urban system, one other concept
plays a part in Castells's theoretical framework, namely, *social
organization*. He uses this as a broad term to cover the various
historically-produced social forms which provide the context within
which general social structural and urban systemic determinations are
set. He identifies three aspects of 'social organization' as being
relevant to 'urban problems': the stratification system, the
organizational system, and ecological forms. This concept is thus a
way of taking into account the influence of the past on the present.

Having presented the basic concepts in Castells's theoretical
framework, we can now examine how this framework is applied to the
study of urban social movements.

A *social movement* is defined as:

> an organization of the system of actors (conjuncture of class
> relations) leading to the production of a qualitatively new effect on
> the social structure. . . . (p. 151)

[35] On this, see Castells, *op. cit.*, 295–8.

A 'qualitatively new effect' may be — at the level of structures — a change in the structural law of the dominant system; or — at the level of practices — a change in the balance of forces such that working-class organizations are strengthened. The definition of *urban social movement* (p. 155) simply replaces 'social structure' in the above definition by 'urban system'.

Two points must be noted about the definition of urban social movement: firstly, it refers to the level of actors (practices), and secondly, the term is only appropriate if a particular type of effect ('qualitatively new') results. If a different (lower) level of effect occurs, a different name (not 'urban social movement') is appropriate, e.g. 'regulation', 'reform', etc. (p. 163).

The analysis of urban social movements requires that they be seen within the framework just outlined, i.e. that they be related to the urban system, 'general social structure' and 'social organization'.

First, *urban system*. The (urban) practices which urban social movements link together are by definition related to the structural elements and relations (of the urban system) on which they are based. To make the connexion between abstract elements of the urban system and their concrete expression in urban practices requires that these elements be broken down into sub-elements, and the latter into the 'places' (i.e. 'levels' and 'roles') actually occupied by actors. Thus, for example, the structural element consumption contains housing as a sub-element, which in turn contains 'levels' (luxury dwellings, public housing, etc.) and 'roles' (owner, tenant, etc.) occupied by actors. In this way a connexion can be made between the contradictions existing at the level of basic elements, relations, systems, etc., and concrete urban practices. For example, an urban social movement in the housing sphere is based on elements, etc., related to the contradiction between the requirement that the labour force be concentrated in agglomerations (for reasons discussed in chapter 5) and the unprofitability of providing the housing and collective means of consumption necessary to its maintenance. Thus the *stake* (e.g. rent reductions, rehousing, access to public housing) or issue around which an urban social movement forms is *structurally determined*.

It follows from this that analysis of an urban social movement will have to take into account the type and number of contradictions involved. Castells suggests that mobilization will be greater, the larger the number of accumulated contradictions, the more they are concentrated in the economic or urban system (rather than in the political or ideological systems), the more urban practices are articulated with other practices (if the latter relate to fundamental contradictions), etc.

The last point relates to '*general social structure*', i.e. those aspects excluded from a particular urban system, for example, the *general* economic and political struggle. Castells advances a basic hypothesis in this connexion: that *purely* urban practices cannot be more than reformist in their effects, and that only if practices 'imported' from other spheres are joined to them can a 'qualitatively new effect' result. Thus, paradoxically, a purely urban social movement, defined by its actual rather than potential effects, is a contradiction in terms.

Finally, the link between urban social movement and '*social organization*'. The main aspect of the latter Castells focusses on is organizations. For him the role of an organization is crucial, since it enables actors occupying 'places' in one or more structural elements of the urban system to unite, and − in certain cases − link their practices to those 'imported' from other spheres. Thus organizations give social expression to categories (or classes) of actors sharing common positions. They canalize the otherwise 'wild' expression of contradictions. (This does not imply that *all* occupants of a given place will participate in a organization: hence Castells's distinction between the 'membership horizon' (actual) and 'reference horizon' (potential) of a movement.) Given an organization expressing and/or linking structural contradictions in this way, variation is possible according to whether the *political line* of the organization is reformist, contestatory, or utopian (revolutionist). An urban social movement will only result if the first and last extremes are avoided.[36]

These, then, are the main features of Castells's approach to the analysis of urban social movements. Their success or otherwise is related to the urban system (or system of urban actors) and the contradictions within it, the importation of practices from other spheres ('general social structure') and the line of the organization concerned.

Clearly, the above discussion does not do justice to the ideas contained in chapter 6 − in particular we have not referred to the important discussion of the limits of planning in the capitalist mode of production (pp. 166−7) − but hopefully it will assist an understanding of them.

In order to facilitate such an understanding we will now turn to a

---

[36] This aspect of the framework is crucial in that it indicates a source of 'openness' in the system. Political lines are not structurally determined, though of course they are not random products either.

discussion of Olives's study of protest movements — mostly against
urban renewal — in one district of Paris, which employs Castells's
framework. Further studies which also employ this framework are
discussed in chapter 8.

Olives's aim is to 'identify the conditions under which urban social
movements emerge' (p. 175), and he does so inductively by analysing
the various struggles occurring in a particular district of Paris.

We saw earlier that urban social movements were defined by their
(potential) success in bringing about 'qualitatively new effects' either
at the level of structures or at the level of practices. Olives
distinguishes between 'urban effects', e.g. success in resisting eviction,
and 'political effects', e.g. the formation of a political group whose aims
are not restricted to a particular urban system. His interest is thus in
determining what conditions bring about such effects.

The first condition is the *size of the stake*, which, he argues, must
be large for urban or political effects to result. In most of the
successful cases he considered, the stake — attempted eviction in the
course of renewal operations — was indeed large. However, the size of
the stake, which reflects the real intensity of the underlying
contradiction (i.e. in this case, between capitalist profitability and the
reproduction of labour power) has its effect in a certain *political
conjuncture*. In other words, in a certain conjuncture of the
development of working-class organization. And this conjuncture as
well as the size of the stake itself is crucial. For example, Olives argues
that in the present political conjuncture (Paris in 1972), few organizations
existed in the field of urban struggle (as opposed to work-based or
general political struggle) and that this meant that the ease with which
stakes could be grasped was an important factor conditioning their
ultimate effect (p. 179). (The importance Olives is attributing here to
perceptions is related to the specific state of development of
organizations, i.e. the 'social organization' factor.)

The second condition Olives identifies for the emergence of an
urban social movement is — as has been implied — the presence of an
organization. This is necessary to link urban practices, and in every case
studied where an urban effect resulted, one or more organizations
were present. Thirdly, this organization must *mobilize the social base*
affected by the stake. Thus outside organizations which had no such
local mobilizing effect were failures: only those with support from the
local base were successful. In most cases a high level of mobilization was
a necessary condition for the production of an urban effect: Olives
argues that this was because without mobilization counter-action by
the police or other authorities would crush the movement.

The fourth condition is the *type of action* engaged in. Here Olives
follows Castells and argues that legal, reformist action is unlikely to be
successful, whereas direct, contestatory action is.

Thus in the majority of cases analyzed by Olives where urban
effects did result this was attributable to the large stakes (threatened
eviction) and presence of organizations mobilizing the social base and
adopting contestatory action. According to Olives, the fact that the
population concerned consisted of African immigrant workers
facilitated the implantation of such organizations. And the same fact
is, he argues, responsible for the link made with work-based struggles
(given the exploitation undergone by immigrants in the work
situation) which explained the ultimate success of the various actions
in halting evictions in the area and strengthening working-class political
organization.

In chapter 8 I discuss some points arising out of the analysis of
urban social movements by Olives and others. To summarize, I argue
that (1) the attribution of 'urban effects' to the actions of
movements, which tends to take movement claims at their face value,
is problematic, and may derive from the analyst's identification with the
movement and/or from the historical materialist conception of the
State (in so far as local authorities are the adversary of the
movement); (2) the attribution of urban effects must take into
account processes internal to local authorities (e.g. inter-departmental
conflicts), and pressure from central government, and from other urban
actors (e.g. property developers, financial institutions) in addition to
that from urban social movements;[37] (3) the stress on popular
mobilization and 'direct' action as a pre-requisite for urban effects is
not consistent with all of Olives's own data, and not with studies
carried out in Britain in recent years;[38] (4) finally, the 'structuralist'

[37] The level of perceptions is of course important in itself; local authority
officials may — for their own purposes (e.g. to contain future protest) — present
a change as a victory for a local group, in the same way that the persistence of a
group will depend on its leaders being able to present certain changes as
victories.
[38] For a resolution of this apparent incompatibility it would be necessary to
relate the means adopted by different movements to the stakes involved and to
the *local* as well as national political conjunctures. For example, it might be
argued that the British studies concern stakes which present less of a challenge
to the urban system, and that the achievement of success in certain cases
without popular mobilization is due to greater working-class pressure on the
State (reflected in extensive public housing and *public* sector urban renewal, for
example) and a perhaps greater degree of local government autonomy
(compared with France).

approach tends to under-emphasize the role of organizations — except as a means of linking urban practices together, and to other types of practice. The crucial role of organizational resources in producing urban effects is thus ignored.

Furthermore, it may be argued that Olives's account of the mobilization process has certain weaknesses.[39] Firstly, it conceptualizes the social base in purely demographic terms. It does not refer to the social structure or value-orientations present in the social base. John Rex's analysis of the factors affecting the formation of housing classes is an excellent example of work which *does* take into account social structure and value-orientations (e.g., in his case, ethnicity and the 'urban value system').[40] And secondly, it fails to analyse the factors affecting the participation in organizations of the population affected by a stake. Apart from such mundane matters as time and money, I would suggest that the 'terms of entry' imposed by an organization are a crucial factor affecting participation. Two particularly important 'terms of entry' are the form (and formality) of the organization, and the obligation to interact with others of different value-orientations, social backgrounds, political lines, degrees of trustworthiness, etc. Both these factors may prevent a social base from becoming a social force.

The above comments on the studies of urban social movements do not imply a rejection of Castells's theoretical framework, but rather a more detailed analysis, essentially complimentary, of certain aspects of the processes involved.

V Conclusion
Having completed our discussion of the various historical materialist approaches outlined in chapters 2 to 7, it remains for us to assess the likely contribution of these approaches to urban sociology in the future. Strictly speaking, of course, only future developments will permit such an assessment, but certain indications of the direction of these developments exist.

[39] The following arguments are set out in full in my paper: From 'social base' to 'social force'; some analytical issues in the study of urban protest, to be published in a collection of papers presented to the Eighth World Congress of Sociology, Toronto: Michael Harloe (ed.), *Captive Cities* (Wiley, London and New York, 1976).
[40] J. Rex, The concept of housing class and the sociology of race relations, *Race* 12 (1971) 293—301; see also J. Rex and R. Moore, *Race, Community and Conflict* (Oxford University Press, London, 1967), esp. pp. 1—18, 272—85.

First, it is necessary to look at the relation between historical materialism and the 'social sciences' in general.

One important feature of historical materialism to emerge from our discussion is that it does not respect conventional 'social science' discipline boundaries. For example, Lamarche's analysis is primarily 'economic', Lojkine's straddles the 'economic' and the 'political', and Castells's the 'political' and the 'sociological'. This is because these disciplines are distinguished from one another not so much by their exclusive claim to different slabs of reality, as Durkheim imagined, but by the concepts which constitute them and the questions these concepts permit to be posed. Now the real objects of historical materialism (i.e. the aspects of reality it analyzes) overlap considerably — but by no means totally — with those of economics, political science and sociology, as its (putative) claim to be 'the science of social formations' implies. It follows that the relation between historical materialism and the social sciences is one of competition in many respects, but not in all.

Let us examine this relation in the case of 'sociology' and 'urban sociology'.

Historical materialism, by definition, emphasizes the material basis of human society and its ultimate role in determining the development of society. This is not to say that the political, education, cultural, etc., superstructure has no importance in this respect, but rather that its role is partly determined and partly determining. (In other words *one aspect* of an analysis of urban politics, for example, must relate to the reproduction of capitalist production, in both the material and social relations senses.) However, unless one accepts the contention that the material base has a uniform effect on all superstructural 'institutions' and affects both the broad trends of development and individual and group variations around these trends equally, then it must be admitted that the role of the material base (and hence the relevance of a materialist analysis) is a matter of degree and will vary from one object of study to another. This suggests (assuming the materialist thesis is correct) that historical materialist concepts will have the most purchase in those fields most closely concerned with the reproduction of social formations, and in respect of those institutions most concerned in this process, and least purchase in those fields and institutions most marginal to it, e.g. interpersonal relations in informal contexts, artistic production, social movements on 'moral' issues.

Thus we may conclude that as far as 'urban sociology' is

concerned, historical materialist analyses are likely to be most relevant
to those features of the city and its institutions which are closely
related to capital accumulation, the reproduction of the material and
social pre-conditions of capital accumulation, and attempts to subvert
these processes and establish new ones. Thus, for example, analyses of
(public or private) housing will relate it to the reproduction of labour
power (and of capital); to the political and ideological control over
the labour force brought about by the financial imposition of rents
and mortgage repayments, to the dispersion of the labour force of
particular factories (whether by individual-based allocation procedures
in the public housing sector, or by the 'free market' in the private
sector); and to the emergence of action against established modes of
housing, its allocation and financing.[41] But such examples — which
could be multiplied — are not exhaustive of analyses in this field.
Analyses of housing as a physical form with effects on social
interaction (e.g. neighbouring), social control of children's play, etc. —
without falling into the trap of physical determinism — constitute a
traditional field of sociological study which is not evidently related to
the material and social conditions of capitalist accumulation. (Indeed
there are notable similarities between such analyses in Eastern and
Western Europe.) Similarly, to refer back to Castells's distinction
between historical, functionalist and semiological approaches, there is
no reason why analyses of institutions such as local authorities or
schools should not focus on organizational structure as a feature
having distinctive effects irrespective of the functions of the
institution concerned (e.g. control/legitimation; control and training,
respectively).

In sum, historical materialist approaches in urban sociology open
up new avenues of enquiry, which posses a unity of their own, but
which are not exhaustive of the space occupied by urban sociology.

---

[41] See, for example, on the political function of urban renewal in Paris,
F. Godard *et al.*, *La Rénovation Urbaine à Paris: Structure Urbaine et Logique
de Classe* (Mouton, Paris, 1973); on public housing developments as a capitalist
product, E. Preteceille, *La Production de Grands Ensembles* (Mouton, Paris,
1973); on the economic functions of owner-occupation, C. Topalov, *Capital et
Propriété Foncière* (Centre de Sociologie Urbaine, Paris, 1973) Part One; on
public housing and the reproduction of labour power, S. Magri, *Politique du
Logement et Besoins en Main-d'oeuvre* (Centre de Sociologie Urbaine, Paris,
1972). For a discussion of the latter three studies, see my article forthcoming in
Antipode, special number on Urban Political Economy.

2

Manuel Castells

Is there an urban sociology?*

'It is not the 'actual' interconnections of 'things' but the *conceptual*
interconnections of *problems* which define the scope of the various
sciences. A new 'science' emerges where new problems are pursued by
new methods and truths are thereby discovered which open up significant
new points of view'.

Max Weber†

1 Social demand and scientific crisis

It is a well-known fact that there are fashions in sociology, usually
produced in response to some demand of society. The growing
awareness in France of the problems created by urban growth is
leading to an increasing demand for research in this field. As a
consequence there has been a mushrooming in recent years of what is
termed 'urban sociology', perhaps less evident as yet in completed and
published studies than in research proposals.

A systematic assessment of this work would be not only premature
but also beyond our capacity. What we do wish to attempt is an
examination of the scientific relevance of a research field which has
developed primarily in response to social changes. The question
appears with all the more force as this expansion of urban sociology in
France coincides with its almost complete disappearance as a distinct
field in Anglo-Saxon research, due not so much to a lack of interest in
'urban problems' as to the fragmentation of urban sociology into a
variety of separate fields of study.

In general it may be said that apart from the mass of technical,
economic and planning studies of spatial policy problems the
sociological or quasi-sociological research falling under the heading
'urban' includes on the one hand: (1) studies of urbanization as a
world-wide process, seen in more or less demographic terms, in the
manner of Hauser, or, better still, as in the work carried out by
International Urban Research (Berkeley) under the direction of
Kingsley Davis; (2) studies of social disorganization and acculturation

*[Translated with permission of Editions du Seuil, Paris, from M. Castells,
Y a-t-il une sociologie urbaine?, *Sociologie du Travail* 1 (1968) 72–90.]
†Max Weber, '"Objectivity" in Social Science and Social Policy' (1904), in
E. A. Shils and H. A. Finch (eds), *The Methodology of the Social Sciences* (Free
Press, New York, 1949), 68.

following the approach of the Chicago school,[1] or the more recent
developments from it by researchers such as Srole,[2] Clinard,[3] Killian[4]
or Glass;[5] and (3) the old 'community study' tradition, which has
finally received proper recognition and which may be devoted to the
exhaustive study of a small town, or, as is more common, an area
within a city. The work of the Institute of Community Studies
(London)[6] represents a systematic approach to the study of social
interaction within a spatially defined area, while the American studies
of suburban life, in particular those of Seeley,[7] Berger[8] and
Dobriner,[9] display a concern to explore a spatial area as such, even
when the validity of such an approach is challenged by the
conclusions reached.[10] On the other hand, political science has made
the residential community a privileged field for the study of decision-
making processes, leading either to the depiction of local systems of
power or to the delimitation of local systems of influence.[11]

Somewhat on the fringe of sociology, there has been renewed

[1] Good illustrations of this approach are to be found in the recently published
collection of the Chicago school's work: E. W. Burgess and D. Bogue (eds),
Contributions to Urban Sociology (University of Chicago Press, Chicago, 1964).
[2] L. Srole *et al.*, *Mental Health in the Metropolis: the Midtown Manhattan Study*
(McGraw Hill, New York, 1962).
[3] M. B. Clinard, A Cross-Cultural Replication of the Relation of Urbanism to
Criminal Behaviour, *American Sociological Review* 25 (1960), 253–7, and also
Slums and Community Development (Free Press, New York, 1966).
[4] L. Killian and C. Grigg, Urbanism, Race and Anomia, *American Journal of
Sociology* 57 (1962) 661–5.
[5] R. Glass, *London's Newcomers: the West Indian Immigrants* (Harvard
University Press, Cambridge (Mass.), 1961).
[6] The most 'urban' of which are: M. Young and P. Willmott, *Family and Kinship
in East London* (Routledge and Kegan Paul, London, 1957; Penguin,
Harmondsworth, 1962); P. Willmott and M. Young, *Family and Class in a
London Suburb* (Routledge and Kegan Paul, London, 1960; NEL Mentor, 1967);
P. Willmott, *Adolescent Boys of East London* (Routledge and Kegan Paul,
London, 1966).
[7] J. R. Seeley, R. A. Sim and E. W. Loosley, *Crestwood Heights* (Basic Books,
New York, 1956; Science Editions (Wiley), 1963).
[8] B. M. Berger, *Working Class Suburb* (University of California Press, Berkeley,
1960).
[9] W. M. Dobriner, *Class in Suburbia* (Prentice-Hall, Englewood Cliffs, 1963).
[10] In our view the most interesting American attempt to develop a sociology of
community is that of researchers at Brandeis University. See, in particular,
M. R. Stein, *The Eclipse of Community: an Interpretation of American Studies*
(Princeton University Press, Princeton, 1960; Harper Torchbooks, New York,
1964; A. J. Vidich and J. Bensman, *Small Town in Mass Society* (Princeton
University Press, Princeton, 1958; revised edition, 1968), and, in particular,
A. J. Vidich, J. Bensman and M. R. Stein (eds), *Reflections on Community
Studies* (Wiley, New York, 1964; Harper Torchbooks, 1971).
[11] See on this subject the excellent critical note by C. Schmidt in *Sociologie du
Travail* 2 (1965) 190–6.

interest in human ecology, instigated by Schnore and others at the University of Wisconsin.[12] The significance of this work is much greater than its apparently descriptive character would suggest. The important problem of the theoretical status of human ecology is one we shall return to later.

This brief survey, which is merely an attempt to show the theoretical fragmentation of urban research into several branches each with a quite different scientific object, could leave one with the erroneous impression that there is an abundance of such research, even despite its variety. In fact, a rapid review of the recent Anglo-Saxon literature reveals a very small proportion of articles on urban subjects in the leading journals and a very small number of reports published of original research. On the other hand, one finds numerous textbooks and readers on urban life which are in fact concerned with general processes either in the form of a systematic exposition of 'social reality' presented in terms of classical functionalist categories,[13] or else in the form of historicist accounts of social evolution.[14] The ease with which reference is shifted from 'urban society' to 'global society' is a good illustration, from another point of view, of the disappearance of urban sociology as a distinct field of research: the identification of this field with urban society has the consequence of making society *tout court* its field of study. As a matter of fact this is precisely what Martindale was referring to when he linked the disappearance of the city as an autonomous social unit with the disappearance of urban sociology as a theoretical corpus.[15]

The fact of the scientific crisis of urban sociology is emphasized by one of the leaders of the field in the United States, Albert Reiss Jr, in his introduction to one of the best known readers on the subject.[16] It is stressed again by Scott Greer when he describes brilliantly what for him is an intellectual crisis.[17] As Louis Wirth stated, and as indicated

[12] Schnore has recently published a collection of his work under the title *The Urban Scene* (Free Press, New York, 1965). For an example of the work of other members of the team, see K. E. and A. F. Taeuber, White Migration and Socio-Economic Differences between Cities and Suburbs, *American Sociological Review* 29 (1964) 718–29.

[13] In particular, N. P. Gist and S. F. Fava, *Urban Society* (Cromwell, New York, 1964), and in a very Mertonian style, Alvin Boskoff, *The Sociology of Urban Regions* (Appleton Century Crofts, New York, 1962; second edn, 1970).

[14] The most recent such account is J. Sirjamaki, *The Sociology of Cities* (Random House, New York, 1964).

[15] D. Martindale, Prefatory remarks: the theory of the city, in M. Weber, *The City* (Free Press, Glencoe, 1958) 62.

[16] 'The sociology of urban life: 1946–1956', in P. K. Hatt and A. J. Reiss (eds), *Cities and Society* (Free Press, Glencoe, 1957). See p. 21 of the 1964 edition.

[17] See S. Greer, *The Emerging City* (Free Press, Glencoe, 1962) chapter 1.

more recently by the young English sociologist Peter Mann, the basic
issue is the problem of the hypothetical existence of a scientific
object. However even writers, like those mentioned above, who have
identified the problem, have not been able to find a satisfactory
solution to it. This would seem to suggest that it is not sociological
imagination which is lacking but that a real difficulty exists.

The problem is not a purely academic one. The question, whether
the city is simply a real object which has to be reconstituted out of
scientific objects or whether it is a sociological entity itself, has to be
answered before any research is undertaken. In a field where, in our
view, a purely deductive approach is as useless as it is pretentious at
the present time, it is necessary to examine what has really been
achieved in urban sociology up till now, paying particular attention to
recent research in France. The significance of the latter will be judged
in relation to the problematic we shall try to outline.

II The city as a sociological variable

Few disciplines have been so dependent on a particular theoretical
school as urban sociology has been on the Chicago school. Thus it is
not surprising to find that the two main theoretical perspectives which
have dominated the field up till now have been logical developments
from the two pioneer texts of the school: Park's article, 'The city:
suggestions for the investigation of human behaviour in the urban
environment',[18] and Burgess's article, 'The growth of the city: an
introduction to a research project'.[19] The two texts could be
summarized in two words: urbanism and urbanization. Urbanism as a
way of life, urbanization as a process determined by the interaction
between man and environment: these are, in sociological terms, the
real object of urban sociology both in the past and in the present.

1 The city as an independent variable[20]

The research programme put forward by Park includes almost all of
the real processes ever studied by sociology. The field of study is

[18] In R. E. Park, E. W. Burgess and R. D. McKenzie, *The City* (1925) (University
of Chicago Press, Chicago, 1967) 1–46.
[19] *Ibid.*, 47–62.
[20] For the best general picture of the state of research in urban sociology in the
United States, see G. Sjoberg, Comparative urban sociology, in R. K. Merton, L.
Broom and L. S. Cottrell (eds), *Sociology Today* (Basic Books, New York,
1959; Harper Torchbooks 1965) II, 334–59. This picture is developed further
in Sjoberg's contribution to P. M. Hauser and L. F. Schnore (eds), *The Study of
Urbanization* (Wiley, New York, 1965). These two articles have been of
considerable help in guiding us through the bibliographical jungle.

everything which takes place within an urban context. Now, given that the urban population in industrial societies is constantly increasing, this would imply that sociology and urban sociology are becoming identical. An argument of this kind underlies community studies — especially the first major studies (Lynd, Warner, Hollingshead, W. F. Whyte, etc.) — which seek to make exhaustive analyses of local societies following the ethnological tradition.

However, a close examination of the main works of the Chicago school shows that their central focus is not so much everything that takes place in the city but (as is well known) the processes of social disorganization and individual maladjustment, the persistence of autonomous subcultures, deviant or otherwise, and their resistance to integration. It is easy to imagine the striking effect which the social life of the city of Chicago must have had on observers, as it grew by 500,000 persons per decade between 1900 and 1930, immigrants for the most part. But the exceptional character of Chicago resulted not only in the restriction of research to certain aspects of reality, but also in the adoption of a particular theoretical orientation. It was Wirth who was able to make explicit what was implicit in the classical studies by Zorbaugh, Anderson, Thrasher, Reckless, etc.[21] The city was not simply a setting for research, a convenient laboratory, to use Park's description. The city, expressed sociologically in the notion of urbanism (as in the phrase 'urbanism as a way of life'), was also an explanatory variable. The permanent settlement of a human population of high density and with a sufficiently high degree of heterogeneity results in the emergence of a new culture[21a] characterized by the transition from primary to secondary relations, role segmentation, anonymity, isolation, instrumental relations, the absence of direct social control, the diversity and transience of social commitments, the loosening of family ties, and individualistic competition. It is this socio-cultural context which is the ultimate explanation of the new forms of human behaviour.[22] Clearly, urbanism has to be contrasted with another pre-existing culture, rural culture or ruralism.

[21] See L. Wirth, Urbanism as a way of life, *American Journal of Sociology* 44 (1938) 1–24; also in A. J. Reiss (ed.), *Louis Wirth On Cities and Social Life* (University of Chicago Press, Chicago, 1964).
[21a] [The French term for urbanism, *culture urbaine*, brings out the cultural basis of the definition of urbanism.]
[22] See R. Redfield, The folk society, *American Journal of Sociology* 52 (1947) 293–308; H. Miner, The folk-urban continuum, *American Sociological Review* 17 (1952) 529–37.

Despite the flimsiness of this argument, the highly polemical nature of the criticisms directed against it have failed to draw sufficient attention to a basic misunderstanding. Thus, after demonstrating that these studies lack a scientific basis, a number of sociologists have been unable to resist reacting against the reactionary and ideological character of Wirth's writings, or against the rural nostalgia of Redfield; but without however subjecting them to adequate theoretical criticism. Thus Wilensky, after pointing out Wirth's confusion between the effects of industrialization and urbanization, limits himself to denying the effects of social disorganization in cities by describing new forms of social control, thus linking the Chicago school to the theory of mass society.[23]

Now the fundamental point is this: everything described by Wirth as 'urbanism' is in fact the cultural expression of capitalist industrialization, the emergence of the market economy and the process of rationalization of modern society. A writer like Stein, analyzing the works of the pioneers of the community study (Park, Lynd, Warner), shows how they were in fact studying, respectively, the processes of urbanization, industrialization and bureaucratization[24] of American society. Gist and Fava have no hesitation in equating the terms urbanization and modernization — the meaning of the latter term becoming quite clear when it is used synonymously with Westernization to apply to the development of non-modern and non-urban societies.[25] This principle underlies more or less explicitly the whole of 'culturalist' urban sociology, with its heavy emphasis on the 'urban context' — especially when it tackles problems of social disorganization.

Thus the logical deduction may be made that *not only does this branch of urban sociology have a non-specific theoretical object* (viz. everything which takes place within an urban setting) *but it has a different and non-explicit scientific object: the process of acculturation to modern society, i.e. to American society.*

It is this which distinguishes urban sociology from, for example, industrial sociology. Some of our criticisms of urban sociology could in fact apply equally to any branch of sociology which focusses on particular aspects of reality and which lacks a theoretical field.

[23] H. L. Wilensky and C. N. Lebeaux, *Industrial Society and Social Welfare* (Sage Foundation, New York, 1958; Free Press, New York, 1965) chapter 5, Industrialism, Urbanism and Integration.
[24] Stein is referring to Volume IV in the Yankee City Series. W. L. Warner and J. O. Low, *The Social System of the Modern Factory* (Yale University Press, New Haven, 1947).
[25] *Ibid.*, 270—5.

However, it may be possible to argue for the value of a division of labour among researchers in which 'urban sociologists' focus on aspects of reality described as urban but which have to be broken down and reconstituted theoretically according to the particular research problem. As we shall see below, this notion is not without its problems. But even if we were to accept this criterion it would not alter the fact that a good proportion of the research done in urban sociology has an object, scientific this time and not only real, which is in no sense urban, viz. *a sociology of integration.* Despite appearances, we are not criticizing the ideology, albeit manifest, of such a sociology. Social integration is a perfectly legitimate field of study. However, in studying it one must not claim to have obtained a full understanding of urban social life.

At a lower theoretical level the use of urban context as an independent variable may derive from the fact that different urban areas are characterized by different types of behaviour. But the findings to this effect in fact tend to demonstrate the irrelevance of context as an explanatory variable. Thus, if we consider for example research on the variation of interaction patterns according to urban context, we discover that Sweetser found that the determinants of interaction within a small neighbourhood were age and sex,[26] Form showed how the intensity of interaction varied according to the social status of the residential area,[27] and Dotson argued that the pattern of local social participation was restricted to the middle and upper classes;[28] Willmott and Young drew attention to class differences in friendship and kinship behaviour even within the same urban context,[29] while Dobriner in his brilliant study of suburban life asserts that the characteristics of urban areas *are dependent on* their social characteristics.[30] Similar conclusions — which it would be tedious to enumerate — are reached in studies of social participation by Ross, Catton and Smircich, and Axelrod,[31] in Boggs's research on

[26] F. L. Sweetser Jr, A new emphasis for neighbourhood research, *American Sociological Review* 7 (1942) 525–33.
[27] J. Smith, W. H. Form and G. P. Stone, Local intimacy in a middle-sized city, *American Journal of Sociology* 60 (1954) 276–84.
[28] F. Dotson, Patterns of voluntary associations among working-class families, *American Sociological Review* 16 (1951) 687–93.
[29] *Ibid.*
[30] W. M. Dobriner, *op. cit.*
[31] H. L. Ross, Uptown and downtown: a study of middle-class residential areas, *American Sociological Review* 30 (1965) 255–9; M. Axelrod, Urban structure and social participation, *American Sociological Review* 21 (1956) 13–18; W. R. Catton Jr and R. J. Smircich, A comparison of mathematical models for the effect of residential propinquity on mate selection, *American Sociological Review* 29 (1964) 522–9.

criminal areas;[32] and in the very interesting comparative study of
different contexts by Elias and Scotson.[33] In other words, as soon as
the urban context is broken down even into such crude categories as
social class, age or 'interests', processes which seemed to be peculiar to
particular urban areas turn out to be determined by other factors.
However, in those cases where a social unit and a spatial unit coincide,
specific patterns of social interaction may be found. Thus, for
W. H. Whyte, the morning 'Kaffee-Klatsch' pattern found among the
middle-class residents of Park Forest was due to the fact that
people of the same social class and same age group lived together in
spatial proximity and in similar dwellings.[34] Seeley's research on the
middle class in Toronto and Berger's book on the working class come
to a similar conclusion.

These last remarks show that it would perhaps be a mistake to
reject out of hand the notion that spatial factors influence social
behaviour. However, what does now seem quite clear is that space
must be included in the web of social structures, not as a variable
which is independent, but as an element of reality which must be
retranscribed in terms of social processes according to the research
problem in question.

2 The city as a dependent variable

Burgess's work on the concentric zone model of urban growth is the
point of departure for a second theoretical perspective which goes
beyond urban ecology as such. In fact to conceive of the city as a
product of the action of the ecological complex (the interdependent
system of population, environment, technology and social
organization)[35] is equivalent to analyzing it as the product of the
social dynamics of a particular historical and geographical formation.

Where Burgess errs is in (implicitly) presenting as a universal feature
a social process which is found only under particular conditions. Thus
his analysis accounts for a particular type of urban growth, as shown

[32] S. L. Boggs, Urban crime patterns, *American Sociological Review* 30 (1965)
899–908.
[33] N. Elias and J. L. Scotson, *The Established and the Outsiders* (Cass, London,
1965).
[34] W. H. Whyte, *The Organization Man* (Simon and Schuster, New York, 1956;
Penguin, Harmondsworth, 1960) chapter 23.
[35] We do not think it necessary to discuss the human ecology approach in detail.
For a general overview, see the collection edited by G. A. Theodorson, *Studies
in Human Ecology* (Row, Peterson, Evanston, 1961).

by studies in other countries,[36] and in particular Chombart de
Lauwe's study of Paris.[37] Recently, Schnore has studied the fit of
Latin American cities to Burgess's model. By examining seven studies
in depth and reviewing some fifty others,[38] he comes to the
interesting conclusion that they display a different spatial pattern
(with the upper class in the centre of the city and the 'outcasts' in
periphery), but that this pattern and that described by Burgess are
simply two stages in the same process: namely, a process of rapid
industrialization, in a market economy, and without attempts to
control the pattern of urban growth. In fact, Burgess's argument rests
on several implicit assumptions which have been identified by the
orthodox ecologist Quinn: social heterogeneity, a commercial-
industrial city, private property, equally available transport
throughout the city, cheap land available on the periphery of the
agglomeration, and location governed only by the rules of the market.

Within this perspective, Sjoberg's criticism, following Weber, to the
effect that pre-industrial cities are associated with a particular set of
social values,[39] simply requires human ecology to limit historically
what it claimed as biological processes. After all, Firey had clearly
shown the influence of cultural patterns on land use in central
Boston.[40] Similarly, Kolb's analysis of the dynamic structure of the
city as an expression of universalistic and achievement-orientated
values[41] belongs to the same perspective, even if one more factor,
social values, has to be added before the formation of urban space can
be explained.

At this point we are on the verge of rejoining an approach which is
very historicist, very European, and very French: the city is the
product of History, the reflection of society, the action of Man upon

[36] See D. C. McElrath, The social areas of Rome, *American Sociological Review*
27 (1962) 376–91 (esp. 389–90) for one of the most recent studies.
[37] P. H. Chombart de Lauwe *et al.*, *Paris et l'Agglomération Parisienne*, 1,
l'Espace Social dans une Grande Cité (P.U.F., Paris, 1952), see pp. 40–53.
[38] L. F. Schnore, On the spatial structure of cities in the two Americas, in
Hauser and Schnore (eds), *op. cit.*, 347–98.
[39] G. Sjoberg, *The Pre-Industrial City* (Free Press, New York, 1960).
[40] W. Firey, *Land Use in Central Boston* (Harvard University Press, Cambridge
(Mass.), 1947). For a much more sociological approach to the same problem, see
W. H. Form, the place of social structure in the determination of land use,
Social Forces 32 (1954) 317–23. A recent study which follows the same
approach as Firey, but much less convincingly, is by S. Wilhelm, *Urban Zoning
and Land Use Theory* (Free Press, New York, 1962).
[41] W. L. Kolb, The social structure and functions of cities, *Economic
Development and Cultural Change* 3 (1954) 30–46.

space as he constructs his abode. Thus reassured, urban sociology is linked to the future of mankind. And, indeed, how can one take exception to such wise remarks? One cannot. One is obliged to accept the good sense of such a general statement. The real difficulties only start later, when one has to specify a field of study, or, to be more precise, formulate a hypothesis. Having accepted the over-general statement that there is a close relation between social process and space, in urban conditions, it is necessary to specify the nature of this relationship. Is urban space a blank page where social action expresses itself, mediated only by the events of each conjuncture? Or, on the other hand, are there certain regularities in the dialectical process by which social action shapes a context and is in turn influenced by pre-existing forms? The argument according to which space is purely the product of social construction is equivalent to the assertion that culture gives birth to nature, just as the earliest statements of human ecology assume culture to be directly determined by nature. Now it is generally accepted today that sociology understands the social world as an integrated whole in which 'man-made' and 'natural' elements are not only indissolubly linked in reality, but are also impossible to separate analytically. In Park's own statement of the problem, he warns against the twin dangers of a natural history of society and an idealist interpretation of the world:

> The city possesses a moral as well as a physical organization, and these two mutually interact in characteristic ways to mold and modify one another. It is the structure of the city which first impresses us by its visible vastness and complexity. But this structure has its basis, nevertheless, in human nature, of which it is an expression. On the other hand, this vast organization which has arisen in response to the need of its inhabitants, once formed, imposes itself upon them as a crude external fact, and forms them, in turn, in accordance with the design and interests which it incorporates. Structure and tradition are but different aspects of a single cultural complex which determines what is characteristic and peculiar to the city . . .[42]

We have come a long way from the reassuring fields of fact-gathering, so cultivated in urban sociology. However, in our view, a degree of theoretical elaboration is necessary before we can rediscover lines of research enabling us to identify what among the

[42] R. E. Park, op. cit., p. 4.

jumbled mass of studies of the urban phenomenon can be considered as scientific. Clearly the scope of this note is much more limited. Its aim is simply to pose certain problems without being able to advance solutions. And what better to make a splash in the self-satisfied pool of French urban sociology than a 'partisan' examination of the latest products of our factory?

III Some recent contributions by French sociology

We shall not attempt to answer questions such as whether the growing importance of urban sociology in France has any other significance than the devotion of (relatively) large amounts of funds to research on urban problems; as to the extent to which any of the recent French studies contains new theoretical approaches, or shows the way to new approaches; or, on the contrary, whether they are total failures, intellectually speaking. Clearly it would be too difficult to give immediate answers to these questions. Instead, we have preferred to adopt an 'empirical' approach, and review those studies which in our view are the most interesting to have appeared in France in the last two years.

Our reading of these studies has been selective in two senses. Firstly, in terms of our research aims: we have sought to identify the point of theoretical anchorage of each study, rather than make a necessarily over-schematic attempt to describe the discoveries realized.[43] Secondly, we have neither examined the vast mass of planning and descriptive studies of urban social structure,[44] nor a small number of extremely important works which do not however lend themselves to our purposes.[45]

[43] We would be pleased to think we have been able to read these studies in the spirit of, and according to the method set out by, Althusser in L. Althusser and E. Balibar, *Reading Captial* (New Left Books, London, 1970) 13–34.

[44] In particular, we consider as indispensable the studies by research workers at the Institut d'Aménagement et d'Urbanisme de la Région Parisienne, some of which have been published in the *Cahiers de l'I.A.U.R.P.* Similarly, the survey by Paul Clerc on the *'grands ensembles'* [i.e. large housing estates consisting of blocks of flats] constitutes the first rigorous study in this field. See P. Clerc, *Grands Ensembles, Banlieues Nouvelles*, CRU-INED, 'Travaux et Documents' series 49 (P.U.F., Paris, 1967).

[45] Starting with those of the pioneer of urban sociology in France, P-H. Chombart de Lauwe. We have already reviewed in this journal his book, *Paris, Essais de Sociologie, 1952–1964* (Éditions Ouvrières, Paris, 1965); we shall shortly be reviewing the collection of his articles, *Des Hommes et des Villes*, (Payot, Paris, 1965). However, his 'inspiration' is a strong influence in the work of the C.E.G.S. and of Henri Coing, which is included in our analysis. Less directly related to sociology, but of indisputable theoretical relevance are the works of Pierre George, *Sociologie et Géographie* (P.U.F., Paris, 1966) and, in particular, of Jean Labasse, *l'Organisation de l'Espace* (Hermann, Paris, 1966).

To start with, let us leave the city. In the shadow of the historical
city a new society is emerging in the suburbs around the old core. But
are these suburbs autonomous? Should one describe them as *cities*?
Or, on the contrary, as one city and several sub-cities? In order to
measure the pull exerted by Paris on the surrounding suburbs, a
research team from the Centre d'Etude des Groupes Sociaux (now the
Centre de Sociologie Urbaine) carried out a questionnaire survey
among 1,053 households, using a sample stratified by five variables:
distance from the centre of Paris, ease of access to the centre of Paris,
type of dwelling, age and socio-economic status.[46] Technically, the
standard of execution and analysis of this study seems to have been
well above average, for France. Lamy studies the variations in people's
images of Paris according to their area of residence and socio-economic
category. The suburbs were preferred as residential areas, the central
areas of Paris were preferred for shopping and leisure. The historical
buildings of Paris exerted little pull. The centre of the agglomeration
would thus appear to be purely functional, despite Lamy's statement
in the mimeographed report concerning its symbolic role. In a
subsequent study[47] Lamy has attempted to show how people's use of
the centre of Paris depends on social and ecological stratification.
Imbert's work on leisure activity adopts the same approach. While
suburban dwellers make less use of leisure facilities, given the lack of
such facilities in the suburbs, distance from the centre of Paris
strengthens the selective character of the pull exerted by each type of
facility: the higher a person's social status, the less the deterrent effect
of distance in respect of use of certain leisure facilities only found in
the city-centre, especially theatres. But essentially the attractive
power of Paris as opposed to the suburbs is based on its possession of
more extensive leisure facilities. As a logical consequence, there is a
general feeling that such facilities should be de-centralized in favour of
the suburbs. Among suburban dwellers, then, there is an attitude of
indifference to Paris itself and an awareness of the shortage of facilities

[46] C. Cornuau, M. Imbert, B. Lamy, P. Rendu and J. Retel, *l'Attraction de Paris
sur sa Benlieue, Etude Sociologique*, 'L'évolution de la vie sociale' series
(Editions Ouvrières, Paris, 1965), and also C.E.G.S., *l'Attraction de Paris sur sa
Banlieue, Observations Complémentaires* (Paris, 1964—5) (mimeo.) [The studies
referred to in the next three paragraphs are all described in these publications.]
[47] B. Lamy, La fréquentation du centre-ville par les différentes catégories
sociales, *Sociologie du Travail* 2 (1967) 164—79. (Translated as The use of the
inner city of Paris and social stratification, in University of Amsterdam,
Sociographical Department, *Urban Core and Inner City*, Proceedings of the
International Study Week, Amsterdam, 11—17 September 1966 (Brill, Leiden,
1967) 356—67).

and the handicap imposed by material obstacles (distance, family situation, etc.).

The potential autonomy of the suburban centres is also referred to in the meticulous report by Cornuau and Rendu on the places used by suburban dwellers for large and infrequent purchases: the proportion of these purchases made in Paris varies inversely with the range of shopping facilities available in the residential locality. However, the crucial (and cumulative) determinants of shopping for large items in Paris are: working in Paris, having a middle-class occupation, and having been born in Paris.

The study which, in our view, is the most sociological is that by Retel on social relationships in the Paris agglomeration. After demonstrating the importance of kinship relations, he asks the basic question, how are social relationships spatially structured? He discovers two patterns; in the first, which is characteristic of residents in the former villages now enclosed within the suburban area, and in particular of working-class districts, social interaction is restricted to a very small area. In the second pattern, which is characteristic of residents of Paris and to a lesser extent of residents in newly-developed suburban areas, family and friendship relations are dispersed throughout the agglomeration as a whole — despite the dissatisfaction caused by long journeys. For people in this second category, it is better transport facilities throughout the agglomeration which are sought, rather than improvements in the immediate residential area. As Retel puts it,

> urban social activity, after passing through a phase of territorial structuration, is going to be reinvigorated by a period of sociological structuration in which relations between groups with no necessary territorial basis will become crucial. (p. 116)

This amounts to a recognition that social activity is not restricted within particular areas of the city and consequently that the analysis of urban social relations is identical with that of social relations *tout court*.

If social relations are becoming dispersed throughout space, if the pull of the city centre is more functional than symbolic, if the use made of leisure facilities depends on accessibility rather than the existence of an urban core, if shopping for large items in Paris also depends on daily accessibility, then one is witnessing the disappearance of every factor which makes an urban centre a social nucleus. The urban centre is thus nothing more than the cumulation

in a geographical area of a collection of functions which should be
decentralized to improve access to them. The authors' conclusion that
new urban centres should be created in the Paris region is thus, in our
view, a purely personal option. In effect, there is no necessity for a
new cumulation of functions apart from the *parti pris* against a
'human unit which has become too large and too anonymous because
poorly structured' (p. 274).

Whilst this extensive study throws much new light on
socio-ecological processes in the Paris region and on attitudes and
images regarding various parts of the agglomeration, it is ultimately
disappointing in that from the very outset it makes no attempt at
sociological explanation: it constructs nothing more than 'ad hoc'
variables and uses for analytical purposes what should only be
sampling categories. In the absence of a specific theoretical
framework, it is impossible to link socio-economic categories and
spatial behaviour unless one has recourse to the vague notion of
sub-cultures whose existence is neither generally demonstrated nor
established in particular cases. Finally, then, explanation is in terms of
a theory of needs and aspirations, frustrated or satisfied by natural
obstacles (such as distance) or social barriers (such as socio-economic
status).

In order to show the lack of coordination and deep-seated
particularism of the various teams working in the field of urban
sociology, let us enter another world which has almost no theoretical
connexion with the one we have just explored. Let us be guided by
the Institut de Sociologie Urbaine through the world of the detached
home.[48] This study is based on a semantic analysis of 265
non-directive interviews with owners of detached homes in eleven
localities spread throughout France; a small number of inhabitants of
collectively or jointly-owned homes was also interviewed. The sample
was designed to include a variety of social situations but not to be
representative, the statistical analysis serving only to help grasp the

[48] Institut de Sociologie Urbaine (Paris), *l'Habitat Pavillonaire. Attitude des Citadins* (Centre de Recherche d'Urbanisme, Paris, 1966) (mimeo.). (Report; Appendix 1, The historical development of the detached house in France, and analysis of ideologies; Appendix 2, The sample; Appendix 3, Analysis of interviews). While the authors of this first report on the study are unnamed, the team was directed by Henri Lefebvre and the main researchers were Antoine Haumont, Nicole Haumont, Henri Raymond and Marie-Geneviève Raymond. (See also N. Haumont, *Les Pavillonaires. Etude Psycho-sociale d'un Mode d'Habitat* (C.R.U., Paris, 1966), and M. G. Raymond, *La Politique Pavillonaire* (C.R.U., Paris, 1966).)

ideology of owners of detached homes and not to explain their
behaviour. However, in the first part of the study, based on a very
thorough historical and documentary analysis, the development of the
detached home in France is related to State policy and social forces,
and also to ideologies expressed in planning literature. By placing the
detached home in a historical context it is easy to see the links
between uncontrolled urbanization and the success of the myth of the
detached home, at once a reformist reaction against collectivism and
the instrument of an ideology of order and austerity. Centred on the
notion of the family as a self-sufficient unit, this myth is the product
both of a bourgeoisie seeking social integration and of the deficiencies
of a style of collective housing lacking any real collective life.
However, while it is a simple matter to link the development of the
detached home to general social changes when policy or doctrinal
statements exist, it is less so when no such organized statements of
intention exist, i.e. when the features which connect social dynamics
with a particular fact, attachment to the detached home, have to be
detected through an analysis of the social structure. For the I.S.U.
research team such an analysis meant not an analysis of motivations,
but a study of the social roots of an ideology, the ideology of the
detached home. Hence the research project described, which appears
to be the first stage in a larger research programme, and which consists
primarily of analyses of the detached home as an expressive object, of
the interior of the detached house as a symbolic system, and of the
ideology of the detached home as a communication code for messages
between inhabitant and society. This symbolic system is meticulously
reconstructed through the coding of interviews. While the method is
not in our view very rigorous,[49] especially in the absence of a
definition of the semantic field of each term prior to the choice of the
term as a signifier or signified, one cannot but be seduced by the
penetration of certain of the analyses.

This study belongs to what might be called the 'clinical sociology'
group of studies, more concerned with depth observation than with
the establishment of regularities. Now, the value of observation of this
type depends on its being made within a theoretical system. And in
the present case this system is not made fully explicit. Nevertheless, a
picture of the internal space of the detached house is built up little by
little, revealing a world which is closed but capable of being invested

---

[49] This comment is based on intuition rather than firm conviction given our
admitted lack of competence in semantic analysis.

with meaning. The detached house represents order and
self-sufficiency: it acts as a stable and thus secure receptacle for the
expression of an individuality whose limits are set differently
according to the pattern of interaction chosen. But this does not
imply a straightforward identification with conservative ideology. In
fact, the difficulty of linking the symbolic system of the detached
house with the ideology of the detached home is due to the difficulty
of analysing the latter without linking it to a general analysis of
societal ideologies. Simply by examining the associations made in
everyday life we can get a glimpse of the links between the ideology
of order and stability represented by the ideology of the detached
home, on the one hand, and the deliberately and wisely restricted
world of the internal space of the detached house on the other.
However, we doubt whether it is possible to use the same approach to
study the connexion between symbolic system and social practice. A
system of signs can only refer back to other signs, i.e. in this case to
other ideological systems. If the origin of the link between these
ideological systems and actors is to be grasped directly, an analysis in
terms of structures of social action is required, since a straightforward
historical analysis would merely mean once again placing the systems
of signs 'in context' and the link could not be more than a statement
of belief.

In our view, the importance of the study, or at least of those parts
of it discussed above, is that it breaks with the purely functional
approach of studies within the main tradition of housing research. A
dwelling is more than a way of satisfying needs. Even if one were to
improve the quality of collective dwellings there are still certain
internal layouts with an expressive quality which satisfies people's
'impulses' and 'frustrations' better than others. (There appears to be
an implicit reference here to a psychoanalytic interpretation which
seeks to link the symbolic system of the dwelling with the personality,
just as the analysis of the social structures of ideology would link this
world with society as a whole). In our view the major innovation of
this study lies precisely in the way in which aspects of the
dwelling-space are transcribed into units of analysis themselves related
together as a system, without leaving the chosen level of analysis, i.e.
the level of signs. The detached home is thus no longer a social fact
but a sign, and its world a world of signs. Is this an example of a truly
urban semiology? Perhaps. But only in so far as aspects of space need
to be specifically retranscribed at the level of signs. To go on to prove
that a closed system of signs coincides with an urban community

could be a possible way forward for the urban semiology initiated by this study of the detached style of dwelling.

From a quite different perspective, another team at the I.S.U., under the direction of Henri Lefebvre, has studied the place of the neighbourhood in the city.[50] After a vigorous denunciation of the neighbourhood ideology as an integrationist ideology, Lefebvre poses the real sociological problem. Is the neighbourhood a unit of social life or not? Is there a coincidence between 'social space and geometrical space'? Does the local community have a social network equivalent at the level of the neighbourhood? In our opinion, a real theoretical problematic is involved here. Unfortunately the research which follows not only fails to supply any answers but even fails to provide itself with the means to do so. The study consists of two historical and geographical monographs, one on the urban development of Argenteuil and Choisy-le-Roi, the other on a typology of neighbourhoods in Suresnes, Vitry and Choisy-le-Roi. The first study describes the disruption caused by rapid urban growth induced by industrialization, and the opportunities for local social activity (conceived largely in terms of participation in associations). But local social activity is approached in terms of institutions. Now given that institutional decision-making centres are located outside the neighbourhood, at the district level, it is concluded that neighbourhood activity is non-existent, and that opportunities for contact based on local facilities should be improved. In our view, the purely descriptive character of the study and the restriction of the analysis to the manifest level rules out any possibility of verifying the initial hypothesis.

The second study, of three neighbourhoods, leads to a typology based on land-use. We are then told that the next and essential step is to link the differential use of land to the strategies of the social and economic forces throughout the history of the locality. At this point we encounter a truism which is fairly widespread in French urban sociology. It has become customary to produce, with almost mechanical regularity, studies in which demographic and urban changes, as reflected in employment, land use and housing density, are linked to the dates at which factories opened, local elections took place, etc. Now this tells us strictly nothing for no one is foolish

[50] I.S.U., Le quartier et la ville, *Cahiers de l'I.A.U.R.P.* 7 (March 1967), comprising Neighbourhood and neighbourhood life by H. Lefebvre, City and neighbourhood by M. Coornaert and C. Harlaut, and Neighbourhoods in three localities in the Paris region by A. Haumont.

enough to deny that the pattern of change in a given area can be
divorced from the wider pattern of social change (or if such people
still exist, they can be safely ignored . . .). Real research starts
afterwards. In what way does a particular social structure contribute
to the creation of the area concerned? To answer this, it is not enough
to describe particular events; one must first have a theory of the
creation of space which cannot be a social history of that space. While
the notion of totality is fruitful for situating a problem and ensuring
the mutual consistency of partial approaches, it is tautologous merely
to juxtapose totality and event. It is this which seems to have
prevented the study from succesfully pursuing the very rich approach
indicated at the start.

Perhaps the most seductive of recent French urban sociological
studies is Henri Coing's study of the renewal of Block No. 4 in the
13th *arrondissement* in Paris.[51] Beautifully written, very much in the
style of an Oscar Lewis, the book attempts to reconstruct a process of
social change in quasi-experimental terms. What happens when the
bulldozers arrive in an old and dilapidated neighbourhood which
forms a veritable hub of social activity, and the foundations are laid of
the skyscrapers-to-be.

Coing starts by reconstructing a picture of the neighbourhood
community. This is based on an examination of documentary and
statistical material, on the observation of several families and on
semi-directive interviews with a non-representative sample of sixty
households. The community depicted is based not on images but on a
number of ecological and social characteristics: multiplicity of
activities, residential stability, proximity of workplaces, the
importance of retail shops with highly personalized relations between
shopkeeper and customer, and, in particular, working-class
occupations. Ultimately it is the presence in the area of a
working-class sub-culture which is conducive to the existence of the
complete system of social relations observed. Coing is not entirely
successful in distinguishing between the somewhat mythical and
over-harmonious image of the community held by the residents (who
were questioned, remember, after the renewal process had started)
and the actual social relationships existing in the neighbourhood.
Oscar Lewis gives a quite different picture in *Children of Sanchez*, and
his study of Tepoztlan is an attempt, succesful in our view, to uncover

---

[51] H. Coing, *Rénovation Urbaine et Changement Social* 'L'évolution de la vie
sociale' series (Editions Ouvrières, Paris, 1966).

social conflicts in the very place Redfield claimed to have found a prototypical integrated community.[52] In any case, Coing gives an accurate definition of the neighbourhood from the sociological point of view since he presents a picture of a single complex of relationships, in which cultural and material elements are closely interdependent. The equilibrium of this world is shattered by the renewal operation since, when the houses are demolished, changes occur throughout the whole structure. But a different set of changes might have come about, and in fact another process of dissolution was already taking place as the sub-culture of the block was penetrated by what Coing calls 'urban life', i.e. the dominant culture of urban society. The specific product of renewal is an accelerated rate of disintegration of the pre-existing world — with the attendant difficulties of adjustment for certain individuals. But Coing rightly rejects the hasty and paternalist interpretation which underlies explanation in terms of resistance to change. Renewal is a process of social mobility. For those who are capable of perceiving the opportunities it offers, mobility is upwards. For those who are not, it means being thrown into the lower strata of the urban agglomeration where those who are left aside by economic growth are becoming concentrated. The differential ability to perceive opportunities for mobility is explained not in terms of psychological adjustment but in social structural terms. First, one needs economic resources, and, secondly, a high proportion of these resources must be disposable: this depends on family size, the age of the couple and whether the wife works, much less than an occupational category. But Coing indicates that differences in economic level are not the whole explanation. Attitude to the new urban life is also important. In between those who react by withdrawing into the former mode of life on the one hand, or by unreservedly embracing innovation on the other, there are also those who see the new urban culture as a consumption race and devote themselves to keeping up their position in it. It is at this point, in our view, that a descriptive typology proves insufficient and it is necessary to grasp the orientations to modernity which govern these different reactions. However, the picture is complete, the problem clearly stated. The neighbourhood community loses its distinctive identity and is swallowed up in the wider urban culture. For Coing this is an inescapable fact. This change occurs all

[52] O. Lewis, Tepoztlan restudied. A critique of the folk-urban conceptualization of social change, *Rural Sociology* 18 (1953) 121–34.

the more easily when the group is parted from its particular
sub-culture, in this case a working-class sub-culture; and when
individuals are linked to global society through a variety of relations
and in a variety of settings. Those who cannot accept change either
become withdrawn or crack up.

The only serious criticism we would make of this study is that the
argument is not rigorously demonstrated. By this we are not simply
referring to the lack of quantification or lack of statistical analysis.
Even a 'field study' must start from a clearly-defined theoretical
framework and then go on to derive indicators, provide relevant
evidence for each observation, and establish a logical link between
observations and hypotheses. Coing presents a consistent account
which we personally find convincing. But, in order to contribute to
the accumulation of knowledge which every science aims at, this is
not enough. The study results in a very useful set of hypotheses.
They still require verification, either statistically or by systematic
observation. Moreover, it is worth pointing out that it is in no way
inconsistent to use statistical techniques to verify the conclusions of
'qualitative' studies.

The most important recent contribution to the theory of the city
made by French-language sociology is the work of a Belgian
economist.[53] Although it is an economic study we shall discuss it
below, partly because it displays a considerable openness towards
sociology, but mainly because its theoretical aim seems to us
exemplary and deserves to be followed in sociology.

Rémy poses at the outset the question of the distinctiveness of the
city within economic theory.

> Is the city simply a field in which theories developed to account
> for other aspects of the economic system may be applied, or is the
> city an original economic unit irreducible to any other? (p. 13)

For Rémy this question must be answered before any concrete
research is undertaken or any measuring instruments constructed. He
then proceeds to a systematic analysis of the mass of economic and
sociological studies of urban and spatial questions in order to be able
to determine some of the respects in which the city is a distinctive
entity from an economic point of view.

To start with, the city is defined in terms of juxtaposition deriving

[53] J. Rémy, *La Ville, phénomène économique* (Editions 'Vie Ouvrière', Brussels, 1966).

from economies of scale. The latter refer to the advantages ؛
from the spatial clustering of functions and firms, which coulᵈ
otherwise gained. What is crucial is this juxtaposition and the
interdependent set of fixed and moveable elements which constitᵘ
it — rather than the particular space in which it is located — and wh
can be explained in historical, but not economic, terms. These
advantages can be summed up in two words: *exchange* and, in
particular, *innovation*. From this point of view the city is seen as a
source of knowledge. In so far as information and innovation are the
basis of the most advanced industries in the most technologically
developed societies, the city becomes not a dysfunctional 'urban
monster' but a prerequisite of economic growth. Rémy also sees the
city as a general form of organization of space favouring the creation
of collective goods which in turn determine the value of individual
goods. The city is the realm of choice, the context for processes of
social and geographical mobility. But these advantages to the
individual are the product of the urban environment as a whole, i.e. of
the juxtaposition of productive units and exchange centres, and the
functional diversity of urban space enabling people to move from one
environment to another within the same system of interdependences.
In other words, the city is characterized more by a flexible pattern of
social organization resulting from the complexity of the system than
by a distinctive urban culture.

What we find most interesting are Rémy's comments on urban
social life. Thus, if the city is the realm of centrifugal forces such as
choice, exchange, and innovation, these forces must be re-integrated at
the level of the consumption process itself, viz. through the housing
system. Thus, for example, role segmentation is accompanied by the
symbolic differentiation of urban space which facilitates the choice of
associates, opportunities for interaction, and hence the creation of
environments which are relatively homogeneous in terms of social
status, if not of life-style. We have thus moved from considering the
function of an urban area as a neighbourhood to its symbolic
function.

Furthermore, the city is not a locus of social disorganization, as is
often asserted, but on the contrary it is the locus of acculturation to
'modern life', i.e. to the process of rapid change characteristic of
industrial society. What characterizes the urban environment is
precisely its two-fold capacity to produce the innovations necessary to
economic growth, and, at the same time, to provide a form of social
organization which is not only receptive to innovation but ensures its

re-integration. Conversely, industrialism is a source of change in the urban environment: it too is a structured system whose main features are a recognition of innovation and exchange as driving forces and its necessary counterpart a capacity for social absorption.

It is in terms of such broad theoretical perspectives that the problem of urban sociology deserves to be posed.

IV In search of the lost object

We would like to introduce some order into the ideas arising out of our reading of these studies as a first and provisional result of our critique. We simply wish to take some steps towards an approach which has so far been too little explored for a definitive statement to be near at hand.

To start with we must stop using terms such as 'urban behaviour' or 'urban attitudes'. Such phrases are, if not confusing, at best umbrella terms. They presuppose an *urban culture* which derives its character from its urban origin and which is thus necessarily contrasted to a rural culture. Now, as we have seen, 'urban culture' is a misleading description for the culture of industrial societies. Sjoberg's study, for example, shows that even large pre-industrial cities exist which do not display the supposedly urban characteristics. Similarly, Weber concluded that the Western city was unique in spite of the fact that urban agglomerations existed elsewhere. Mann shows that quantifiable differences between city and country are much smaller when the comparison is made *at the same date* and not, as is generally the case, for the same settlement at different points in time.[54] And moreover it is readily admitted that the characteristic features of urban culture are to be found in rural villages: but this is attributed to the penetration of rural culture by urban culture. . . . It would be absurd to deny that differences exist between city and country. What we do maintain, however, is that the fundamental features of this urban culture are the direct consequence of industrialization, and, in certain cases, of capitalist industrialization. It is true, nevertheless, that the concentration of a large population, the diversity of social milieux, and the juxtaposition of a variety of functions in space favour the emergence of a pattern of social relations different from that possible in the village community. But this is part of the movement towards industrial society. Too often

[54] P. H. Mann, *An Approach to Urban Sociology* (Routledge and Kegan Paul, London, 1965) 28–68.

social change is analyzed in terms of single factors such as industrialization or urbanization. In fact, what is necessary is to reconstruct the complex system of social elements, including both values and the 'material' base which is transformed in the process of producing change. Let us consider two examples. Firstly, the arrangement of housing in large cities is such as to encourage role segmentation. But rapid urbanization is the result of industrialization. And capitalist industrialization is based on the treatment of labour as a commodity which presupposes and causes a breakdown in social ties and an atomization of the labour force. [Thus the spatial arrangement of housing cannot be understood in isolation from the process of capitalist industrialization: it is both affected by and congruent with the demands of the latter.] Secondly, social classes emerge as actors as industrialization proceeds. But their organization is based on actual social groups, one of whose sources is precisely socio-ecological segregation. And so on. The purpose of these examples is simply to indicate the impossibility — even analytic — of treating in isolation the effects of urbanization *at the level of the total culture* of so-called 'urban' society.

We saw earlier that the mass of studies — in particular those of the Chicago school — focussing on processes of adjustment to urban culture, formed a vast sociology of integration, extended by a sociology of change presented as a transition from rural (traditional) society to urban (modern) society. However, while we deny that the urban context in general has any specific effects, we recognize that particular urban contexts and also certain non-urban contexts (such as villages) may have such effects. This might suggest a possible basis for a sociology of community, a possibility we shall return to later.

While the urban context does not constitute a specific scientific object for urban sociology, the city can still be analyzed as an aspect of reality, making use of the theoretical approach appropriate to the particular question posed. But even a definition of urban sociology based on the idea of the city as an aspect of reality is by no means clear, as it might be, for example, in the case of the sociology of the firm or the sociology of education. Thus, having agreed to study the 'city-as-it-is', it remains unclear what precise entity is being referred to: the city, the agglomeration, the urban region? And which aspects are to be studied. Social classes? The use people make of the city-centre? Housing satisfaction? The symbolic attraction of historical buildings? Transport? Air pollution? Neighbourhood social participation? Voting in local elections? Residential mobility?

Industrial location? Urban renewal? Clearly such a list is theoretically disparate. And yet all these subjects are referred to as 'urban sociology'. As the spatial setting of social life becomes almost entirely 'urban' the subject-matter of urban sociology becomes limitless and urban sociology becomes general sociology.

So be it. However, two things remain to be done. On the one hand, different levels of analysis must be distinguished; and on the other hand, for each level isolated, space must be coded in order to explicate the link between social processes and the ecological system.

First let us consider the different levels of analysis. The study of a city can be conceived as the study of 'society' as seen through a particular spatial entity, in the same way that sociology has usually been conceived as the study of social action via a particular historical entity. The aim is to uncover through a spatial cross-section the same processes which are usually revealed through a temporal cross-section.

Four levels of analysis may be distinguished.

At a pre-sociological level the history of the spatial entity as such may be studied. This is the particular field of human ecology which attempts such an analysis both in terms of change over time and in terms of synchronic interdependence.

At a second level, the local society may be analyzed as a social system. The residents of a house or street, for example, may be analyzed by coding them as actors and studying their system of interaction. Sometimes the residents of a street will not be linked together into a social network. In this case the real object (residents of the street) cannot be transformed into a scientific object (the social system of the street) — unless the street were to disappear and the social networks of each individual were made the subject of study. Clearly the logic of this approach is to search for a system of interaction rather than to study separate individuals as such.

In the same way, at a third level, if we wish to understand some aspect of a system of historical action,[55] e.g. a social movement, it would be pointless to search for social classes in the *grands ensembles*.

[55] Although there is no room to discuss it further here, the term 'system of action' derives from work in progress around Alain Touraine's seminar. The absence of research illustrating the concepts derived from this work should not prevent us from recognizing the level of sociological analysis involved, which in our view is fundamental though barely begun, viz. the scientific study of the processes of formation and transformation of a society. The importance of this approach is in no way thrown into question by the difficulties and contradictions of particular theoretical constructions which adopt it.

Rather the subject of the social movement [e.g. social class on which it is based] must be defined beforehand in relation to the issue one wishes to study, and then reconstructed in reality.

It must be noted that the penetration of 'urban society' by 'society' *tout court*, i.e. the disappearance of the city as a scientific object and even as a real object, is not equivalent to the widespread image of the city as a projection of society on space. This approach implicitly refers to a fourth level of analysis, namely a semiological approach. In fact, if the city is a *projection* the approach necessary is the reverse of that usually adopted. Instead of studying a system of social relations or a process of action which occurs, like everything else, in this social agglomeration described as the city, one would *read* the city. The physical objects and ecology of the agglomeration would be treated as signs. At this point three possibilities are open: (1) one could remain at the semantic level and attempt to uncover an internally consistent system of signs, (2) one could assume that the city exists as a local society with its own organization, and attempt to verify this assumption by examining the correspondence between the organization of signifiers and that of signifieds, or (3) one could carry out a sort of social archaeology (the most usual choice) and reconstruct past society through the traces it has left in buildings, streets and factories.

Whichever of the four approaches we adopt, the term 'urban' is irrelevant. However, for the time being we would not wish to push our iconoclasm regarding urban sociology to the extreme limit. Particularly in view of the fact that here and there we have uncovered some faint indicators that urban sociology might after all have some specific object. What we would like to examine, though, is under what conditions a sociology could be defined as urban from the point of view of its scientific object.

In our opinion this possibility exists when there is a coincidence between a spatial unit and a social unit, whether the latter is a social system, a system of action, or a system of signs [i.e. whichever of the last three levels of analysis described is adopted].

To give a clearer picture of this possibility let us compare the city with the firm. Like the city, the firm too is a real object and penetrated by general social processes. And yet the sociology of the firm is a recognized field. But sociologically, a sociology of the firm exists because there exists a sociology of organization, and, though this may be less clear, because there exists a sociology of the

institution. In other words, because a real entity, the firm, coincides
with a system of statuses and roles; and in addition because this real
entity is also a collection of means orientated towards a specific end.

Let us transpose this to urban sociology. We felt we had found a
specific object for urban sociology wherever we referred to
community, i.e. whenever an ecological unit coincided with a 'unit of
social life', with a social system usually consolidated by a sub-culture
which was itself reinforced by the spatial boundaries of the area.
Coing's study undoubtedly concerned an urban community. But the
coincidence of spatial units with social units is not exclusive to urban
sub-cultures. It is also characteristic of what is often described as a
village, e.g. by Redfield. The term 'urban villagers',[56] for example,
causes no surprise. Thus, we are not dealing with a transition from
rural to urban but with the process by which community sub-cultures
are destroyed by 'mass culture', i.e. by the socially dominant
culture. Viewed in terms of social change one might refer to the
separation between spatial units and social units. But the sociological
study of this phenomenon requires that one start from a particular
sub-unit and analyze its penetration by global society, either
culturally (as described by Retel) or through the disintegration of the
ecological base (as described by Coing).

The question of an autonomous urban sociology can also be
approached at another level of analysis: one could speak of *urban
institution* (or more simply, city) whenever an ecological area
coincided with an autonomous system of action. By the latter we
mean a system in which the production process on which every
institutional system is based is re-integrated through a complimentary
process of organization. The complete lack of urban studies
undertaken from this point of view makes it difficult to imagine what
this would imply. But this approach is foreshadowed by Weber's
definition of the city in terms of political-administrative autonomy
within a given economic base and spatial agglomeration.[57] The
political-administrative system is the institutionalized expression of a
system of action.

Referring back to the ideas of Rémy, the environment of
innovation and the complementary process of social reorganization
enabling accelerated change to be assimilated which exist in industrial

[56] H. J. Gans, *The Urban Villagers* (Free Press, New York, 1962), a study of a
working-class Italian neighbourhood in Boston.
[57] Max Weber, *The City*, 74.

societies represent a system of action since they are at the root of the process by which such societies are formed. If the city is indeed the spatial form of this complex, is it not an example of that ecological-spatial compound that might be termed urban institution?

The study of the existence or otherwise of communities and urban institutions, of the conditions contributing to their formation, and of their links with other elements in the social structure, might then be a relatively distinct field of study.

However, the precarious bases of such an approach are easy to see. On the one hand, urban communities of the type described are on the whole vague recollections in industrial societies and by studying them it would be very easy to restrict oneself to an analysis of social change conceived in terms of the imposition of 'external' forces on actors. Only the discovery of new forms of spatially-delimited systems of social relations could rekindle interest in this line of research. On the other hand, it is very difficult to imagine an 'urban system of action'. Even the example given above, that of Weber, shows the historical particularity of such a situation. Only the study of New Towns would enable this question to be answered. Can New Towns be seen as the spatial expression of systems of action? Or are they merely mediated expressions of one element of the system of action underlying the policy followed by a society? Perhaps a last major research project for urban sociology would be one in which the impossibility of its having any scientific autonomy would be empirically demonstrated.

The questions we have discussed are merely isolated examples of a possible commentary on the possible scientific content of this sociology which seeks to link social processes and elements of space. The difficulties we have encountered in doing so are a good illustration of the severity of the crisis indicated. If a sociological paradox were still necessary it would not be the least of paradoxes, namely, that after fifty years existence only one subject for research in urban sociology remains untackled: its subject-matter.

3 Manuel Castells

Theory and ideology in urban sociology*

A science may immediately be distinguished by its possession of a specific theoretical object, itself a response to a social demand for knowledge of some aspect of concrete reality.

The scientific object of a discipline is constituted by the set of concepts developed to account for the various real objects the science is claimed to analyze. It is thus possible to conceive of the application of a science to a particular domain of reality: in such a case one would talk of specialized theoretical activity. However, a science either general or particular which has neither a specific theoretical object nor a specific real object does not exist as a science. This does not mean that it may not have an institutional existence, in so far as it is socially recognized as capable of producing knowledge.

However, if its only distinctiveness is institutional, this is because it produces not knowledge but misknowledge or displaced knowledge, i.e. which concerns theoretical objects other than those it claims to be analyzing. Such an activity is not theoretical but ideological. Every science in fact consists of a mixture, which varies according to circumstances, of ideology and theory. Sometimes ideological activity receives the institutional consecration 'science', in order to legitimate it. In such a case the little theoretical knowledge it produces is produced *in spite of* the straightjacket of ideology. *Urban sociology is an ideology.* We shall attempt to demonstrate and define this ideology and describe the social function it fulfills.

I. The misadventures of a pioneer: from social worker to technocrat

To start with we shall give a rapid outline of the main features of urban sociology as it has existed in the past.

While analyses of industrialization from Marx to Durkheim and Weber certainly took the existence of cities into account, and even emphasized their role (e.g. Weber in *Economy and Society*), the

*[Translated with permission of Less Presses de l'Université de Montreal, Montreal, from M. Castells, Théorie et idéologie en sociologie urbaine, *Sociologie et Sociétés* 1 (1969) 171–90.]

formulation of a sociological theory of the city as such had to await the Chicago school, and in particular the publication of Park, Burgess and McKenzie's work, *The City*, in 1925.[1] The first three chapters of this book in fact foreshadow all the subsequent developments of the discipline.[2]

Park saw in the city a new society, a laboratory offering the sociologist the full range of new social phenomena, and, in particular, the problems linked to the integration and cohesion of a social formation undergoing very rapid change. He foreshadows the urbanism theme which, when taken up later and developed by Wirth, is to serve as one of the foundation stones of urban sociology and as favourite theme in discourses on social change.

Burgess establishes the existence of a relationship between economic development, social transformations and the organization of space, by means of his famous concentric zone theory of urban growth, a theory which does not seek any naive empirical generalization but rather a demonstration of the dependence of space, and hence of the city, on a given social structure.[3] The notion of the city as a product of society underlies the historicist approach in urban sociology in the United States (Mumford, Sjoberg, Firey, Form, etc.) and has had a particular attraction for European and especially French sociologists (Chevalier, Lefebvre).[4]

McKenzie uses the organic analogy of Malinowskian functionalism and treats the city as an ecological system whose conditions of functioning he attempts to establish. Hawley provides a new systematization of the ecological approach initiated by McKenzie, which goes beyond the analysis of relationships to space to a conception of society as a hierarchy of spatially defined human

[1] See Don Martindale, Prefatory remarks: the theory of the city, Introduction to Max Weber, *The City* (Free Press, New York, 1966) 9–62.
[2] R. E. Park, The city: suggestions for the investigation of human behaviour in the urban environment; E. W. Burgess, The growth of the city; and R. D. McKenzie, The ecological approach to the study of human community; all in Park, Burgess and McKenzie, *The City* (1925) (University of Chicago Press, 1967).
[3] See, on this subject, Schnore's discussion of the concentric zone theory: L. F. Schnore, On the spatial structure of cities in the two Americas, in P. M. Hauser and L. F. Schnore (eds), *The Study of Urbanization* (Wiley, New York, 1965) 347–99.
[4] See, in particular, Lewis Mumford, *The City in History* (Harcourt, Brace and World, New York, 1961); Gideon Sjoberg, *The Pre-Industrial City* (Free Press, New York, 1960); Walter Firey, *Land Use in Central Boston* (Harvard University Press, Boston, 1947); W. H. Form, The place of social structure in the determination of land use, *Social Forces* 32 (1954) 317–23; Henri Lefebvre, *le Droit à la Ville* (Editions Anthropos, Paris, 1968).

communities.[5] Later, Duncan develops the notion of ecological
complex[6] which is, in fact, also a theory of regulation and change of
the community as a social system in terms of the interaction of the
four component elements of the ecological complex: environment,
population, technology and social organization.

A specific cultural system, producing the new norms and values
characteristic of modern societies; space as shaped by the
transformations of the socio-economic structure; a self-adjusting
ecological organism responding to new needs created inside it or
induced from outside; these then are the themes around which urban
sociology's attempts at theoretical definition have focussed.

In addition to these central themes there have been analyses of
other real objects from theoretical perspectives related to one or other
of the three perspectives mentioned. For example, the analysis of
urban social disorganization (and, in particular, of individual
pathology and marginality) is part of the tradition of urban sociology
in so far as one accepts the existence of an urban culture (urbanism),
produced by population density and heterogeneity, and which
explains the disappearance of mechanical solidarity or the eclipse of
community, and the consequent high rate of social disorganization.[7]

On the other hand, community studies, which are often confused
with urban sociology, have been able to assert their independence,
either by emphasizing their links with the anthropological tradition
(the holistic study of social microcosms),[8] or, as is increasingly the
case, by specializing in the study of power and influence networks in
the management of the local system, an easier task than at the
national level.[9] It is quite clear, in fact, that the central notion in
these studies is not 'urban', but 'community', conceived as a closed
system of social relations. Moreover, the notion of community has
been rediscovered in units which are not spatially defined, such as
industrial firms and organizations (e.g. occupations, or social

[5] A. H. Hawley, *Human Ecology* (Ronald Press, New York, 1950).
[6] O. D. Duncan, Human ecology and population studies, in P. M. Hauser and
O. D. Duncan (eds), *The Study of Population* (University of Chicago Press,
Chicago, 1959) 681–4.
[7] See M. B. Clinard, The relation of urbanization and urbanism to criminal
behaviour, in E. W. Burgess and D. J. Bogue (eds), *Contributions to Urban
Sociology* (University of Chicago Press, Chicago, 1964) 541–59.
[8] See J. Bensman, M. Stein and A. Vidich, *Reflections on Community Studies*
(Wiley, New York, 1964).
[9] See in particular the excellent synthesis by N. W. Polsby, *Community Power
and Political Theory* (Yale University Press, New Haven, 1963).

institutions).[10] However, communities whose boundaries *seem* to coincide with those of particular spatial — or, to be more precise, residential — units also exist. The problem they raise is that of the existence of socially distinctive urban environments — neighbourhoods or suburbs, for example — which could be treated as analytically autonomous.[11]

Institutionally, urban sociology has enjoyed two golden ages in the United States: (1) the inter-war period, devoted to the study of social disorganization and mechanisms of integration in large cities undergoing rapid growth (directed by the Chicago school); and (2) the period immediately after the Second World War devoted to the study of urban diffusion and the constitution of interdependent and hierarchically linked metropolitan regions (directed by the Michigan school, but also continued at Chicago under Bogue).

But during the 1960s there has been a slowing down of production within urban sociology. Not because urban problems have become any less important. On the contrary, they are still central. But it is precisely because of this that sociology is separated from the treatment of urban problems. This has to be stated since it is a highly significant *index* of the social role played by the discipline.

On the one hand, as industrial societies are becoming almost entirely 'urban',[12] urban sociology becomes a general sociology applied to the study of the framework of particular social formations.[13] The numerous urban sociology textbooks which have appeared in recent years are in fact textbooks of social organization marked by a very strong (American) ethnocentrism despite (and perhaps especially because of) their references to 'traditional' societies.

On the other hand, the urban problems requiring solution are no longer problems of integration, but problems of management of the system as a whole: the organization of spatial interdependences within a complex technological environment, public sector intervention to

[10] See M. R. Stein, *The Eclipse of Community. An Interpretation of American Studies* (Harper and Row, New York, 1964; Harper Torchbooks, New York, 1971).
[11] For a useful discussion of this problem see A. J. Reiss, The sociological study of communities, *Rural Sociology* 24 (1959) 118–30.
[12] See D. L. McElrath, Introductory: the new urbanization, in S. Greer, D. L. McElrath, D. W. Minar and P. Orleans (eds), *The New Urbanization* (St Martins Press, New York, 1968) 3–12.
[13] See Alvin Boskoff, *The Sociology of Urban Regions*, Appleton Century Crofts, New York, 1962 (second edition, 1970).

organize the consumption of collective goods, attempts to manage the social tensions produced by the spatial expression of processes of ethnic and social integration. Appeals for help in the solution of these problems are made to a variety of disciplines, but particularly to urban planners on the one hand and political analysts on the other.[14]

The emphasis has shifted from social reform to urban planning: from social worker to technocrat. At the same time political science has benefited from the recognition of the issues at stake as political issues.

And what of Europe? In fact, urban sociology is primarily American. The reasons for this are simple: the superiority of the information-producing machines represented by American universities, paralleling the economic, political and technological dominance of that country; and, in particular, urban sociology's intellectual origin within an empiricist epistemological perspective, which underlies American sociology generally, but which is less predominant in Europe, and particularly in France.

However, wherever urban sociology as such has developed, especially in England and Scandinavia, its evolution has paralleled that described above. Even in France, the pioneer of urban sociology Chombart de Lauwe, and his team, have followed through the same stages in this evolution over the last twenty years.

What characterizes urban sociology in France is that the social demand, which is primarily that of the State technocracy, is formulated in new terms, e.g., technical rationality and political stakes, and the sociologists' response is simply a little ahead of or a little behind this formulation. The development of urban sociology in France has been arrested by the continuing dependence of the urban sociology produced on the Chicago school and hence on the problematic of integration, or else has been directed towards the creation of a unified social science, with a consequent rejection of the divisions proposed by the State. Hence a relation of manipulation or confrontation exists between administration and sociology, the former relation being generally more common than the latter.[15]

---

[14] It is thus interesting to note that the two best recent urban sociology readers published in the United States — S. Greer *et al.*, *op. cit.*, and L. F. Schnore (ed.), *Social Science and the City* (Praeger, New York, 1968) — are characterized by an interdisciplinary approach and by the emphasis they give to political analyses.
[15] The recent conference on Sociology and Planning, held at Royaumont in 1968, provided a striking proof of this division.

Our aim here is not to set out a history of ideas but to situate an intellectual production within a theoretical field and within a social structure. This is why it has first been necessary to define our object of analysis. We can now examine one by one the real and apparent foundations of the theoretical practice of urban sociology.

II Urban sociology has no specific theoretical object

1 The myth of urbanism

It is indisputable that the concept of urbanism provides the essential theoretical basis of urban sociology. The term urbanism[16] refers to a particular system of norms or values, or, at the level of actors, of behaviour, attitudes and beliefs. This system is the expression of a particular form of activity and social organization characterized by: a high degree of differentiation between individuals, social and personal isolation, role segmentation, superficiality and utilitarianism in social relations, functional specialization and the division of labour, the competitive spirit, a high level of mobility, the market economy, the predominance of secondary relations over primary, the shift from community to association, the subordination of the individual to organization, control of the political process by mass appeals, etc.

It is immediately clear that this does not constitute a theoretical definition but rather identifies a socio-cultural type; and this is even true of Wirth's[17] rigorous formulation which remains the best statement of the urbanism thesis. Ultimately, urbanism is the cultural system corresponding to what is termed 'mass society'.[18] Hence the phrases urban attitudes, urban behaviour, urban values, etc. And hence the definition of urban sociology's task as the study of the phenomena thus labelled.

Many of the criticisms made of the above characterization of urbanism are directed at its lack of correspondence with the picture of

[16] The definition derives from the notions of culture of E. B. Tylor, Parsons, Park and Wirth.
[17] Louis Wirth, Urbanism as a way of life, *American Journal of Sociology* 44 (1938) 1–24. A recent discussion, supporting Wirth's argument, has just appeared: S. S. Guterman, In defence of Wirth's urbanism as a way of life, *American Journal of Sociology* 74 (1969) 492–9. In fact this is an empiricist work which makes a somewhat crude attempt to contrast 'reality' with the 'theoretical' criticisms.
[18] As described by David Riesman and Harold Wilensky. David Riesman, *The Lonely Crowd* (Yale University Press, New Haven, 1950). H. L. Wilensky and C. N. Lebeaux, *Industrial Society and Welfare* (Sage Foundation, New York, 1958).

reality revealed by empirical research, according to which, for example, new forms of social solidarity have developed and primary groups still retain their cohesive force in large cities in industrial societies.[19]

In fact, these criticisms do not pose any problems for the 'culturalist' approach in so far as it never claimed a close 'fit' to reality, but simply to describe the general tendencies of change of modern society. Certainly, it is true that the characterization of urbanism offers a rough description of social evolution in the first phase of industrialization at the *level of forms*. And moreover it was on these transformations that the earliest sociologists — Tönnies, Simmel, Durkheim, etc. — focussed their attention.

The nub of the question lies elsewhere — in the fact that the presence of the term urban in the definition of urbanism is not accidental. One can accept initially the empiricist assertion: the new features did indeed first emerge in cities. Hence the term urban describes their place of emergence but does not define them. But the notion of urbanism implies much more than this. Implicitly or explicitly, there is an underlying theory which seeks to deduce urbanism from the ecological characteristics of cities, in other words, a theory of production of social forms. And, in particular, there is linked to it a theory of social change: the folk-urban continuum thesis.[20] According to the latter, the history of humanity is the history of the movement from folk societies to urban societies, through a series of intermediate stages, impelled by transformations in the size, density and heterogeneity of the community. Urbanization thus becomes synonymous with modernization, and modern society equivalent to liberal capitalist society.

Thus the theory of urbanism is based on, and can be summarized in the form of, two theses: (1) 'modern' (i.e. capitalist industrial) societies have a distinctive cultural system.[21] This system is the end

---

[19] For example, the research by Morris Axelrod in Detroit, or that of the Centre d'Etude des Groupes Sociaux in the Paris region.

[20] Robert Redfield, The folk society, *American Journal of Sociology* 52 (1947) 293–308. Horace Miner, in a discussion which supports Redfield, criticizes this notion: The folk-urban continuum, *American Sociological Review* 17 (1952) 529–37. For an excellent discussion, see Richard Dewey, The rural-urban continuum: real but relatively unimportant, *American Journal of Sociology* 66 (1960) 60–6.

[21] A major objection to this interpretation of urbanism may be raised. Since Soviet, non-capitalist, cities display analogous characteristics to capitalist cities, does this not tend to prove that these characteristics are in fact linked to the urban ecological form as such? This argument can be answered at two levels.

point of the process of development of the human species. However, its establishment does not come about without difficulties so, in addition to defining its characteristics, one must study its diffusion and the 'resistance to change' of unintegrated sub-cultures. (2) This system is the product of a particular ecological form, namely the city. Society is transformed from rural to urban through the increase in size, density and heterogeneity of the territorial collectivities which

---

Certainly if one means by capitalism the *juridical* private ownership of the means of production then one would not expect different cultural systems to result according to whether capitalism was present or not. But in fact we are using the term 'capitalism' in the sense in which Louis Althusser has demonstrated it was used by Marx in *Capital*: as a particular type of matrix for the basic systems of a society (economic, political, ideological). However, even if we were to use the vulgar definition of capitalism, the similarity between cultural types might be due, not to the existence of a common ecological form, but to the social and technical complexity underlying population concentration and heterogeneity. This would be more a case of 'industrialism'. The technological character of industrialization would thus be the major element determining the evolution of social forms. This argument would be similar to the theses on industrial society advanced by Raymond Aron. But, on the other hand, if we adopt a scientific definition of capitalism, it may be asserted that, in those historical societies where studies of the transformation of social relations have been carried out, the way in which the dominant mode of production called capitalism is articulated can account both for the production of such a system of of relations and, *at the same time*, for the emergence of a new ecological form.

The fact that similar behaviour is observed in *societies* where it may be presumed that the capitalist mode of production is not dominant, in no way invalidates the above assertion, since the crude dichotomy capitalism/socialism must be rejected. On the other hand, it does raise a question and necessitate the undertaking of research in order to: a) determine whether, in fact, the real content, and not merely the formal content, of this behaviour is the same, b) examine the way in which different modes of production are concretely articulated in Soviet society, since it is indisputable that the *capitalist mode of production is present there*, even if it is not dominant, c) establish the outlines of the new post-capitalist mode of production, for, whereas the scientific theory of the capitalist mode of production has been partly developed (in *Capital*), an equivalent theory of the socialist mode of production is lacking, and the latter term is still largely ideological, and d) develop a theory linking the way in which the various modes of production are concretely articulated in Soviet society with systems of behaviour in that society.

It is obvious that once conclusions had been reached on these questions the problematic of urbanism would cease to be relevant. However, until the necessary research on non-capitalist societies has been carried out, we can say intuitively: that similar technological determinants can lead to similarities in behaviour; that these are strengthened by the very real presence of capitalist structural elements in such societies; and that formal analogies between types of behaviour are only meaningful when related to the social structure in which they are found. For, if one were to follow this line of argument, one would end up by asserting the unity of all societies from the fact that everyone eats and sleeps more or less regularly!

constitute it. Once a certain level of development is reached, urban society exerts its influence and imposes its values even on rural settlements.

Rural and urban are two ends of a continuum. The varied situations observed empirically can all be placed on the continuum, and are all evolving from rural to urban.

The first thesis in our view must be subjected to thorough-going criticism: a discipline cannot take as its theoretical object a particular historical cultural type, unless it is defined as a *final form* which exists not only in one historical conjuncture but is implicit as a germ in other situations. To put it more clearly, for urbanism to be the specific theoretical object of urban sociology rather than merely the culture of liberal capitalist society, it would be necessary to identify it with modernity, and assume that all societies are moving towards it as they develop, despite secondary differences, e.g., those concerning their economic systems.

We are now in a position to describe the ideological significance of urban sociology. We have already referred to the emphasis placed on the study of social integration. While the scientific analysis of such a subject is quite unobjectionable, a discipline which restricts itself to the study of social integration to a particular culture — in this case the culture produced by capitalist industrialization — gives itself very limited scope for theoretical development.

As for the second thesis, the position is even clearer, The idea that a form of social organization (urbanism) could be produced by ecological changes represents too impoverished a vision of sociological theory to be seriously defended.

Wirth's attempt to demonstrate the specific links between size, density and heterogeneity, on the one hand, and urbanism, on the other, is, despite his intellectual ability, a collection of common-sense hypotheses lacking internal theoretical coherence. It can hardly be disputed that social organization and cultural system depend on something other than the number and diversity of individuals who constitute the society. Characteristics such as these must not be neglected, but rather must be incorporated into the technico-social structure underlying the organization of any society. Although this is not the moment to present a theory of production of these social forms, we nevertheless believe it possible to reject a view as simplistic as that which underlies the assertion that urbanism is the product of the 'city'.

Empirical studies have shown the existence of 'cities' with very

diverse cultural systems.[22] It is true that some writers go on to
suggest restricting the term 'cities' to agglomerations in industrial
societies,[23] while others use the terms urbanization, modernization
and 'Westernization' interchangeably.[24] The differences between
cities and countryside became blurred: Gottman has demonstrated the
interpenetration of activities in these social forms.[25] Hence the term
urban diffusion![26]

If we move from general considerations to particular urban
contexts and attempt to link types of behaviour with the particular
ecological environment (e.g. the neighbourhood) in which they are
observed, we find that multivariate analyses invariably come to the
conclusion that it is social characteristics (individual or contextual)
which are decisive influences on types of behaviour and that spatial
proximity merely reinforces their effect.[27]

The coincidence between certain characteristic types of behaviour
and the constitution of large agglomerations in industrial society can
often be misleading. In fact this is a typical case of spurious
correlation. Transformations in the technico-social base of society
lead *both* to new types of social relations *and* to a new form of spatial
organization. The theoretical coherence of the process cannot be
discovered by inter-relating the elements which co-exist on the surface
of reality, but only by establishing the relations between structural
elements through which this surface is itself organized.[28] One might
thus be inclined to accept the term urbanism to describe what
happens in cities. But, on the other hand, as we have shown, the
'confusion' is not as innocent as it seems: it carries, *implicitly*, an

[22] See G. Sjoberg, *op. cit.*; R. C. McC. Adams, *The Evolution of Urban Society*
(Aldine, Chicago, 1966); G. Sjoberg, Cities in developing and in industrial
societies: a cross-cultural analysis, in P. Hauser and L. F. Schnore (eds), *op. cit.*,
213–65.
[23] For example, Leonard Reissman, *The Urban Process* (Free Press, New York,
1964).
[24] N. P. Gist and S. F. Fava, *Urban Society* (Cromwell, New York, 1964).
[25] Jean Gottmann, *Megalopolis* (Twentieth Century Fund, New York, 1961;
M.I.T. Press, Cambridge (Mass.), 1967); J. Gottmann and R. A. Harper,
Metropolis on the Move (Wiley, New York, 1967).
[26] Achille Ardigó, *La Diffusione Urbana* (Ave, Rome, 1967).
[27] For a very useful synthesis of research results, see J. M. Beshers, *Urban Social
Structure* (Free Press, Glencoe, 1962). See also W. M. Dobriner (ed.), *The
Suburban Community* (Putman, New York, 1958), and J. O.Retel, Quelques
aspects des relations sociales dans l'agglomération parisienne, in C. Cornuau *et
al.*, *l'Attraction de Paris sur sa Banlieue* (Editions Ouvrières, Paris, 1965).
[28] We shall leave aside, for the time being, discussion of the elements concerned,
this being the central problem of sociological theory.

ideology of the production of social forms. And, moreover, urbanism is not a theoretical object or specific concept which urban sociology could use to provide itself with a specific theoretical field.

Urbanism is not a concept. It is a myth in the strictest sense since it recounts, ideologically, the history of mankind. An urban sociology founded on urbanism is an ideology of modernity ethnocentrically identified with the crystallization of the social forms of liberal capitalism.

2 The social organization of space

The study of urbanization has focussed both on the description of new forms of spatial arrangement of activities and populations, and on the establishment of the link between social structure and the organization of space. While this perspective has its origins in human ecology, especially in the work of Burgess, continued today by Schnore,[29] it is also present in the historicist Marxist approach to urban problems, as indicated by the research of Lefebvre and Pizzorno,[30] among others.

Two aspects of this work must be distinguished: (1) the treatment of space as an object of analysis; (2) the theorization of the relation between society and space.

In fact, the sociological analysis of space appears to us to be a quite legitimate field of study. However, it is not a theoretical object, but a real object, since space is a material element and not a conceptual unit. We shall thus deal with it later as an attempt to found urban sociology as a discipline specializing in a specific domain of reality.

In principle, the statement of the relation between society and space should be unobjectionable: it is obvious that space, like every other material element on which human activity is exercised, receives a particular form according to the technico-social complex of which it is part. But too often a sort of 'reflection theory' is used to tackle this problem. Now, society cannot be 'reflected' in space since it is not external to space. What is necessary, rather, is to show how space and other material elements of social organization are articulated within a coherent theoretical or conceptual whole which accounts for the processes or conjunctures to be explained. To take a concrete example, the formation of metropolitan regions in industrial societies

[29] L. F. Schnore, *The Urban Scene* (Free Press, New York, 1965).
[30] H. Lefebvre, *op. cit.*; A. Pizzorno, Développement économique et urbanisation, *Transactions of the Fifth World Congress of Sociology* (International Sociological Association, Louvain, 1962).

is not the 'reflexion' of 'mass society' but the spatial expression, at
the level of forms, of the processes of centralization of management
and decentralization of execution, in both production and
consumption spheres.[31] But the very fact that space is thus of little
importance in terms of distance is due to the predominance of the
'technical environment' over the 'cultural environment' and to the
type of social organization and technical progress which have
produced the new agglomerations. The analysis of social forms
(including space) requires the reconstruction of the significative
structure of the relationships between the concrete elements
(including space) which constitute a society. Space must thus be
incorporated into this structure, with its specific effects, and at the
same time display in its characteristics the concrete way in which the
structures and levels of the social formation of which it is part are
articulated.

We thus find ourselves in a concrete problematic, that of
development, which is not dependent on an autonomous set of
concepts. Similarly, urban stratification refers to the spatial dimension
of the theory of social stratification, and thus does not require new
intellectual tools.[32]

The sociological treatment of the organization of space, as a
material element of human existence, does not, thus, lead to a specific
theoretical field but to the uncovering of the relationship maintained
by this space with the rest of the technico-social complex.

3 The ecological system

An urban unit is a system structured by elements whose changes and
interaction thereby determine its composition. Within this
perspective, the attempt to explain territorial collectivities by the
notion of an ecological system constitutes the most serious attempt to
give urban sociology a specific theoretical field in conjunction with
the functionalist approach.[33]

Let us take a closer look. According to, for example, the fairly

[31] See J. Bollens and H. J. Schmandt, *Metropolis* (Harper and Row, New York,
1965), and L. F. Schnore, Urban form: the case of the metropolitan community,
in W. Z. Hirsch (ed.), *Urban Life and Form* (Holt, Rinehart and Winston, New
York, 1963) 169–201.
[32] See J. M. Beshers, *op. cit.* and O. D. Duncan and B. Duncan, Residential
distribution and occupational stratification, *American Journal of Sociology* 60
(1955) 493–503.
[33] See on this subject the excellent anthology edited by G. A. Theodorson,
Studies in Human Ecology (Row, Peterson, Evanston (Ill.), 1961).

elaborate formulation of Duncan,[34] urban phenomena depend on the inter-relations between four basic elements: population, environment, social organization and technology. On the other hand, the different collectivities are inter-linked by hierarchical relationships and the whole is a complex network whose basic elements are linked both inside and outside each individual collectivity.[35]

The schema can be made more complicated by adding other elements, e.g. the 'psycho-social element' or culture[36] or by making one element dominant, e.g. technology, which then acts as the driving force of the system.[37]

But, whatever the case, it is clear that the ecological system schema is not a specific theoretical object, but a general theory of social structure. It is not only the city or relationships to space which are explained by this schema, but society as a whole, at least as far as its structural elements and tendencies to change are concerned.

Moreover, this is precisely the conception of human ecology held by McKenzie[38] and especially by Hawley.[39] The central notion, that of community, is prior to that of territorial community; it can be applied to space, but originally had no spatial referent. For Hawley, the organization of space is a special case of the general processes which shape the structure of a community and which are based on relationships of symbiosis and 'commensuality'. The fact that human ecology has been particularly used in the study of space is due to the historical link between this theme and the theory of its founders (a link which, moreover, is by no means arbitrary).[40] But this combination must not mislead us as to the character of human ecology, i.e. a veritable attempt at a general theory of society, with close connections with the organicist current of functionalism.

The ecological system does not thus represent a specific theoretical

---

[34] See p. 62, fn. 6.
[35] O. D. Duncan, *et al.*, *Metropolis and Region* (Johns Hopkins Press, Baltimore, 1960).
[36] Gist and Fava, *op. cit.*
[37] For example, J. P. Gibbs and W. T. Martin, Towards a theoretical system of human ecology, *Pacific Sociological Review* 2 (1959) 29–36.
[38] R. D. McKenzie, The scope of human ecology, *American Journal of Sociology* 32 (1926) 141–54.
[39] A. H. Hawley, *op. cit.*; compare in particular chapters XIII and XIV, concerning space, with chapter XII, concerning the general theory of community structure. The former are an application of the latter in relation to one domain of reality.
[40] This connexion is due both to the way in which administrative divisions are reflected in research units and to the influence of the biological sciences on the first empirical social science research.

object, but is rather a particular approach to social structure as a whole.

Urbanism is not a conceptual unit but an ideology of social integration to 'modern' society. The relationship between society and space is not a theoretical object but a specific domain of reality. The ecological system, rather than being a specific corpus of sociological theory, is a particular attempt to explain social structure.

The three themes around which urban sociology has historically attempted to constitute itself as a science do not therefore possess the characteristics of theoretical distinctiveness. Urban sociology has no specific theoretical object.

III Urban sociology has no specific real object

The immediate reaction of the sociologist who refuses to adopt the divisions of administrative practice in his theoretical work is to conceive urban sociology along the lines of other specialized sociologies (industrial sociology, sociology of education, medical sociology, etc.), as the application of the theoretico-technical corpus of sociology to a particular domain of reality.

Now, *what characterizes urban sociology is precisely the absence of any clear delimitations of its real object.* Certainly, industry describes a certain type of productive activity, education refers to the set of processes of apprenticeship, socialization, institutionally established selection, etc. But what of the urban? In current usage, urban is contrasted to rural; thus everything must be either urban or rural. But the rural-urban contrast lacks distinguishing criteria, since in terms of social content the contrast refers primarily to the distinction between industrial society and agrarian society, and as far as the spatial forms of society are concerned, their diversity cannot be reduced to a dichotomy, nor be placed on a continuum: one has merely to remember that the city is indissolubly part of the metropolitan region, and that the small town is as distant from the village as it is from the large city.[41]

Recently there has been a growing awareness of the difficulty of defining the urban by contrasting it with the rural in so far as

[41] See the excellent discussion of the definition of urban in H. T. Eldridge, The process of urbanization, in J. Spengler and O. D. Duncan (eds), *Demographic Analysis* (Free Press, New York, 1956). Pierre George has demonstrated the arbitrariness of empirical criteria of delineation in his *Précis de Géographie Urbaine* (P. U. F., Paris, 1964) 7–20; see also D. Popenoe, On the meaning of urban in urban studies, in P. Meadows and E. H. Mizruchi (eds), *Urbanism, Urbanization and Change* (Addison-Wesley, Reading (Mass.) 1969) 64–76;

'industrial societies are becoming completely urbanized', i.e. as
previously separate activities and functions are becoming spatially
mixed in a network of interdependences which has no need for
geographical proximity. Since 'rural' and 'urban' are becoming
integrated, the definition of the latter must be sought elsewhere.[42]
And once again, it is the urbanism theme to which implicit reference
is made.

Thus, if 'urban' social classes, 'urban' bureaucracy, 'urban' politics,
'urban' participation, leisure activities, friendship relations, transport
problems, etc., are studied under the same label it is because they are
all regarded as aspects of social life belonging to a new type of society,
almost a 'new way of living' (urban . . .) whose ideological contours
have already been outlined.

On this argument, urban sociology would simply be the *sociology*
of 'modern' society, of mass society. Despite the apparent simplicity
of this possibility, it amounts to an ideological displacement of the
whole problematic — which is the very basis of the researcher's
activity — in so far as its point of departure lies within a theoretical
field which is disorganized, or, rather, organized in terms of an
ideological rationality.

Must one conclude, then, that urban sociology is identical with
sociology *tout court*, and that the term urban is ideological and must
be denounced? Yes and no. The term urban as it is used is certainly
ideological, even though one is obliged to continue using it in
everyday language. But the institutional distinctiveness of urban
sociology does derive from its specialization in certain aspects of
reality despite the facts that (a) it embraces not one, but *several*
distinct domains and (b) that their variety is concealed rather than
brought out by the umbrella term urban sociology.

Thus, while, as has been shown, there is no field of reality which
can be termed 'urban', urban sociology has in fact tended to tackle
two types of problem: (1) *relationships to space*; and (2) what may be
termed the *process of collective consumption*.

We have seen that relationships to space, i.e. the concrete way in
which the material element 'space' is articulated with the social
structure as a whole, can and must be the subject of sociological
analysis. The study of urbanization processes and the study of the

---

[42] Raymond Ledrut provides a very clear statement of the problem in the
introduction to his latest work, *l'Espace Social de la Ville* (Editions Anthropos,
Paris, 1968).

arrangements and transformations of social elements and processes in relation to a given spatial unit represent a field which human ecology and social history have made serious efforts to analyze, but without reaching any theoretical systematization capable of giving direction to the mass of individual research projects carried out.

On the other hand, urban sociology has tackled a multitude of problems whose connexion is that they belong to the sphere of collective consumption, that is to say, of consumption processes whose organization and management cannot be other than collective given the nature and size of the problems: e.g. housing, collective facilities, leisure provision, etc. Moreover it is this particular problematic which is the source of the ideological bias prevailing in urban sociology. Urban sociology plays in the consumption sphere the same role as industrial sociology in the production sphere. Now whereas industrial sociology has been the object of some respect because of its assistance in detecting bottlenecks to growth, urban sociology from the very outset was conceived as a search for the mechanisms of adjustment to a given order, to a given type and level of collective consumption. This difference of status is simply an expression of the dominance of production over collective consumption and the difference between the interests in the two processes.

Thus, as well as ideological themes and highly diverse real objects, the urban sociology tradition includes *a sociology of space* and *a sociology of collective consumption*. Urban sociology, as such, has no specific real object. Its institutional unity derives not from its theoretical work but from the ideological function it fulfills.

IV The legacy of urban sociology
1 A new theoretical field
There are two themes, then, lost in the murk of urban sociology, which deserve a fresh theoretical approach. The mass of information and incomplete analyses already available concerning them can and must be systematized within an explanatory framework. Research projects, organized within such a framework, may be able to throw light on the intervention of individuals and groups on these problems in the context of a particular society.

However, having defined these two domains of reality, it is still necessary to spell out the analytical approach by which they are to be studied. In fact, three different approaches are possible according to whether one wishes to study the *production of social forms*, the *functioning of the social system* or the *structure of the semantic field.*[43]

Thus, for example, an analysis of space could be devoted to (1) the study of transformations of the relationships between society and space, and hence of changes in the latter, (2) the integration of the functional system within a particular spatial unit, following the ecological system approach, or (3) the reading of the semantic field of an agglomeration, in the manner of Claude Lévi-Strauss.

Each of these three *approaches* cuts up the same real object in a different way, corresponding to its theoretical viewpoint. Each appeals to a specific set of concepts, appropriate to the particular theoretical problem it poses.

While these three differentiated theoretical objects oblige one to refer to three approaches, the real object, space, may be analyzed at different *levels*. One may study (1) a more or less arbitrary spatial unit, delimited in terms of the social demand underlying the research; (2) the overall system of interdependences at the spatial level, in which case each unit would be interpreted in terms of the overall spatial structure; or (3) the relationship between space and social structure, in which case space is only one element in the total system. It is obvious that everything is inter-connected and that even an isolated spatial unit expresses determinations of the whole. But when such a unit is studied, the focus of interest is more on the effects visible in the unit than on a reconstruction of the structure as a whole. The need to distinguish between levels of analysis is even more basic since not to do so would amount to having to reconstruct the totality of structures of a social formation in order to situate each particular research study. Now obviously the main point is not to analyze the whole but to show the specific effects of this whole on a particular practice or structure. In fact, social structure is a theoretical notion and thus only has any value if it is capable of accounting for particular processes.

If instead of remaining at the level of structures (space) we wish to analyze actors, the same three approaches (historical, functionalist, semiological) must be applied at each of the three corresponding levels (personality, groups or collectivities, global society).

Thus, *the study of space and of the process of collective consumption, at these three levels, in relation to structures and in*

[43] Following the definitions given by Alain Touraine, *Sociologie de l'Action* (Seuil, Paris, 1965) chapter II.

relation to actors, and following the three approaches indicated, constitutes a new theoretical field. This field is not that of a new urban sociology, but is simply a redefinition of the real problems tackled and discoveries made within the ideological field described as urban sociology.

We shall adopt one particular approach: historical analysis, or the study of the production of social forms. While we shall not attempt to resolve the problems raised by this approach within the space of this article, we would like to attempt to take the first steps in this direction, by stating a number of propositions for research concerning the two real objects mentioned above, analyzed from within our chosen approach. In other words, to be more precise, what is meant by a sociology of the production of space? What is meant by a sociology of the production of the social forms of collective consumption?

2 The sociological analysis of the production of space
By production of spatial forms we mean the set of processes which determine the concrete way in which material elements are articulated on a particular space. Or, to be more precise, the determination of the organization, in relation to space, of individuals and groups, workplaces, functions and activities, etc.

This analysis becomes all the more important as technical progress reduces the importance of space as a determinant. This is not to argue that space is external to the social structure and unaffected by it, but that in the relationships it maintains within this structure, in respect of which it is both determining and determined, its specific importance is becoming less and less.

Does this mean that space is becoming a blank sheet on which the action of social groups is inscribed? Or that space is constituted by actors? The theoretical issue here goes beyond the problematic of the study of space. What is at issue, in fact, is whether studying the production of social structures is equivalent to analyzing their origin in the action of subjects crystallized in institutions.

Our answer to this must be unambiguous. To identify the production of forms with their origin in action presupposes acceptance of the notion of actor-subjects, constructing their history in terms of their own values and aims and leading, through a cooling process, to society, seen as containing struggles and conflicts between opposites. This requires that one take as starting point actors and combinations of actors, and thus that one accept the existence of primary essences, not deduced from social structures. More precisely, historical actors, irreducible to a combination of structural elements, would have to be seen as an *absolute* in so far as they are placed in history asserting themselves of themselves and constituting social forms through their confrontation.[44] The theoretical issue is this: historical actors founding society through their action, or support-agents expressing particular combinations of the social structure through their practice. We will take for granted that the first approach belongs to the philosophy of history, and that only the second is capable of founding a science of society[45]

Transformations of space must thus be analyzed as specifications of transformations in the social structure. In other words, one must see how, in relation to the spatial unit being considered, defined in terms of the requirements of the research, the fundamental social processes constitutive of social structures are articulated and specified spatially. We shall use the term *spatial structure* (or 'urban system' to conform to tradition) to describe the particular way in which the basic elements of the social structure are spatially articulated.

It would be tedious to discuss here the processes and elements in question for the social structure as a whole. But we can suggest the precise content of the 'urban system'.[46] The transformation of a spatial unit is determined by changes in the elements of the urban system and in the relations between them. The elements of the urban system are as follows:

[44] It is scandalous to treat as rapidly as this the central problem of sociological analysis, which is currently the subject of great debate. But the very fact that we are forced to mention it in order to tackle the problems of research in a particular area shows that it is not an esoteric question, but is the source of daily difficulties in empirical research. While Alain Touraine seems to us to be the sociologist who is most aware of the problem, Nicos Poulantzas has been bold enough to present a first anti-historicist theoretical formulation in his remarkable work *Political Power and Social Classes* (New Left Books, London, 1973).
[45] It would be erroneous to identify Touraine with the first perspective, even though the confused and even contradictory statement of this problem in *Sociologie de l'Action* gives rise to ambiguity. It is rather historicism on the one hand and liberal analysis on the other that we are referring to.
[46] A confused statement of the notion of urban system, which does not coincide with our own, but shares the same approach to the analysis of urban structure, can be found in the unpublished research report of Alain Touraine on *La Création des Villes Nouvelles* (Laboratoire de Sociologie Industrielle, Paris, 1968). The fact that this report adopted a normative approach (what elements and relationships can give rise to urban autonomy?) shifts the meaning of the notion considerably. The notion of urban system suggested here has a different social content, while sharing the same theoretical approach.

P (Production): spatial dimension of the set of activities involved in the production of goods, services and information (e.g. industry, offices, mass media).

C (Consumption): spatial dimension of the activities comprising the (individual and collective) social appropriation of the product (e.g. housing, cultural and recreational facilities, etc.).

E (Exchange): spatial dimension of the exchanges between P and C, within P, or within C (e.g. transport, commerce, etc.).

M (Management): process of control of relationships between P, C and E (e.g. urban planning agencies, municipal institutions, etc.).

These elements are not simple elements but social processes, i.e. interventions by social agents on material elements. The way in which these elements are combined is not arbitrary but is an expression of the structural laws of the social formation of which the urban unit is part. However, in explaining a particular situation it is not necessary to refer back to the social structure as a whole to determine the specific relationships at the level of the urban system. On the other hand, it is necessary to refer back to the overall social structure (as a concept) to be able to define the urban system and give it a historical content.

In order to illustrate this approach, let us take as an example the results of the study we carried out on industrial location trends within the Paris region.[47] We discovered three main types of spatial behaviour which varied according to the technical and economic characteristics of the industrial firm. In brief, we can say that: (1) firms dependent on a localized market follow the growth patterns of the central (residential) core of the agglomeration; (2) firms using mass production methods, concerned about problems of operation and profitability, seek a location with good access to transport networks; and (3) technically advanced firms create new industrial zones located in areas of high social status, i.e. in accordance with the spatial expression of status stratification.

This means that in the Paris region, the element P can be broken up into three parts: the first governed by changes in the spatial distribution of element C (residence), the second governed by changes in E (exchange-transport), and the third initiating a new spatial trend but governed by a non-spatial factor linked to the state of dominant social values.

[47] See the research report, La mobilité des entreprises industrielles dans la région parisienne, Cahiers de l'I.A.U.R.P. (1968), 2 vols; and the article which appeared in Sociologie du Travail 4 (1967).

The correspondence between these three types of relationship and the technical and social division of labour within the economic system can be shown as follows: for example, (1) the economic dependence of the first type of firm is reflected in its dependence on spatial forms; (2) for the second type of firm, purely economic rationality alone leads to a choice of location on the basis of exchange advantages and not on the basis of changes in the spatial structure of the agglomeration, thereby creating an increase in the overall productivity of the system; (3) the fact that the third type of firm is technically independent of space does not mean that it is 'free', but that its location is governed by ideological factors linked to the essentially political role of the large firm in advanced capitalism.

All this is simply an illustration of one possible approach. In fact, the analysis of the urban system of the Paris region would require identification of the state of each element and of changes in the relations between them. The network of relations thus established would then permit predictions to be made. Certainly this schema is a complex one. But how could it be otherwise?

One final remark: technical and social change in industrial societies is leading to a progressive increase in the importance of element M (i.e. political interventions) over the other elements of the system. This does not mean that society is becoming more 'voluntaristic', but simply that the dominant instance is shifting towards the political as the State progressively becomes not only the centre but the driving force of a social formation whose complexity requires centralized decision-making and control of processes.

Consequently, a sociology of the production of space must increasingly be focussed on what is termed urban planning. But this intervention by M must be analyzed to discover and take account of the other elements of the system and their inter-relations.

3 Towards a sociology of urban planning[48]
Analysis of the processes of collective consumption involves confronting some of the central problems of our society. We are thus far from being in a position to offer a theoretical systematization, even as rudimentary as that presented above concerning the production of space. However, we can set out the terms of the problem.

[48] For a more detailed discussion of this subject, of which only an outline is given here, see my article, Vers une théorie sociologique de la planification urbaine, *Sociologie du Travail* 4 (1969) 413–43.

To start with, let us clarify what is involved. In the process of social appropriation of the result of human labour, i.e. of the product, certain needs exist whose characteristics make their satisfaction necessarily collective, due to the quantity of material means needed to meet them, for example, housing, education, physical and intellectual development, health, etc.

Since the product is distributed in a differentiated manner, according to the position of individuals and groups in the social structure, i.e. according to the organization of social classes, it follows that consumption processes are sufficiently specific to merit separate analysis.

To study the question of housing is not to contrast popular 'needs' with the 'wickedness' of capitalists, but to reveal the structural limits of the solutions to the problem of shelter, and the complex set of correspondences between the practices of agents and their place in the social structure.

While the present state of our thinking prevents us from answering the vast question thus posed, we may make a number of analytical points concerning the essentially indirect manner in which the problems referred to have been tackled in urban sociology, namely, through the study of the actions and organizations described by the term urban planning. In fact focus has been not on the question of collective consumption itself, but on the deficiencies of the system and the possibilities of remedying them by the intervention of the political instance.[49]

If, on the other hand, we recall the growing importance of the *management* of the urban system as far as the production of space is concerned, we reach the conclusion that the *essential legacy of urban sociology, from the point of view of an historical approach, concerns the study of urban planning.*

Let us sketch in a few research areas. The basic idea is that one must start with an analysis at the level of social structure, while at the same time specifying the concepts in relation to the domain of reality (urban planning) which is the object of research.

Any historical society represents the particular intertwining of several *modes of production,*[50] of which one is dominant. By mode

---

[49] See L. F. Schnore and H. Fagin (eds), *Urban Research and Policy Planning* (Sage, Beverley Hills, 1967).
[50] See L. Althusser, Contradiction and over-determination, in *For Marx* (Penguin, Harmondsworth, 1969); L. Althusser and E. Balibar, *Reading Capital* (New Left Books, London, 1970); N. Poulantzas, *op. cit.*, Introduction.

of production we are not referring to the economic system but to a specific form of articulation of the fundamental elements of a social structure, namely, economic system, political system, ideological system, and possibly other systems.

Within the structural limits of a given society, urban planning is generally the intervention of the political system on the economic system in an attempt to remove the bottlenecks produced in the latter. This intervention bears primarily on two problems: the reproduction of labour power and the reproduction of means of production.

However, sometimes, urban planning, under the cover of a regulative action on the economic, is a direct intervention of the political system on the political system itself, as, for example, in most urban renewal operations in the United States.[51]

The effect of such an intervention on a particular social unit can be seen analytically as a modification in the state of relations in the urban system, in the system of actors (supports) involved in it, and in the relations between these two systems.

To conceptualize the system of actors we require a set of concepts expressing the state of social relationships regarding the concrete stake in question. One might imagine three systems of opposed interests as being present in a planning operation: (1) opposition between Authority (public) and Organizations (private); (2) opposition between Production interests and Consumption interests; (3) opposition between Local and Global interests.

The various possible combinations of these three dichotomies could be used to describe the actors present. For example, the combination Authority-Consumption-Local corresponds fairly well to local government, whereas the combination Organization-Production-Global could be represented by a large international firm. Thus meaningful concrete examples of the eight combinations can be given.

Each particular combination of the urban system and the system of actors around an urban 'problem' giving rise to a planning intervention results in a particular practice, i.e. the making of a decision governed by the combination concerned. This decision modifies the system according to the characteristics of the decision and of the state of the system.

---

[51] See S. Greer, *Urban Renewal and American Cities* (Bobbs-Merrill, Indianapolis, 1965).

However, not all the combinations are possible, and some relationships give rise necessarily to others. *The relationships between urban system and system of actors are the specific expression of the relationships between the various global systems of the particular society being studied. The state of the social structure is the hidden structural cause of the relationships between the two systems which give an urban planning operation its specific content.*

At this level of generality, it would be pointless to go into any further detail. We have presented a set of theoretical concepts with which *concrete sociological analyses* of urban planning may be carried out. In our opinion this is the most accessible immediate investment of the collection of information and knowledge inherited from urban sociology.

Conclusion: the end of urban sociology

A basically sound reaction to the above analyses would be one of astonishment at such great insistence on locating the distinctiveness of urban sociology. Is such a concern not reactionary at the very time when an interdisciplinary approach is in favour?

In reality, one must beware of false protestations of sociological innocence. There is no such thing as a direct relationship between researcher and real object. All thought is more or less consciously shaped by a pre-existing theoretico-ideological field. To seek to avoid facing problems is to repeat ideas or even phrases without having understood their full implications. To deny the need for theoretical definition prior to any concrete research is to adopt a perspective which is narrowly empiricist and thus devoid of any scientific value.

In fact the indeterminacy of the theoretical status of urban sociology is clearly displayed in its 'interdisciplinary' role. Properly defined interdisciplinarity is a necessity: i.e. the communication and inter-relating of results obtained *independently* by each discipline in relation to the same real object. In fact this is not usually what obtains: more often the term refers to the collaboration of *specialists* from various disciplines in the examination of a problem or the making of a decision. The scientific role of the urban sociologist in such company is as undefined as his political role is clear. This role is to plan mechanisms of adjustment to decisions, to regulate the integration of the whole, or to resolve tensions produced at the level of collective consumption, when it is not simply that of 'social animator', or, in other words, agent of political manipulation.

It is clear that sociology cannot be other than a discipline applied to different domains of reality. But we have shown that, taken as a whole, urban sociology lacked any specific real object. Thus, before burying it as a theoretical field applied to a domain of reality, one must establish in what sectors researchers within this tradition have produced knowledge. This work of demarcation enables one to identify the real problems tackled by urban sociology, which may then be analyzed within the general framework of sociology. We have tried to indicate several of the possible areas for such analysis.

In no way do we wish to claim to be writing a death certificate for urban sociology, though the theoretical preconditions for this are met. The beginnings of a science, the end of an ideology, are not the work of individuals or institutions but are expressions of a given state of the social structure.

However, analysis can conclude that an intellectual activity lacks scientific rigour and point the way towards a clarification of the conditions which contribute to its perpetuation as an institutional entity.

The 'end of urban sociology' is only an ideological expression seeking an awareness of the unresolved theoretical problems in the sociological analysis of consumption processes.

François Lamarche

4

Property development and the economic foundations of the urban question*

At a time when urban space, 'centrality', or 'dwelling-space' are for some the nodal point of *new* social relations, and when, moreover, certain working-class organizations (hardened by experiences such as that of the F.R.A.P.[1] in Montreal) are declaring struggles limited to the municipality to be a blind alley . . ., it would appear relevant to enquire as to the foundations of urban dynamics.

These foundations are, among other things, economic in nature, since the city is not simply the product of the preconceptions of planners or even of politicians. It is a response to specific economic requirements which we shall attempt to define in part in the present article.

In industrial and capitalist societies, the city develops according to the requirements of the circulation of capital and commodities, and according to the subordination of labour to capital. It presents itself as the place in which the factors of production and demand are concentrated. In such a context, as has been stated clearly by Freitag, it is difficult to speak of urban social relations:

> Formally, it is primarily through the generalized mediation of labour-capital relations, relations based in turn on the institutions of private ownership of the means of production, of the salariat and market competition, that the inhabitants of a city enter into relation with one another.[1a]

*[Translated with permission of Les Presses de l'Université de Montréal, Montréal, from F. Lamarche, Les fondements économiques de la question urbaine, *Sociologie et Sociétés* 4 (1972) 15–40.]

[1] [The Front d'Action Politique (F.R.A.P.) was formed in 1970 by existing neighbourhood citizen action groups and trade union and student activists in order to oppose the urban policies of Mayor Drapeau. The Quebec political crisis in Autumn 1970 and the holding of elections led the F.R.A.P. to take up a more radical political stance, which in turn led to internal conflicts based on prior divisions and to a decline in support. See M. Castells, *Luttes Urbaines* (Maspero, Paris, 1973) chapter III.]

[1a] M. Freitag, De la ville-société à la ville-milieu, *Sociologie et Sociétés* 3 (1971) 25–57, at 48.

However, one must recognize the existence of problems which are specific to the city as such. For example, the insalubrity of a relatively large part of the housing stock, the high level of 'rents',[1b] expropriation, etc. (in brief, what certain authors rightly or wrongly call problems of collective consumption). But do these problems relate to a specifically urban logic or should they not be seen, rather, as local consequences of capitalist accumulation? Are they manifestations of newly emerging social relations of which the city is the arena, or do they result simply from the widening of the contradiction between labour and capital? These are the sorts of question we shall seek to tackle here.

If the city is considered to start with as a market where labour power, capital and products are exchanged, it must equally be accepted that the geographical configuration of this market is not the result of chance; it is governed by the laws of capital circulation which will be briefly set out at the start of this article. These laws determine the division of social capital into a number of specialized capitals. Among these capitals is property capital. This 'typically' urban capital will be our main focus of attention, and we shall enquire as to the sources of its profitability and as to its functions within social capital. After describing the importance of property capital in urban development, we shall consider the effects it produces on the land market, and then finally on the housing question.

The main hypothesis underlying our argument can be summarized as follows: the urban question is first and foremost the product of the capitalist mode of production, which requires a spatial organization which facilitates the circulation of capital, commodities, information etc. Even if certain problems exist which are specific to the city as such, at the economic level there is no specifically urban social relation. There are only class relations determined by the contradiction between capital and labour.

Preliminary
By circulation we mean exchanges considered in their totality: transactions involving the buying and selling of labour power, of

---

[1b] [The English word rent combines two meanings which in French are distinguished by different words: the sum of money paid by a tenant corresponds to *loyer*, while the analytically separable components of this sum or of the price of land, which can be seen as realizations of present advantages of situation or of anticipated future advantages (see Parts IIA, IIB and IIIB below), correspond to *rente*. In order to preserve this distinction we shall place inverted commas around rent in the first sense. Thus 'rent' refers to the first meaning (*loyer*), while rent refers to the second meaning (*rente*).]

means of production and of finished products. In other words, circulation embraces all economic activities which precede or follow the production process; thus, strictly speaking, it is located outside the sphere of production.

In the case of capital, circulation corresponds to its metamorphoses, $M-C-M'-C'$: conversion of a sum of money into labour power and means of production, reconversion of the commodities produced into an amount of money comprising surplus-value, new investment, etc. In short, it is through circulation that the capitalist converts his fortune into productive capital and extracts, with the sale of commodities, the surplus-value created in production.

Thus at the level of circulation itself, no creation of value takes place. Value is created in the sphere of production, never in the metamorphoses $M-C$ or $C-M$. When a capitalist takes on extra workers or purchases new means of production, he realizes no profit on these transactions; he changes the form of his capital but does not alter its size. Likewise, when he sells his products he does not change their value in any way; he simply converts them into their monetary equivalent. In other words, circulation both prepares the way for and completes the extraction of surplus-value; but taken in itself it does not add any value to the commodity, still less does it create surplus-value for the capitalist. The costs incurred at the level of circulation can be described as unproductive costs, i.e. they slow down the reproduction of capital on an extended scale.

On the one hand these costs include money spent directly on the metamorphoses of circulation. For example, all administrative labour concerned with the employment of personnel, the purchase of equipment, advertising, etc., can be regarded as unproductive labour. It is carried out in order to realize value but, as such, adds no value. The costs of such labour must therefore be deducted from the profits produced by capital engaged in production.[2]

On the other hand, capitalist accumulation is slowed down by the time necessary for capital to carry out its different metamorphoses, i.e. to transform itself from commodity-capital into money-capital, and then again into productive capital (into labour power and means of production). The longer this period of time, the less will capital

[2] A qualification is necessary here. In fact certain types of labour remain productive (create surplus-value), although strictly speaking they are located in the circulation sphere. Transport is one such example. Such labour can be added to that already contained in commodities, in so far as they must be shifted from one place to another before becoming true use-values available for consumption. See K. Marx, *Capital* 2 (Progress Publishers, Moscow, 1967) 152 *et seq.* (Chapter 6, §III).

yield, since in its commodity form or hard cash form it produces nothing at all. In brief, capital is only productive in the sphere of production; the time it takes to return to that sphere thus appears to the capitalist as dead time, not creative of surplus-value.

Consequently, it is to the advantage of the capitalist class, whose objective is the unlimited accumulation of value, to reduce to a minimum the period of time and costs involved in circulation. But how can this reduction be brought about? By following the principles of the division of labour, that is to say, by splitting up the different operations required by the actual extraction of surplus-value among different capitalists. It is undeniable that when an operation ceases to be a secondary task for several persons and becomes the specialized task of a few, it is more efficiently carried out. The same applies to the time and labour involved in buying and selling: they will be reduced if the tasks are taken charge of by specialized capitals. In this way, total social capital can be divided into three types, each with a specialized function: (a) industrial capital which controls the process of production . . . of surplus-value; (b) commercial capital which controls the circulation of commodity-capital; and (c) financial capital which controls the circulation of money-capital.

Let us examine briefly the bases on which commercial capital and financial capital, whose sphere of activity is primarily located at the level of circulation, operate.

1 Commercial capital

The primary function of commercial capital is to convert commodities deriving from production into money. Instead of this conversion being a secondary function of industrialists it becomes the sole task of a particular category of capitalists, merchants. The latter purchase the commodities produced by the industrialists who are thus enabled to return more quickly to the factory to make their new capital bear fruit. . . . In other words, merchants act as intermediaries between capitalist producers and the market and, as such, shorten the distance which the producers' commodity-capital has to cover before being converted into money.

However, the fact that commodities pass through the hands of intermediaries does not give them any higher value when they leave the factory. In so far as the merchant simply buys to sell, he in no way alters the quantity of labour contained in the commodity. Even his investments in the hiring of a labour force or in the equipping of business premises add nothing to the value of the products; the essential function of these investments is the realization of value already contained in the commodity, that is to say, the metamorphosis of this commodity into its monetary form. In brief, even if the labour undertaken by commercial capital is useful from the point of view of industrial capital since it reduces the time and money devoted to the circulation of commodities, it nevertheless remains unproductive labour, not creative of surplus-value.[3]

In these conditions, what is the basis of commercial transactions? Since the merchant sells his products at the value which they have on leaving the factory, what is the origin of his profits? For there must be some small profit to justify his capital investments. . . . More precisely, the problem can be stated as follows: in order for the merchant to realize a profit, he must obviously sell his commodities at a higher price than he paid for them; but, at the same time, he must sell them at their correct value (i.e. that fixed by their production time). This is only possible under one condition: that the merchant buys the commodity from the producers at below its value, and thus captures a part of the surplus-value produced in its manufacture; in other words since commercial capital produces no surplus-value its profits necessarily derive from the surplus-value produced by industrial capital. Marx will say that the size of these profits depends on the share of commercial capital in total social capital.[4] For our purposes the essential point is the following: commercial capital accomplishes a necessary function in the process of reproduction, but it creates neither value, nor product; its utility derives not from the fact that it changes an unproductive function into a productive function, but from the fact that it reduces the costs of circulation which would be relatively much greater if the labour involved in circulation was carried out by each industrialist individually; this then is the utility in terms of which commercial capital is remunerated.

[3] It is interesting to add Marx's remarks concerning commercial workers:

> The commercial worker produces no surplus-value directly. But the price of his labour is determined by the value of his labour-power, hence by its costs of production, while the application of this labour-power, its exertion, expenditure of energy, and wear and tear, is as in the case of every other wage-labourer by no means limited by its value. His wage, therefore, is not necessarily proportionate to the mass of profit which he helps the capitalist to realise. What he costs the capitalist and what he brings in for him, are two different things. He creates no direct surplus-value, but adds to the capitalist's income by helping him to reduce the cost of realising surplus-value, inasmuch as he performs partly unpaid labour. (K. Marx, *Capital* 3 (Progress Publishers, Moscow, 1971) 300 (chapter 17).)

[4] See *Capital* 3, 281–301 (chapter 17).

2 *Financial capital*

The same argument holds true for financial capital. This also operates
at the level of circulation; and is thus not creative of surplus-value.
But unlike commercial capital its function does not directly concern
the circulation of commodity-capital but that of money-capital. Its
utility derives from the fact that it concentrates the money-capital not
engaged in industrial and commercial operations; it contributes so as
to reduce the share of social capital which has to exist in money form
as working capital to finance payments or purchases. In other words,
financial capital speeds up the circulation of capital in so far as it
reduces for each private capital the share which has to be kept in
liquid form to ensure the continuous functioning of its operations;
financial capital thus enables a larger part of these capitals to be
committed as productive capital creating surplus-value, or as
commercial capital extracting this surplus-value. . . .[5]

Consequently the profits obtained by financial capital in the form
of interest, administrative charges, etc., do not derive from a value
which it produces directly through its own operations. As in the case
of commercial capital, its profits originate in the surplus-value created
in the sphere of production. They are a function of the reduction in
costs of circulation brought about by its specialization as banker and
accountant of capital. Or again, one could say that by its function
within total capital, financial capital contributes to the production
and conservation of an increased mass of surplus-value; it is as a result
of this contribution that it shares with industrial capital and
commercial capital the profits of production.

I Property capital

Now it is obvious that the costs of circulation also depend on the
distance separating the different economic agents and, in particular,
on the spatial organization of their activities. For example, it is a
well-known fact that the concentration of shops in very restricted
areas increases their turnover; it is also beyond doubt that
shopping-centres are more economically successful if they are
geographically close to office developments and/or residential areas
capable of supplying a large and varied range of customers. . . .

[5] We restrict ourselves here to the *theoretical* function of financial capital as
defined by Marx (*Capital* 3, 321–2 (chapter 19)). In other words, we do not
take into account for the time being the social power acquired by financial
capital when, in the monopoly stage, it merges bank capital and industrial
capital. On this subject see Lenin, *Imperialism, the Highest Stage of Capitalism.*

Similarly, it is recognized that the efficiency of the administrative sector depends in part on the proximity of certain service establishments such as banks and credit institutions and of information networks and contacts necessary to the operations of capital, etc. Typical spatial expressions of this are Wall Street, rue Saint-Jacques or, previously, rue Saint-Pierre, etc.

It might thus seem that like commercial and financial capital another specialized capital exists with the sole function of planning and equipping space in order to increase the efficiency of commercial, financial and administrative activities. To be more precise, if it is accepted that space is a more important factor in time and labour than the capital invested in circulation as a whole, it is logical to assume that a specialized capital exists whose primary role is to plan this space in order to reduce the indirect costs of capitalist production. This capital is property capital.

To give just one example of this particular type of capital let us take the case of Trizec Corporation Ltd. This corporation, to a very large extent controlled by English interests, is almost exclusively engaged in property development.[6] On the one hand, it is not a construction firm and does not even have any investments in this type of firm; the buildings it finances are constructed by one or more entrepreneurs who, as the expression goes, 'deliver' them at an agreed cost and date. On the other hand, the operations of Trizec are in no way speculative in the usual sense of the term. Most often its operations concern very large buildings which the Corporation has itself had built and which it plans to exploit over a very long period; in most cases the value of the land involved represents only 15 per cent of the total capital invested. Most often the properties controlled and managed by Trizec are located in the heart of the city-centre and are tightly integrated into the administrative and commercial activity of the area. This is the case, for example, of Place Ville-Marie, Trizec's largest investment. Over 20,000 people work in this imposing building on Dorchester Street, in Montreal. Apart from the administrative complex where the main tenants are the Royal Bank of Canada, I.B.M., Esso, Alcan, Air Canada, Montreal Trust, General Trust of Canada, etc., Place Ville-Marie includes a precinct containing sixty shops, eight restaurants and two theatres, the whole unit being

[6] Trizec Corporation Ltd is 61.1 per cent controlled by the financial holding company Star (Great Britain) Holding Ltd of London. This information and that which follows are contained in the documents relating to the takeover bid for Trizec by Great West International Equities Ltd, 30 April 1971.

directly linked (by subways etc.) to five million square feet of office
space, to over two hundred shops, to a network of hotels containing
two thousand rooms, to the C.N.R. and C.P.R. railway stations, and
to the underground railway. . . . The same characteristics can be found
at Place Quebec, a new Trizec project in course of construction in the
'old' capital. Situated close to the provincial parliament building, the
Latin quarter, and the shopping centre of rue St Jean, Place Quebec
will include an administrative complex, a shopping arcade, a 600-room
hotel, a large conference centre. . . . But these examples represent
only a fraction of the property owned by Trizec throughout Canada.
In total, this corporation controls 30 office-blocks (7,184,000 sq. ft
floor area), 7 shopping-centres (2,221,000 sq. ft), 12 residential
blocks (1,849 dwellings) and 18 hotels (with room for 2,500 persons).
This floor area is let, on average, to about 98 per cent of its capacity.
The modes of letting for office space and shops are usually as follows:
renters of office space pay a fixed 'rent' depending on the floor area,
and this 'rent' is periodically revised to reflect increases in taxes and
general maintenance costs; shopkeepers, for their part, have to pay a
basic 'rent' together with a supplement which may be anything up to
15 per cent of their turnover. It is thus that even though Trizec
showed a deficit of $840,000 in 1966, its net profits for 1970
amounted too $2,615,000, 2.3 times those of 1968. The least one can
say is that Trizec Corporation Ltd is quite a prosperous property
development company.[7]

One could give many other examples of property capitalism, such
as Concordia Estate, developer of the famous Place Concordia in
Montreal, Immeubles Delrano Inc., owners of Place Laurier and of the
new Carré d'Youville building in Quebec, and even the Mouvement
Desjardins with its vast project in the centre of Montreal, etc. But for

---

[7] The annual income and expenditure accounts of Trizec as quoted in the
documents mentioned earlier are as follows:

Consolidated Statement of Earnings (in millions of dollars)

Years Ended 31 December

	1966	1967	1968	1969	1970
Income					
Property operations	20.5	24.4	27.0	36.7	40.4
Interest and miscellaneous income	0.5	0.6	1.0	1.1	1.3
	21.0	25.0	28.0	37.8	41.7

our purposes the essential point is the following. In the strict sense, property capital does not carry out any productive labour; it thus creates no surplus-value. It plays the same role at the level of property as does commercial capital at the level of movable goods: buying in order to sell at a higher price (M—C—M'). Its own commodity is floor-space let (i.e. sold over a very long term) by the square foot. It can thus be distinguished from capital invested in the building industry in that the latter produces a concrete good, the building, whereas property capital merely realizes the metamorphosis of the building into money form. Since property capital produces neither value nor surplus-value through its operations, it may be asked, as for the other capitals operating in the sphere of circulation, whence come its profits?

1 The building industry

At first sight it would be logical to assume that the profits accruing to property capital derive from the surplus-value produced in the very construction of buildings. Indeed, one of the obvious functions of the property developer is the conversion of builders' commodity-capital into its money form; he buys buildings from entrepreneurs in order to sell them on the market. Thus one might say that through this specialized activity he contributes to the speeding up of the circulation of the capital invested in the building industry and thereby benefits from a part of the surplus-value created within that industry. In other words, if we see the function of property capital as restricted to the buying and selling of property, its profits must be explained as

Expenses					
Operating and rent	4.0	4.7	6.4	˙11.2	12.8
Salaries, general and					
administrative	2.1	2.0	1.8	2.0	2.4
Property taxes	3.8	5.3	5.7	7.0	7.5
Interest on long-term debt	10.9	11.5	11.6	14.0	15.2
	20.8	23.5	25.7	34.2	37.8
Operating Profit					
before depreciation	0.2	1.5	2.4	3.6	3.8
Depreciation of fixed assets	1.1	1.2	1.3	1.5	1.7
Earnings (loss) before					
extraordinary items	(.1)	0.3	1.1	2.0	2.2
Extraordinary items	—	—	—	.7	.5
Net earnings (loss)	(.8)	0.3	1.1	2.7	2.6

[N.B. Errors are due to rounding]

for commercial capital, by reference to industrial capital whose productivity it increases.

However, to state that the profits of property capital derive *solely* from the building industry raises at least two major objections. Firstly, in order for property capital to have as its sole function the circulation of capital invested in construction, it would be necessary for the latter to be sufficiently productive to make such specialization economically possible. In fact it appears that this is not the case. On the one hand, the building industry is one of the industrial sectors where monopolies are almost non-existent. It comprises a multitude of very small locally orientated firms, but very few large firms with high concentrations of capital and operating over a wide area.[8] As a corollary of this low degree of concentration, the building industry shows, on the other hand, a considerable technical lag in relation to other sectors of manufacturing industry. Its working methods still to a large extent involve a division between the various trades and are ultimately very expensive in relation to the average cost of production for the economy as a whole. Consequently, it would seem that the capital invested in this sector is of relatively low productivity compared to industrial capital as a whole. By itself it would thus not justify the existence of a capital exclusively specializing in the buying and selling of its commodities.[9] In other words, if property developers simply acted as salesmen for builders, their investments would be difficult to explain, since the share of surplus-value which they could obtain from entrepreneurs would be relatively small, especially taking into account the size of the capital immobilized.

Secondly, in order for the profits of the property developer to originate exclusively in the surplus-value produced at the time of construction, 'rent' levels would have to be fixed solely in terms of building costs. The developer, as a good businessman, would have to

[8] An American study has even demonstrated that the development of the building industry does not proceed by mergers between firms as is usual in other sections of industry (see J. Herzog, Structural change in the house-building industry, *Land Economics* 39 (1963) 133–41). On the fragmented state of the building industry in Quebec, see F. Lacasse, *Politiques du logement: analyse économique* (C.E.B.E.Q., Montreal, 1971).

[9] A clear distinction must be made between property capital and financial capital. The latter facilitates the circulation of money-capital and at the level of property does so indirectly via the mortgage market: its profits are expressed in terms of interest. Conversely, property capital specializes not in the circulation of money but in the metamorphosis of a particular commodity: floor space. Its profits are thus to be explained as a function of this specialization; we shall see later that they are expressed in terms of rent.

let his floor-spaces at a value determined solely by their production time. Now if this were the case, how could one explain the increase in residential 'rent' levels as one approaches the city-centre? How could one explain the percentage that the developer takes for himself from commercial activity? In brief, how could one explain the fact that the 'rents' demanded may be up to 30 per cent higher than building costs?[10]

Thus in other words the profits sought by property capital do not originate so much from the enterprise of construction as from the letting of floor-space. To put it more clearly, the profits which the developer has in view do not depend on the difference between the price he pays for his buildings and their value determined by their construction cost; his profits are primarily dependent on the divergence between this cost and the amount he extracts in the form of 'rents'. It is as if simply by letting his buildings the developer was realizing a value over and above that contained in the physical structure erected by the builder.

We are thus entitled to enquire as to the origin of this value which makes property capital relatively independent of the level of productivity of the building industry. Or again, we may ask ourselves what are the conditions which enable the developer to demand 'rents' which do not correspond to the cost of his buildings.

2 Resident tenants

Let us remember to start with that in the capitalist mode of production value can only be explained by reference to labour. On the one hand, it is created through the labour of production (extraction and transformation of raw material); on the other, its mass is preserved according to the efficiency of the labour of circulation (commerce, administration, etc.).

Now it is quite obvious that a family does not realize any labour simply by living in a dwelling. It creates no value (or surplus-value) by

[10] On this subject, see R. M. Williams, The relationships of housing prices and building costs in Los Angeles from 1900 to 1953, *Journal of the American Statistical Association* 50 (1955) 370—6. In order to illustrate the difference between the capital invested in the construction of a building (including land) and the level of 'rents' demanded, we might quote the words of the broker who stated that with the profits obtained at Place Ville-Marie ($19,493,000 gross income in 1970) Trizec could complete payment on this complex ($70 million) in 30 years. When one bears in mind that such a building will be usable for at least 100 years one can see the gap between its construction cost and its rental value.

so doing; still less does it obtain any financial advantage. It simply consumes a particular good in the same way that it consumes bread or other items necessary to the satisfaction of its needs. In short, the resident tenant plays no active role in the production-reproduction of capital, apart from that of having needs and being the final consumer of a particular commodity: housing.

In these conditions, the amount of 'rent' the resident pays should be determined as for all other commodities by the quantity of labour contained in his dwelling. More precisely, since a dwelling does not acquire any value solely through the fact of being lived in (on the contrary, its value falls with use) its 'rent' should correspond to construction costs, plus, obviously, interest on the capital which the owner has immobilized in it.[11]

But a dwelling can offer other advantages than those contained within its own four walls. It may be situated in a pleasant area, close to work-places, large stores and other services considered necessary, etc. In brief, depending on the location of his dwelling, a tenant may enjoy a more comfortable life and in particular need to waste less time in travel. And these advantages must be paid for!

One can thus understand now in what conditions the property developer will invest in residential property. Since, strictly speaking, he is not a financier, that is to say he seeks something other than the average rate of interest on the capital he advances, the developer will not operate in the field of housing unless he can convert the advantages provided by the environment into profits. And how is he able to do this?

We have seen that the advantages paid for by the tenant are paid for over and above the minimum 'rent' corresponding to the cost of construction plus interest on the capital immobilized in the dwelling. If one were to take into account these factors alone, the advantages paid for over and above the basic 'rent' would represent a net profit for the owner. But we shall see later that in the price of land the owner too has had to pay for some of the situational advantages that he now extracts in the form of excess 'rent'. Now for these excesses to really represent a profit, the developer owner must maximize the

[11] A further point on the subject of interest. One may say that the owner of residential property gets back the capital invested, in small amounts, in the form of 'rents'. It is thus logical to think that he includes in his 'rents' interest on the capital he has yet to recover, i.e. on the capital immobilized in his dwellings that the tenants use in a sense on credit. See F. Engels, The housing question, in K. Marx and F. Engels, *Selected Works* 2 (Progress Publishers, Moscow, 1969) 359 (Part III, §II).

advantages he can get from the environment. In order to do this firstly
he will order high-rise buildings, because it is quite obvious that the
greater the number of dwellings on his piece of land, the greater the
excess 'rent' he will be able to obtain. Secondly, the developer will
maximize his profits by adding to the price an amount reflecting the
advantages supplied by the environment. He will be able to demand a
higher price if these advantages are not equally distributed in space,
i.e. if they are found concentrated in certain places and almost
non-existent in others; in other words, the developer will be able to
demand for his dwellings what Marx calls a monopoly price, in so far
as he controls the advantages available to a limited extent in a given
area.[12]

In short, we can say that the property developer will only invest in
residential property if luxury dwellings are involved. It is only on this
condition that he can make his capital profitable and maximize his
profits. But such a practice runs up against certain limits, on the one
hand, because of the low elasticity of demand for this type of
dwelling (not many people can afford a 'rent' of $200–300 per
month); and, on the other hand, because the profitability of this
practice is due precisely to the exceptional, exclusive or restricted
character of the advantages it offers. Property capital must thus find
additional investment outlets.

3 Commercial, financial and administrative enterprises
In reality, the field of housing is only a sub-product, a sideline of
property capitalism, since the profits it yields are primarily a function
of its proximity to and integration with shopping-centres and office
developments. It is thus in the planning and equipping of the latter
that the primary interests of property capitalism lie. In particular, it is
by carrying out this function that property capital plays its true role
within social capital.

As we have hinted, this role is related to that of commercial and
financial capital in so far as the principal effect of the activity of
property capital is to speed up the circulation of commodities and the
execution of financial operations and certain administrative tasks . . .,

[12] When we refer to a monopoly price, we mean in general a price determined
only by the purchaser's eagerness to buy and ability to pay, independent of
the price determined by the general price of production.

K. Marx, *Capital* 3, 775 (chapter 46). On monopoly elements in the housing
market, see J. J. Granelle, La formation des prix du sol dans l'espace urbain,
Revue d'économie politique 78 (1968) 52.

ultimately reducing the costs inherent in the circulation of productive capital. Conversely, one might say that it is in so far as property capital has such effects that it is profitable for its owners.

In order to clarify the origin of the profits pocketed by developers, we should first enquire as to the reasons which lead businessmen, bankers and administrators to establish themselves in the developments planned and equipped by property capitalists. We have already indicated some of these reasons by saying that both by their internal organization and their location these developments facilitate commerce, financial operations and certain administrative tasks. For example, the person who controls the large shopping-centre at Place Laurier is well aware that the concentration of businesses there has a favourable effect on their turnover figures: the large stores attract a large clientele which then visits the dearer and more specialized shops; conversely, the latter shops attract people with well-lined pockets who then complete their purchases in the large stores, etc. It is the same logic which underlies the demands of the traders of Saint-Roch for the construction of a covered precinct and the plans of certain developers for a commercial development in zone 2 in Quebec. In fact, one could say that the more that businesses accede to the plans of the developers and become concentrated in narrowly delimited areas, the less safe their prospects become outside these concentrations; traders who are geographically isolated have to ask themselves increasingly whether paying a doubled or trebled 'rent' is not preferable to risking a fall in turnover from a level which not so long ago was enough to provide them with an adequate standard of living! And what is to be said about office developments such as Place Ville-Marie or Place Quebec? To start with, that they are not simply products of the imagination of some ambitious architect. They are first and foremost the physical expression of the concentration of capital and of the close ties linking the headquarters of industry and the financial world. They represent a geographical answer to the provision of the services, information and contacts required by the interconnected activities of capital. . . . In the case of Place Quebec, the office-block currently being constructed also enjoys proximity to government buildings; such proximity will not be in vain, since we shall see the embassies of large firms and a whole cohort of sub-entrepreneurs, so-called management advisers, establishing themselves there to benefit from the double patronage thus created.

In reality there is only one reason which pushes businessmen, administrators and bankers to become concentrated in the centres prepared for them by the property developers: greater efficiency in their activities. For some this means a higher turnover, for others better access to a mass of services and to information useful in management, in financial transactions, etc. In brief, through their location and internal organization these developments contribute to a reduction in the cost of activities linked to the reproduction of capital or, what amounts to the same thing, to an increase in efficiency at a given cost. Theoretically they should thus give rise to excess profits for those established in them.

In fact the property developer reserves all rights of ownership relating to the office-blocks or shopping-centres he has built for him. The 'rent' levels he demands for his floor-spaces thus depend on the economic advantages the tenant businessmen, administrators, etc., obtain from them — as well as on building and maintenance costs, interest on the capital immobilized in the building, land taxes, etc. For example, when the owner of a shopping-centre adds, as an element in the 'rents' he charges, a percentage of turnover, he is reckoning to appropriate the excess profits which his shopping-centre brings to the traders. In brief, the profits the property capitalist has in mind when he invests in the construction of office-blocks or shopping-centres, correspond to the excess profits which the developments he owns create for a given firm.

In these conditions it would seem that since the developer does not strictly speaking create either value or surplus-value (any more than do businessmen, administrators or bankers), the profits yielded by his property intervention on the administrative, commercial or financial sectors, originate ultimately in the surplus-value created at the level of production. It is because it contributes to a reduction in the time and labour involved in circulation that property capital, like the other specialized capitals, is entitled to share in the surplus-value created by productive capital. . . .

II The planning role of property capitalism
In reality, the profits captured by the property capitalist are not to be explained solely by his ownership rights over urban space. These rights give him the power to make his tenants pay for advantages which he has often had absolutely no part in creating. For example, the tenants living along the Abraham plains in Quebec pay a very high 'rent' for the quietness of the area and the beauty of the countryside; but these advantages have in no way been created by their owners. In the same way, Trizec will extract fat profits from Place Quebec, principally

because of the development of Parliament Hill and the construction of
the Dufferin highway; but these situational advantages are nothing to
do with the corporation, they are the product of public investments. . . . However, considered as a whole, we may say that the more
property capitalism develops on a large scale, the more it creates the
conditions of its own profitability itself. For example, by linking
residential and commercial developments geographically, the property
capitalist acts simultaneously on two levels: he pockets on the one
hand the price paid by residents to be close to the shopping facilities
and on the other the tribute of the shopkeepers for the access to a
large clientele which he has himself created. . . .

   The profits yielded by the right of ownership over urban space
appear in the form of rent. As Marx said, rent is 'that economic form
in which landed property is realized'.[13] It presents itself as a sum of
money that the owner extracts from the occupation 'of certain
portions of our planet . . .'. A consideration of the different forms of
rent obtained by the property capitalist will enable us to get a better
grasp of the role of the latter in planning the development of modern
cities.[14]

1 Differential rent I

This first form of rent is a function of the advantages offered by the
site of a property, and which do not depend directly on any action by
the owner. An example of this would be the cases already quoted of
the luxury dwellings built along the Abraham plains or of Place
Quebec on Parliament Hill. This rent is termed differential because the
situational advantages on which it is based are not evenly distributed
throughout space. It is constituted by the excess 'rent' that the owner
demands in exchange for these advantages (which, moreover, do not
belong to him). As we have already said the size of this excess in the
field of residential property will depend on the desire to rent and
ability to pay of the residents; in the case of shopping-centres and
office-blocks, this excess will be directly proportional to the increase
in profits created by the location of these developments for their
tenants.

[13] In *Capital* 3, 634 (chapter 37).
[14] The forms of rent defined here are based essentially on the definitions given
by Marx for agricultural land (*Capital* 3, 614—813 (chapters 37—47)). On the
application of Marx's definitions to land for building, see the articles by
F. Alquier, Contribution à l'étude de la rente foncière sur les terrains urbains,
and J. Lojkine, Y a-t-il une rente foncière urbaine?, in *Espaces et Sociétés*
2 (1971) 75—94.

Considered from the point of view of an individual developer, differential rent I may originate from two sources which are by definition (i.e., according to this type of rent) external to his property development activity. We are excluding here natural causes, since in an urban environment greenery and even the beauty of the landscape, etc., are, for the most part, the fruit of economic and political action. On the one hand, the differential rent I extracted by an individual developer may derive from other private investors. For example, a developer who has an apartment-block constructed in the vicinity of a shopping-centre, will profit from its proximity to the shopping facilities; conversely, the owner of the shopping-centre will benefit, because of the method by which he calculates 'rents', from the arrival of the new clientele, etc. In short, it is as if, in a given district, each private developer provides the others with an opportunity to increase their differential rent I. . . . On the other hand, this form of rent may be made possible by public investments. The most obvious example of this is that of investment in transport facilities. For example, a developer whose property is situated on the edge of a main road will profit through his 'rents' from this advantage which brings residents closer to their work-places, expands the catchment area of businesses, etc.

It is hence easy to see the importance of public investments for property capital as a whole; because, by increasing geographically the opportunities for private investment, they simultaneously expand the opportunities for property capital to hold on to this first form of rent. One could even say that from the point of view of property developers as a whole, the size of differential rent I is proportional to the amount of public investments in collective facilities. . . .

2 Differential rent II

Unlike the first type of rent, differential rent II is not strictly speaking brought about by the location of a property. It is based, rather, on advantages contained within the limits of the property, advantages which depend primarily on the characteristics of the occupants. With certain qualifications, one could say that this second form of rent corresponds to the profits the developer obtains for the advantages offered by the 'proximity' between the tenants occupying his property.

Obviously it is difficult to envisage any such advantages in purely residential developments; because as a general rule the convenience and comfort of one resident are not increased by the presence of his neighbours. The sole advantage a resident could derive from his immediate neighbourhood, and for which he might be led to pay an excess in his 'rent', lies in the prestige or status of living in such an environment. . . . It is primarily in commercial and office developments that the role of differential rent II becomes apparent; because it is in this type of case that the activities of the various tenants can be mutually advantageous. Thus, head offices of large companies, financial institutions, and administrative services of all sorts (management consultants, public relations consultants, lawyers, accountants, brokers, etc.) can obtain numerous advantages from the clustering of their activities in the same place. In the same way, the nature and size of the shops in a shopping-centre help the sales of each of them. . . . In these fields, differential rent II corresponds to the excess profits created by the proximity of different capitalist agents within a given property. In the strict sense, it is thus not the owner developer who creates these benefits, but rather the nature and mutual advantage of the activities carried out *intra muros*. The only action for which he is responsible is that of having had the walls erected and geographical framework created which make possible the production of such benefits. It is by virtue of the right of ownership he exercises over the development that he can subsequently capture the profits in the form of rent.

It is now easier to grasp the planning role of property capitalism; for the more this specialized capital develops on a large scale, and becomes concentrated in a small number of hands, the greater the role of differential rent II in the profitability of its investments.

In fact, as we have seen, this second form of rent is based on advantages lying within the limits of a private property. Now, if this property increases in size, so do the advantages it contains. For example, an apartment-block or a small commercial building can offer few situational advantages of themselves; the rent obtained by their owner is primarily a function of the characteristics of the environment over which, moreover, he has no control. But if he also owns the entire group of buildings of which they form part, some of what appeared before as differential rent I now becomes differential rent II; what was previously an external advantage is now within the limits of the property. The owner developer thus increases his control over the production of these advantages, in that he is in a better position to plan the organization of his property so that the nature and activities of the tenants increase the profitability of his capital.

In other words, the more property capital becomes concentrated and extends its control over urban space, the more it is in a position to itself create the conditions of its own profitability, that is to say, to plan the organization of its property so that the nature and activities of the tenants of a given site are more mutually advantageous and, hence, maximize its profits.

As we have already indicated, the types of activity for which the developer intends his property to be used are principally commerce, administration and finance . . . in short, activities concerned with the circulation of capital. This is because, on the one hand, these are the activities which economically profit most from their mutual proximity, thereby increasing the profitability of property capital; and, on the other hand, it is in this field that the developer finds the most extensive investment opportunities. The residential sector constitutes a source of profits for property capital primarily in so far as it is linked to commercial and office developments, since the situational advantages on which the profitability of residential property is based are to a large extent due to the proximity of shopping facilities, work-places . . . in short, to the reduction of time spent on travel. Obviously, the higher the price demanded in exchange for these situational advantages, the more the developer's profits swell. Now, this price will be all the higher if the clientele the dwellings are directed at is a privileged one, i.e. 'able to pay'. This is why it is more profitable for the developer to invest in luxury dwellings. It is as if the high 'rent' implied at the outset by the sumptuousness of the dwellings was aimed at selecting a rich clientele capable of subsequently paying a high rent for the advantages of the surrounding environment.

Finally, one may ask what role is played in the urban question by the political authorities which boast loudest that they are the sole masters of their territory. We shall return to this important question elsewhere. Let us say for the time being that planning by the political instances is real in as much as it forms part of the logic of property capitalism. The development plans drawn up by municipal planning departments can only be realized if they are subordinated to the interests of developers. The gradual modifications made to what the planners learnedly called 'the general concept of redevelopment of Parliament Hill in Quebec' [sic], provide a perfect example of this subordination. In reality, a city's control over the planning and equipping of its territory is more or less limited to the creation of the situational advantages (transport facilities, public buildings, absorption of costs due to land speculation, etc.) on which part of the profits of property capital are based. To put it another way, it is as if the role of the city was to clear and plough its own land in order for others to sow and harvest the best fruit. That is the meaning of the 'highly rational' planning of the municipal technocrats! At least that is what is unequivocally revealed by the story of Place Quebec; and it is the same story repeated again and again almost everywhere, particularly in the old quarter of Saint Roch in Quebec. . . .

III The urban land market

Prior to the activity of property capital is a special phenomenon, the land market; because property does not travel through space like fruit from California. It is necessarily fixed to a plot of ground which can acquire a value independently of what is built on it. It is the realization of this value which is sought in the land market. This economic phenomenon is worth studying, especially as it seems not entirely unrelated to the gradual deterioration of certain quarters of the city.

1 The formation of land prices and the profits of land speculation

To start with, how is the price of urban land determined? At first sight one might be tempted to answer that it is determined by the value of the facilities placed on it (buildings, etc.). But this would be short-sighted, since a piece of land with only poor facilities or even without any facilities also has a price which can often be very high. For example, many people have learnt to their cost that a piece of land on which an ancient hovel is falling apart is sometimes worth more than a piece of land containing the perfect house. . . . In other words, there are factors other than the building which influence the price of a piece of land.

According to the indications given by the price curve in the land market, these factors are due primarily to the site of the parcel, both in relation to the urban area as a whole, and in relation to the immediate environment. Thus a vacant urban lot located close to a business district is usually worth much more than another of the same size further from it. . . . In the same way, experts on this subject consider that, as a general rule, taking the urban area as a whole, land prices fall from the city-centre to the periphery, more slowly along main roads, and with slight humps around secondary centres. . . . Thus Vieille concludes that:

The price of each parcel of urban land is a function of neighbouring parcels. Micro-ecological structures thus exist, as well as the global structures of the agglomeration as a whole.[15]

In order to be able to proceed further we need to make a distinction between what we shall call the land market and the property market. Following from what was said earlier, the property market is mainly concerned with the buying and letting of floor-space; the profits obtained by the property owner in the form of rent derive from the use made by the tenants of the advantages provided by the internal organization and/or location of his properties. In other words, the profitability of property investment is made possible by the occupation of a given space. Of course the developer's operations also include plots of land, but solely as favourable sites for his property investments. The same is not true for what we have called the land market. This market may be seen as principally concerned with plots of land, any property standing on it being of only secondary importance in the operation. Thus the land-owner is not involved in investing in the opportunities for use provided by the sites he owns. The most striking example of this is the owner of a vacant lot close to the city-centre.

Now it is obvious that the owner who owns a piece of land with the sole aim of re-selling it, seeks a profit at the end of the transaction. Since the profit sought does not, strictly speaking, derive from the exploitation of any property that may be on the site, it is relevant to enquire as to its origin. To put it more clearly what is the source of the profitability of capital invested in a piece of land if, as is sometimes the case, it lies completely unused?

One element of the answer has already been established. In order for the land-owner to realize a profit he must obviously sell his land at a higher price than he paid for it, although he is not at all responsible for this difference in price. Since the land-owner does not invest any money in the equipping of his land, the value acquired by the latter on the market must come from elsewhere.

This 'elsewhere' is, in a sense, the more or less immediate environment which, as it is developed, increases the number of possible uses of a given piece of land or, to be more precise, makes it a more and more favourable site for profitable property investment. This is why Vieille says that the land-owner

[15] P. Vieille, *Marché des Terrains et Société Urbaine* (Editions Anthropos, Paris, 1970) 89.

... speculates on urban dynamism and the provision of facilities by the community, and takes today the value expected tomorrow,[16]

In order to have a clearer picture, let us take the example of a vacant lot close to the city-centre. Let us assume that its owner paid x dollars for it and has spent nothing since to equip it with any sort of building or even a parking lot. Let us assume also that some years later this same owner is in a position to demand $5x$ dollars for his piece of land. We know that this difference in price cannot be explained by the incorporation of capital in the land, since the lot is still vacant. On what, then, is this difference based? It is based on the very simple fact that the piece of land has become a particularly favourable site for property development. Thus, let us say that our land-owner finds a buyer in the person of a developer who wishes to have a very large office and commercial block built upon it. We already know the intentions of such a developer: by realizing his project he expects to obtain fat profits from the site of the piece of land, in the form we termed differential rent I. Now our land-owner is also aware of the intentions of the purchaser. He is so well aware of them in fact that his entire activity has consisted in simply awaiting the realization of such intentions. Thus the profits he obtains by quintupling the price of his piece of land are based on the size of the possible profits which the future developer owner will extract from it. In other words, the more favourable the site of the piece of land for profitable property investment, the better the chance the owner has of increasing its price, and thereby appropriating part of the profits its eventual use will create.

From this perspective the price of land in urban areas can thus be regarded as representing only an abstract value, not yet actualized, i.e. which anticipates on the future profitability of property capital. For example, a developer who sold his property to another developer would set his price according to the amount of capital incorporated in the land and the rent produced by this capital; in this case, the piece of land would have no value other than that of its current use. The same is not true on the land market. If the price of a piece of land does not correspond to the value determined by its current use this is because the owner is speculating on the changes which could be made to it. As Vieille states, the price demanded in this case is based '. . . on a calculation of the capitalised value of expected future incomes'.[17]

[16] *Ibid.*, 96.
[17] *Ibid.*, 6.

This is why the word speculative is often used to describe this type of market, or the word speculator to describe the land-owner:

> Speculators are those who are quick to see that the uses in a given area, the types of building to be found there or not, are becoming inadequate or irrational in the existing spatial-economic context and will necessitate the transformation of pre-urban uses or a change in use of existing neighbourhoods.[18]

To summarize, the land market is prior to property development, and the profits it yields are based on the anticipated profitability of property capital. It is thus most active in geographical areas suitable for commercial, office or luxury residential development, since it is in this type of development that property capital maximizes its profits. Concretely, it is in the areas surrounding the city-centre and the secondary centres, and along the principal roads, that the land-owner will find the most favourable sites for speculation on urban redevelopment and profitable future investment.

2 The right to withhold land and the formation of absolute rent
However, to say that the land-owner's profits rest on the anticipated profitability of property capital is to give an incomplete explanation of them. In addition we must specify what it is that entitles the owner of a piece of land to raise its price and thus appropriate a share of the profits that others will create after him. Well, this right is the same as that which enables the developer to profit from the situational advantages created, for all practical purposes, by the use of his properties and by the surrounding areas: the right of ownership. But whereas for the developer ownership is the result of property investments which actualize situational advantages which are translated into rents, for the land-owner it represents economic and legal control over areas in the process of being (re)developed, his profits being based on the future possibilities of the sites he owns. In other words, the developer's right of ownership enables him to extract a rent for the *real* advantages which his tenants actually benefit from; whereas that of the land-owner enables him to obtain a rent for the *potential* advantages which the property developer will actualize. . . . In a way it is the story of the stealer stolen which repeats itself according to the following rule: the developer is the one who carries

---

[18] J. Lautman, La spéculation, facteur d'ordre ou de désordre économique, *Revue française de sociologie* 10 (1969) 608–630 at 622.

the plan through while the land-owner, fully aware of the plan, demands a share of the loot in exchange for his complicity.

In reality, the right of ownership over land can be summed up essentially as the legal right to withhold a given site from the market (i.e. from free circulation or free use) for a shorter or longer period of time, during which the general development of the city increases the importance of the site in the eyes of property capital and thereby enables its owner to increase its price. For example, we assumed that our vacant lot close to the city-centre was bought at a price of x dollars. Now for it to be resold for a figure five times higher ($5x$ dollars) its owner had to be able to retain possession of it, and even keep it empty, until the growth of the city-centre made its use for property development more profitable. It is this power to withhold land which is conferred by legal ownership of land. In short, as noted by Marx, landed property gives its owner

> ... the power to withdraw his land from exploitation until economic conditions permit him to utilise it in such a manner as to yield him a surplus.[19]

The anticipated profits made possible by the right to withhold land appear in the form of *absolute rent*. Thus, unlike differential rents, this third form of rent does not yield actual and immediate profits to the land-owner. It is based on time and results in fact from the action of the owner who, by withholding his land from exploitation, encourages the increase in expected differential rents (the only ones to constitute hard cash). In other words, absolute rent may be regarded as corresponding to the portion of differential rents (rent I mainly) attributable to the land-owner's action in withholding land. ... Thus the profits obtained by our owner as soon as he sells his land ($5x - x = 4x$ dollars) may be defined as absolute rent. They do not derive from exploitation of the site but from the owner's legal power to retain possession of his land until the growth of the city-centre makes its use for property development profitable. To be more precise, absolute rent corresponds in this case to the portion of differential rent I obtained by the developer from the new advantages created by surrounding developments.

In order to avoid any misunderstanding, it must be emphasized here that while economic agents in the land and property markets are

---

[19] Quoted by F. Alquier, Contribution à l'étude de la rente foncière sur les terrains urbains, *Espaces et Sociétés* 2 (1971) 80 [*Capital* 3, 757 (chapter 45)].

often different individuals, it is not impossible — quite the contrary in fact — for the developer also to play the role of land-owner in respect of his future property development projects, i.e. to slow down the exploitation of the land he owns until the appearance of a more favourable spatial conjuncture. In such a case, he captures the value acquired by the land in the form of absolute rent; but in no way does he alter the general laws governing the land market. More precisely, the land market does not simply consist of transactions relating to pieces of land for (re)development; it also includes the process by which the uses of these lots are transformed. One might even go so far as to say that it is governed by these transformations, since the absolute rents it yields are dependent on the profitability of the future uses.

Furthermore, whether the change from one form of use to another more profitable form of use does or does not coincide with a change in ownership of the piece of land in no way alters the mechanism of the change, which is characterized by a 'postponement' of the new use, and by the formation of absolute rent. The only difference is that in one case the roles of land speculator and property developer are played by the same capitalist whereas in the other they are played by different capitalists. . . . For example, for over ten years Concordia Estate has owned 90 per cent of the land and property in the Milton-Parc district of Montreal, where it is planning to carry out its famous 'Place Concordia' project. The speed with which it bought the sites made it clear that Concordia wanted to avoid paying the costs of land speculation, i.e. avoid giving up any of the value which these pieces of land would have acquired by the time building operations started! But by displacing the land speculators in this way Concordia was not acting any differently from them: like them it is waiting for general conditions to make its project profitable; like them it is letting the buildings it plans to replace deteriorate in the meantime. . . .

3 Urban decay, a source of excess profit
We are now in a better position to grasp the way in which the land market or land speculation speeds up the deterioration of those existing districts which are suitable for future property development.

To start with, at what point can one regard a piece of developed land as becoming the object of land speculation? At the point when the value of the piece of land (or site) exceeds the real value of the property, including the rents deriving from its use. More precisely, when does a piece of developed land pass from the property market to the land market? When the profitability of its current use falls in relation to the growing opportunities offered by surrounding developments.

For example, let us suppose that standing on our piece of land located close to the city-centre is a small apartment building built a long time ago. Let us also suppose that the city-centre is rapidly expanding, in other words that very large commercial and office-blocks and luxury towers are being constructed there and that new roads will soon connect it to the different points of the city, etc. The use made of our piece of land thus appears increasingly anachronistic in relation to the redevelopment which is taking place all around. For the owner this means that the profitability of his small apartment building looks more and more ludicrous in relation to the new possibilities acquired by the site; in concrete terms, this is expressed by an increase in the price of his piece of land which thus ceases to bear any relation to the real value of the building standing on it. In this conjuncture, how will our owner act? Since it is profit which is his primary aim, he has ultimately very few choices open to him. He only needs wait for surrounding developments to make the radical transformation of his site for office, commercial and luxury residential use, etc., more profitable. If he has sufficient financial resources he will carry out these transformations himself; if not he will realize his profit through the increased value his piece of land acquires due to the development of the surrounding districts. In such conditions what becomes of his small building? It loses importance, given that the profits he seeks now rest on the future possibilities offered by the site. Consequently, the owner no longer has much interest in investing in the maintenance of a building which sooner or later will disappear under the pickaxes of the demolition men. The apartments deteriorate but the price of the piece of land continues to rise. The owner rubs his hands with glee, especially as the 'rents' he obtains from his dilapidated property cover his outgoings (land taxes, etc.) and even yield him a profit. . . . Finally, after a number of years of this easily tolerated waiting, the site is cleared to make way for a new building at the height appropriate to a prosperous city-centre!

What is true for a particular case is, with the passage of time, true for a whole neighbourhood. Because, as a district becomes transformed, the different properties successively become suitable for new uses as determined by the development of property capital. In this situation, owners who previously presented themselves as vendors of 'buildings to let' gradually become vendors of land, speculating on the profitability of future investment. It is thus that in an existing neighbourhood the price of land gradually increases while paradoxically the real value of the buildings falls. Though slow in starting, these contradictory tendencies proceed rapidly as property development comes closer.

The fall in the value of the buildings can be explained, as we have seen, by two factors: the low level of profits deriving from their use in the new conjuncture brought about by property capital; and the consequent fact that their owners cease to have any interest in spending anything on their upkeep. But until the buildings are demolished their letting brings in additional income which adds to the profits anticipated from the sale of the land or the future use of the site. This excess profit is all the greater when, despite the gradual deterioration of the buildings, the owners are in a position to demand a situation rent because of the advantages created by surrounding developments. So that in decaying property the proportion of the 'rent' which covers the real cost of the building tends towards zero, while the part based on the advantages of the surrounding environment increases. In other words, it may be said that if the 'rent' level of a slum dwelling stays relatively low, it is due to the obsolescence of the dwelling; but if the level stays the same or even on occasion increases despite its continued deterioration, it is because the owners are increasing the component of the 'rent' extracted in the form of differential rent I.

'The owner's strategy,' writes Castells, 'is thus simple: he waits for the construction of new property or an urban renewal operation which will bring him a profitable sale of his land, and during this period he obtains an adequate rent through the *socially defined* particular conditions of the property market in which he operates.'[20] Moreover, it is this dual strategy of the land-owner which enables one to understand why the redevelopment of an existing neighbourhood does not take place gradually, and why excessive decay is almost always followed by property development on a large scale. For, firstly, the greater the divergence between the price of a piece of land and the value of the building standing on it, the more the owner is able to maximize his profits in the form of what we have termed absolute rent. Secondly, the greater the accentuation of the factors leading to a rise in price of the piece of land (i.e. the greater the

[20] In La rénovation urbaine aux Etats-Unis, synthèse et interprétation des données actuelles, *Espaces et Sociétés* 1 (1970) 107–35 at 121.

number of potential uses of the site), the more the owner is able to increase the excess profits he obtains from the current use of his land. Finally, it may be wondered what would become of an owner who undertook repairs on a building which the logic of property capital destined for demolition. Two things could happen to such an owner — perhaps philanthropic, but certainly a poor capitalist. Either he would quite simply lose the money invested in repairing the building when he sold the land, given that the building counts for virtually nothing in the price of a piece of land that property capital destines to new uses. Or else our owner would continue to exploit his building at a relatively low level of profitability compared with what was possible in the new spatial conjuncture of which it is part. . . .

Conclusion: the housing question
Engels wrote that:

> In reality the bourgeoisie has only one method of settling the housing question after *its* fashion — that is to say, of settling it in such a way that the solution continually poses the question anew.[21]

In other words, this method which properly belongs to the 'thinkers' of the dens of government, even to some trade union leaders, etc., amounts to a wish to treat the symptoms while ignoring the causes. . . . A strange sort of medicine.

However, our discussion so far leads us to *one* conclusion: the housing question — which condenses a good number of urban social problems — cannot be posed in isolation from capitalist production; *its* solution cannot thus be conceived apart from the shattering of the contradiction between labour and capital. This is a short way of saying that the problems experienced by workers in their homes in the large cities depend to a major extent on land speculation and in particular on property capitalism, *the latter only becoming comprehensible by referring to its particular function in the capitalist mode of production.* Consequently, the difficulties encountered by the working class outside work (during the reproduction of its labour power) link up with the exploitation it is victim of at work, *in the sense that the solutions to both radically challenge the capitalist ownership of the means of production.*

The difficulties encountered by workers in living in the urban

---

[21] F. Engels, The housing question, in K. Marx and F. Engels, *op. cit.*, 350 (Part II, §III).

environment are mainly of three orders: (1) expropriation required by what the planners call frankly 'urban renewal'; (2) the insalubrity of housing awaiting 'renewal'; and (3) the shortage of dwellings at reasonable 'rents' after the completion of renewal operations. By considering these three aspects of the housing question one after the other we shall be able to summarize the arguments developed earlier and better support our conclusion.

1 Expropriation

A problem whose subtlety is matched only by its importance is certainly that of expropriation in neighbourhoods undergoing redevelopment. A direct product of property capitalism, this problem is far from being reducible, as the crudest interpretations would suggest, simply to a temporary disturbance occasioned by the physical renewal of deteriorated buildings. Expropriation is rather the signal for a slow exodus which gradually removes the working classes further and further from the nerve-centres of the city and from the mass of services necessary to their maintenance.

In order to understand this gradual process of expulsion undergone by urban workers it is necessary to refer to the foundations of property capitalism. We will attempt to summarize the latter in the following few propositions:

(a) The time and labour devoted by capital as a whole to its circulation are unproductive, i.e. they produce neither value nor surplus-value; their cost must therefore be deducted from the mass of surplus-value created in the production sphere;

(b) One of the ways in which capital reduces these unproductive costs and thereby accelerates its own accumulation on an extended scale consists in dividing the different tasks necessary to its reproduction among specialized capitals. Thus in addition to industrial capital we find commercial capital which specializes in the circulation of commodity-capital, and financial capital which specializes in the circulation of money-capital;

(c) However, the costs of circulation also depend on the distance separating the different economic agents and the spatial arrangement of their activities. Thus one can conceive of the existence of a specialized capital whose function within social capital is to organize spatially commercial, financial and administrative activities in order to increase their efficiency and thereby facilitate a reduction in the indirect costs of capitalist production. This capital is property capital;

(d) It is thus in the development of commercial and office-blocks

that property capital finds its true 'vocation', as well as a very wide
field for investment. The profitability of its investments will depend
on the increased efficiency it produces in commercial, financial and/or
administrative operations;

(e) From the point of view of property capital the field of housing
appears as an allied field of investment, in that its profitability
depends to a large extent on its integration with shopping-centres and
office developments. In exchange for the advantages provided by the
location of residential developments, the developer can demand a
monopoly price. And this price will be higher when luxury residences
are involved since the main effect of this type of housing is the
selection of a clientele 'able to pay'.

The ability to pay 'rents' of $250 or $300 per month is certainly
not the lot of workers or of the unemployed living in old
neighbourhoods undergoing redevelopment. Furthermore, after their
slums have made way for banks, large stores and offices for large
firms, after beautiful houses for the managers of these same banks,
stores and firms have been built, and after new roads have been laid
out, etc., they will be forced to move to other districts which are
deteriorating but which have not yet been affected by renewal,
districts which (for the time being only) are geographically marginal
to urban growth commanded by property capital according to the
laws of capitalist accumulation, i.e. according to the economic logic
which determines market relations and private ownership of the
means of production. As Marx put it so well:

> 'Improvements' of towns, accompanying the increase of wealth, by
> the demolition of badly built quarters, the erection of palaces for
> banks, warehouses, etc., the widening of streets for business traffic,
> for the carriages of luxury, and for the introduction of tramways,
> etc., drive away the poor into even worse and more crowded hiding
> places.[22]

2 The insalubrity of housing awaiting 'renewal'

The activity of property capital is not a gradual process; for if this
were so an urban area would be developed progressively as the spatial
conjuncture of the city changed. Urban redevelopment proceeds,
rather, by jolts, or leaps, so that in existing areas large-scale
developments invariably occur only after an excessive degree of

---

[22] K. Marx, *Capital* 1 (Lawrence and Wishart, London, 1970) 657 (chapter 25,
§ 5b).

dilapidation has taken place. These gaps between periods of property investment (or what one might call delayed redevelopment) raise the whole problem of the insalubrity of housing in older districts awaiting renewal. This problem cannot be explained without reference to the land market or to the land speculation which precedes property development. We can try to summarize our argument on these matters in the following way:

(a) A piece of land has no real value apart from that determined by the capital incorporated in it and apart from the profits produced by that capital. The value of developed land thus corresponds to the capital immobilized in the building and the rents deriving from its use for property development;

(b) If the profitability of a building falls in relation to the new opportunities offered by surrounding developments, the piece of land will tend to acquire a price which bears no relation to its real value. This price represents an abstract value, still to be actualized, which takes into account the profits expected from the future use of the site;

(c) The profits of the land-owner which originate from the increase in value of the plot appear in the form of absolute rent. Basically absolute rent rests on the legal right of an owner to withhold his plot while the development of the city increases its importance in the eyes of property capital and thereby gives him the opportunity to increase its price;

(d) The land-owner who speculates in this way on urban development thus has no interest in investing in the maintenance or repair of buildings which no longer meet the demands of property capital and which, sooner or later, will be replaced by new and more profitable complexes.

In brief, the more a district becomes the object of land speculation (i.e. becomes suitable for property development) the smaller becomes the share of the building in the total price of the land. This fall is not solely due to the new conditions of profitability created by the surrounding environment; it is also caused by the physical deterioration of the buildings arising from the inaction of the owner who withholds his land for other purposes. It is in this precise conjecture that the problem of insalubrity of housing occurs, as, for example, in the case of housing close to the city-centre.

It may be wondered why these dwellings continue to be lived in despite their increasing state of decay; or, again, why the land-owner persists in exploiting buildings which are economically inappropriate in the spatial conjuncture in which they are located. The answers are, however, obvious. On the one hand, since these dwellings are dilapidated, their 'rents' remain comparatively low so that they have many potential users among the poorest section of the working class; on the other hand, they are a source of excess profit for the owner. To put it more clearly, 'rent' can, as we have seen, be broken down into the following elements: building costs + interest on capital immobilized + situation rent. Now, as the material value of a dwelling falls (in other words, as all of the capital invested in the dwelling has been recovered over the years, at the same time as its physical state has been deteriorating), so the magnitude of the first two elements falls in proportion; logically there should be a corresponding fall in the total 'rent'. But of course in areas suitable for urban renewal, owners of slums can compensate for this fall by an increase in the part of the 'rent' based on situational advantages, and do so without changing the level of the total 'rent' which remains relatively low compared with that of new dwellings. In other words, the more a dwelling deteriorates, the more its owner is able to increase the part of the 'rent' which is reckoned as rent; thus while maintaining his 'rents' at the level of his customers' 'ability to pay', he pockets profits additional to those he will realize when his land is sold or reconverted. . . . It is in this light that the following comment by Marx must be understood:

> Everyone knows that the dearness of dwellings is in inverse ratio to
> their excellence, and that the mines of misery are exploited by
> house speculators with more profit or less cost than ever were the
> mines of Potosí.[23]

3 The shortage of dwellings at reasonable 'rents'

It is now easy to understand the reasons for the shortage of dwellings at reasonable 'rents' in the city. Of course, we are not talking here of subsidized housing built by the State which, in any case, comprises an almost negligible part of the total stock of urban housing. By dwellings at reasonable 'rents' we mean, rather, those which are owned by private capitals and whose 'rents' approximate to the building cost together with interest on the capital immobilized, i.e. those whose situation could only give rise to the extraction of a rent with some difficulty. In the case of such dwellings, the owner's profits are thus limited to the surplus-value realized at the time of the actual

[23] K. Marx, *Capital* 1, 657–8 (chapter 25, §5b).

construction of the dwelling (if the owner was also the builder) and/or the interest on the capital borrowed.

This definition leads us rapidly to an observation that many people make every spring: this type of dwelling is almost impossible to find in the city. In fact, the more property capital (which in the strict sense functions neither like industrial capital, nor like financial capital) extends its grip on urban space, the more the profitability of investment in housing comes to depend on the rents extracted. On the other hand, the more the city-centre and secondary centres are developed and the more roads are widened, etc., the greater the extent to which the situational advantages on which the profitability of property capital is based extend to the agglomeration as a whole. Under these conditions, what choices remain for tenants with low incomes? They are crowded together in dilapidated neighbourhoods, paying for dwellings which have no value apart from that of being conveniently located, but since these neighbourhoods will sooner or later be the object of new property investment, only one choice remains for them in the long term: to go into exile in the outer suburbs, cut off from the advantages of the city. . . .

It is for this reason that it is possible to talk of a bourgeois city in the same way that one may talk of a bourgeois society. But we must hasten to add that the city is necessarily made in the image of the society which builds it. Subjectively, this means that urban advantages are appropriated by the same people who monopolize social wealth; objectively, that the development of the city can only be determined by the development of capital.

Specifically urban problems do exist, which diminish as one moves away from the centre of the city; those raised by the housing question are so many examples. But from an economic point of view it would be daring to conclude from this that there exists a specifically urban structure, sufficient unto itself, and independent of the social structure as a whole. In reality, such a conclusion should be judged in the same way as the claim that the problems particular to a firm relate, first and foremost, to a structure particular to that firm. For as everyone knows, the capitalist first of all, the difficulties met by an industry, and even a manufacturing division, depend on conditions determined by the economic structure as a whole. The same is true of the urban question.

It is for this reason that Engels asserted, in the direct manner for which he is well known:

As long as the capitalist mode of production continues to exist it is folly to hope for an isolated settlement of the housing question or of any other social question affecting the lot of the workers. The solution lies in the abolition of the capitalist mode of production and the appropriation of all the means of subsistence and instruments of labour by the working class itself.[24]

[24] F. Engels, The housing question, in K. Marx and F. Engels, *op. cit.*, 352–3 (Part II, §III).

Jean Lojkine

5

Contribution to a Marxist theory of capitalist urbanization[*]

The relationships established by Marx between the industrial revolution, mechanization and capitalist accumulation are well known; on the other hand, it would seem that an analysis of the meaning of the 'urban revolution' for capitalist relations of production lay outside his theoretical field.[1] And yet, far from being a minor phenomenon, urbanization in our opinion plays as important a role in the general development of capitalism, as does the increased use of mechanical labour power in the production unit.

I

Marx demonstrated in *Capital* that the capitalist mode of production was obliged continually to 'revolutionize' its means of production in order to increase the share of surplus labour in relation to that of necessary labour. Far from being simply a technological need, increasing *productivity* is necessary to the development of capitalist accumulation.

Now this well-known analysis of the relationships between the development of productive forces and the accumulation of capital is in no way restricted, as is sometimes thought, to labour in the workshop, or even in the production unit. The 'socialization' of productive forces, consequent on the development of relative surplus-value, is in no way restricted to the training of the 'collective worker' within the work-place; on the contrary, for Marx the concept of socialization extends to the reproduction of social capital as a whole. More precisely, one can say that it refers both to the technical division of labour in the workshop and to the division of labour in society as a whole. Moreover, Marx is led to develop a new concept in

[*] Translated with permission of Presses Universitaires de France, Paris, from J. Lojkine, Contribution à une théorie marxiste de l'urbanisation capitaliste, *Cahiers Internationaux de Sociologie* 52 (1972) 123—46.
[1] Certainly one can find allusions, and even preliminary analyses, in particular in *The German Ideology*. But Marx's systematic study of the principal forms of capitalism (*Capital*) leaves aside urban phenomena.

order to define the relation between the immediate process of production, the productive unit, on the one hand, and the overall process of production and circulation of capital, on the other: the concept he uses is that of the *general conditions* of production.

The hypothesis that we are going to develop concerning the place of urbanization in Marxist theory is to a large extent based on this concept. Moreover, it seems to us necessary to analyze the implications of the concept as rigorously and exhaustively as possible. When Marx uses the term he does not in fact seem to give it a meaning which would enable it to be linked to urban phenomena:

> The revolution in the modes of production of industry and agriculture made necessary a revolution in the *general conditions* of the social process of production, i.e. in the means of communication and transport.[2]

However, in our view this restriction of the scope of the concept is put into question today by the appearance of factors which are of equal importance and which are likewise *necessary conditions* for the overall reproduction of developed capitalist formations. We are referring on the one hand to *collective means of consumption* which must be added to *means of social*[3] and *material*[4] *circulation*, and on the other hand to the *spatial concentration* of the means of production and reproduction[5] of capitalist social formations.

The concentration of means of production and exchange (banking, commerce) is in no way a specific characteristic of the capitalist city in so far as even in the medieval city productive and commercial activities were brought together, though admittedly on a much more limited scale. However, in our opinion what does characterize the capitalist city is on the one hand the growing concentration of 'collective means of consumption' which gradually create a style of life, new social needs — hence the phrase 'urban civilization'; and on the other hand the particular mode of concentration of the totality of

---

[2] *Capital* I (Lawrence and Wishart, London, 1970) 384 (chapter 15, § 1), emphasis added.
[3] By 'means of social circulation' we refer essentially to commercial and banking institutions. Marx laid particular emphasis on the role of credit, but he also showed how commercial capital could be an indirect condition of increased productivity.
[4] i.e. means of communication and transport.
[5] i.e. means of reproduction of capital (see fns 3 and 4) and means of reproduction of labour power, i.e. individual and collective means of consumption.

means of reproduction (of capital and of labour power) which itself becomes an increasingly determinant factor in economic development.

Let us now attempt to analyze these two characteristics more closely.

(A) By 'collective means of consumption' we mean the totality of material supports of the activities devoted to the extended reproduction of social labour power, which is not to be confused either with simple physiological reproduction or with the consumption-destruction by an individual of a material object.

It is from this perspective that Marx in his definition of the 'general conditions of the process of social production' contrasted the satisfaction of needs which the individual 'consumes and feels . . . as a single individual in society' and the satisfaction of 'the *socially posited* needs of the individual' which he 'consumes and feels . . . *communally with others — whose mode of consumption is social by the nature of the thing'.*[6]

Concretely this refers today to the totality of medical, sports, educational, cultural and public transport facilities. One has only to consider the share of health and educational expenditure in the budgets of the major capitalist countries since 1945 to have an indication of the great importance of these new and necessary modes of reproduction of labour power.

Now increases in productivity, like increases in the speed of circulation of capital, occur today more and more through this socialization of consumption. Both the basic education and the extended reproduction (further training, retraining) of complex labour power in fact presuppose not only mechanization (which today means automation of the means of production), the *cooperation* of workers combining their simple labour power into social labour power, but also the concentration of means of education and research and the whole set of preconditions of the new reproduction of labour power = parks, housing, transport facilities, etc.

Let us remind ourselves of the specific characteristics of collective means of consumption.

In contrast to *individual* means of consumption, *collective* means of consumption are not commodities in the strict sense of the word, i.e. material products existing independently of their process of

---

[6] *Grundrisse, Foundations of the Critique of Political Economy* (Penguin, Harmondsworth, 1973) 532, latter emphasis added.

production. Certainly, schools, roads, parks are material objects;
certainly, they have a value, i.e. they are the product of past,
crystallized labour. But their own use value is not crystallized in an
object which can be sold. The product sold in this case is simply the
useful effect of a material process which itself does not create any
product: namely, the management of collective means of
consumption. What is sold is *labour* not a *product*.

The workers responsible for the maintenance of a block of flats or
a park, the teacher dispensing a lesson, etc., are providers of *services*
and not producers of commodities. *Of services*, in other words *of
useful effects, of use values which are inseparable from the process
which produced them*, and, hence, from their *means of production*.

While any individual consumption good is by its nature separate
from its means of production, the 'collective consumption good' is
inseparable from the material means which produced it: medical care
does not exist, it has no material existence independent of medical
care facilities . . . This is what Marx showed in the case of the
transport industry where the *useful effect*, change of location, is
'consumed the moment [it is] produced'; the same can be said of a
lesson given by a teacher or the care dispensed by a doctor.

The second characteristic of *collective* means of consumption is
that the realization of their use value, of their useful effect, is durable;
in other words, their consumption does not involve *destruction* as in
the case of the consumption of food, but rather implies a very
particular type of subjective appropriation which we shall now
attempt to describe.

In our opinion, collective consumption presupposes a social
relationship which is not masked, dehumanized by the objectification
of the use value in a commodity, as in the case of individual
consumption. Whereas the latter tends to cover over the social
exchange lying behind the exchange of two products, two exchange
values, in the provision of a collective service, human exchange cannot
be hidden and thus enters into opposition with the standardization of
use values produced by the laws of the market, as we shall see below.

The third and last characteristic is that the mode of consumption is
collective and is thus by its nature opposed to individual, privative
appropriation. Parks or lessons cannot be consumed individually — at
least not in their current increasingly socialized form.

Similarly, the social needs created by the development of
cooperation are increasingly leading to a shattering of the framework
of liberal medicine, including that in countries with marked 'liberal'
ideologies such as the United States.

And housing, whose appropriation appears to be individual, is becoming increasingly hard to dissociate from the urban environment and can no longer be reduced today to a 'machine for living' in so far as it has become an integral element of an entity which cannot be consumed other than collectively: the city.

(B) The urban agglomeration, a spatial combination of the various elements of production and reproduction of capitalist social formations.

The above analysis of collective means of consumption has enabled us to bring out the novelty of the urban mode of life. It cannot however tell us why it is the *city* which has been the specific centre of the socialization of consumption. Such a question refers to the wider problem of the socio-historical conditions under which not only means of production and circulation, but also the totality of *general conditions* of production, including collective means of consumption, have become concentrated within a limited area.

It is this which in our opinion is explained by the Marxist concept of *cooperation*, provided that it is not restricted merely to the association of workers within the productive unit, but is seen as an *essential instrument* for the development of *social* production.

This in our view is the meaning of the celebrated text in which Marx analyzes the relationships between the use value of social space and the concept of cooperation. According to Marx:

> Cooperation allows of the work being carried on over an extended space. . . . On the other hand, while extending the scale of production, it renders possible a relative contraction of the arena. This contraction of arena simultaneous with, and arising from, extension of scale, *whereby a number of useless expenses are cut down*, is owing to the conglomeration of labourers, to the aggregation of various processes, and to the concentration of the means of production.[7]

Far from being reducible to the concentration of means of production, *developed* cooperation thus extends to include the concentration of workers and the bringing together of the various operations, i.e. different phases, of the production process.

The concentration of population, instruments of production, capital, of *pleasures* and *needs* — in other words, the *city*[8] — is thus in no sense an autonomous phenomenon governed by laws of

[7] *Capital* I, 328–9 (chapter 13), emphasis added.
[8] K. Marx, *The German Ideology* I (Lawrence and Wishart, London, 1970) 69 (Division of labour: town and country).

development totally separate from the laws of capitalist accumulation: it cannot be dissociated from the tendency for capital to increase the productivity of labour by socializing the *general conditions* of production — of which urbanization, as we have seen, is an essential component.

Conversely, what does explain the apparent autonomy of urban phenomena is the fact that they are part of the *division of labour within society* and not of the *division of labour within the productive unit*: now the 'social' division of labour — of which the division between town and country is the *'fundamental basis'* — *is part of the economic formations of the most diverse societies* and not, *like the division within manufacture or that within the workshop, of the capitalist formation alone.*

It is this which accounts for the fact that the emergence of urban forms occurred long before the birth of capitalism and that some of (even) their (present-day) features do not appear to be *directly* dependent on capitalist accumulation (in particular the persistence of small towns whose social and economic life is related more to the feudal mode of production than to the urban civilization engendered by mechanization).

This is why Marx avoids reducing the relation between urbanization and capitalism to a simple, direct and univocal relation of cause and effect. After distinguishing the two spheres in which these two phenomena are manifest (the division of labour at the level of the social formation as a whole and the division of labour within the productive unit) he restricts himself initially to an analogy, to a parallelism whose limits he is careful to state:

> *Just as* a certain number of simultaneously employed labourers are the material prerequisite for *division of labour in manufacture, so* are the number and density of the population, which here *correspond* to the agglomeration in one workshop, a necessary condition for the *division of labour in society.*[9]

In order to make clear that it is not simply a demographic feature (the concentration of population within a limited area) but an *urban* feature which is involved, Marx is at pains to emphasize what for him determines population density: the *communications network*[10]

---

[9] *Capital* 1, 352 (chapter 14, § 4), emphases added.
[10] 'Nevertheless, this density is more or less relative. A *relatively* thinly populated country, with well-developed *means of communication*, has a *denser population* than a more numerously populated country.' (*Loc. cit.*, emphases added.)

More generally we would say today that it is the spatial distribution of means of production, capital, and means of consumption which is determinant, the communications network simply actualizing this distribution. Moreover, Marx uses a closely related expression when he refers in the same text to 'the *territorial* division of labour, which confines special branches of production to special districts of a country'.[11]

Does this mean that no distinction need be made between cooperation in the workshop and cooperation in society? Not at all. And it is for this reason that Marx is careful to state the limits of his analogy:

> In spite of the numerous analogies and links connecting them, division of labour in the interior of a society, and that in the interior of a workshop, *differ not only in degree, but also in kind.*
>
> While within the workshop, the iron law of proportionality subjects definite numbers of workmen to definite functions, in the society outside the workshop, *chance and caprice* have full play in *distributing the producers* and their means of production among the various branches of industry.[12]

In a word, while cooperation implies concerted planning within the capitalist enterprise, it means nothing but anarchy at the level of the capitalist social formation as a whole, a closed field of *competition* between independent commodity producers.

This difference in kind is thus fundamental, since it relates to the very essence of the capitalist mode of production from which it is impossible to eradicate *competition*, especially in an era of international monopolies, without putting an end to capitalist accumulation. But it in no way diminishes the essential place of the *spatial distribution of the means of production and means of consumption in capitalism's search for increased productivity.*

On the contrary, Marx shows the *direct connexion* between the increased productivity of labour and urban development by quoting, among others, James Mill and Thomas Hodgkin:

> *There is a certain density of population which is convenient, both for social intercourse, and for that combination of powers by which the produce of labour is increased.* (James Mill, *Elements of Political Economy* (London, 1821) 50)

---

[11] *Ibid.*, 353 (chapter 14, § 4), emphasis added.
[12] *Ibid.*, 354, 355 (chapter 14, § 4), emphases added.

As the *number of labourers increases, the productive power of
society augments* in the compound ratio of that increase,
multiplied by the effects of the division of labour. (Thomas
Hodgkin, *Popular Political Economy* (London, 1827) 125, 126)[13]

Thus, far from being three independent spheres, the spheres of
production, exchange and consumption are in constant interaction:

Division of labour in manufacture demands that *division of labour
in society at large* should previously have attained a certain degree
of development. Inversely, the former division *reacts upon* and
develops and multiplies the latter.[14]

Marx generalized this interaction to *all historical stages* in the
development of cooperation (manufacturing and factory periods) by
showing how the means of communication and transport were
'revolutionized' to start with by the division of labour in manufacture,
and then by mechanization and modern industry.[15]

However, we cannot limit ourselves to a simple parallelism between
the different stages of development of capitalist cooperation and their
relationships to the *general conditions* of production: for is there not
a contradiction between the very notion of *development* of
cooperation and the idea of static interrelations fixed once and for all,
between the immediate process of production and the *general
conditions* of its reproduction?

Whereas the manufacturing period and the start of modern
industry saw an opposition between the *unit* of production
(dominated by a capitalist agent) and the *plurality* of independent
commodity producers, the development of modern industry has given
birth to vast monopolies whose empires are subdivided into numerous
establishments linked to one another by cleverly-planned savings of
indirect costs and an *overall strategy* of profit maximization.

The difference in 'kind' between the 'order', the organization
within manufacturing and the anarchy of competition thus remains,
but it is manifested today in the opposition between the formidable
organization of each industrial and banking empire on the one hand,
and the competition, the anarchy which governs relations between
rival empires on the other.

An analysis of developed capitalist cooperation thus leads

[13] *Ibid.*, 352, fn. 2 (chapter 14, § 4), emphases added.
[14] *Ibid.*, 353 (chapter 14, § 4), emphases added.
[15] *Ibid.*, 384 (chapter 15, § 1).

necessarily to the opposition between the *technical* necessity of socialization and the *social* necessity of competition. It thereby enables us to grasp the contradictory character of the capitalist socialization of the general conditions of production.

Socialization of (social and material) circulation, socialization of consumption, spatial concentration of the means of production and of reproduction of labour power, developed cooperation corresponds to the current state of development of productive forces and hence to the new forms of increased productivity necessitated by capitalist accumulation. But at the same time this socialization bears all the marks of the contradiction between the socialization of productive forces and the capitalist character of the relations of production.

This is what we are going to attempt to show now by confronting the specific nature of the *economic effects* of urban agglomeration with their social (capitalist) content.

II

So far we have only been concerned with *one aspect* of the relation between urbanization and capitalist accumulation, namely the development of urban agglomeration determined by the constant tendency of capitalism to reduce production time and the time of circulation of capital.

The city thus appeared as the direct effect of the need to reduce indirect costs of production, and costs of circulation and consumption in order to speed up the rate of rotation of capital and thus increase the period during which capital was used productively. But to conclude from this that urban development is in some way ensured by capitalism's constant need to increase the productivity of social labour would be mistaken for two reasons: on the one hand, because every increase in productivity, by raising the organic composition of social capital, ultimately strengthens the tendency for the rate of profit to fall and leads to a counter-reaction which *checks* and 'selects' the development of productive forces; and, on the other hand, because the need for cooperation among the different agents of production in urban space is contradicted by:

(a) the laws of capitalist competition
(b) the parcelling out of urban space into independent fragments which are the private property of *land-owners*. This second limit is that of *urban ground rent*.

Thus capitalist relations of production, at the same time as bringing about — with modern industry — a growing tendency towards urban agglomeration, impress a triple limit on any rational, *socialized*, planning of urban development.

> Firstly, a limit connected with the *financing* of the various elements which give capitalist urban life its particular character;
> Secondly, a limit connected with the social division of labour throughout the territory as a whole and hence with the anarchic competition between the different agents who use or transform urban space;
> Thirdly, a limit deriving from the private ownership of land itself.

1. Capitalist limits to the financing of means of communication and collective means of consumption

Marx showed clearly the contradictory effect of the development of productive forces on the tendency for the rate of profit to fall: on the one hand, increases in productivity augment the mass of surplus-value and the rate of surplus-value; but by raising the organic composition of capital through the growing accumulation of constant fixed capital (machines) they tend to result in a renewed tendency for the rate of profit to fall. This is what Marx meant, for example, in the following pithy and particularly explicit phrase:

> It is by no means equally clear, that *this increased productive force* [i.e. the machinery employed in modern industry] , *is not . . . purchased by an increased expenditure of labour.*[16]

It remains to be demonstrated that urban expenditure plays the same role as regards the organic composition of social capital as does the use of machinery. Which would enable the comparison made above to be extended to the relation between the socialization of the immediate process of production and the socialization of its general conditions.

In order to do this we shall proceed in two stages. To start with we shall attempt to examine the position of the various urban elements in relation to the two spheres of productive capital and unproductive capital. We shall then place ourselves at the level of the social distribution of the mass of surplus-value, i.e. at the level of the collection and appropriation of profit, in order to determine the 'profitability' of the various types of urban expenditure.

[16] *Ibid.*, 387 (chapter 15, § 2), emphasis added.

We defined the capitalist city as the product of the socialization of the general conditions of production, and the socialization of space. Thus one may use the term *urban agglomeration effects* in discussing the global impact of urban activities on the capitalist economy.

By this term we mean:

on the one hand, the *useful effects* produced by the means of circulation and consumption concentrated in the city;
on the other hand, the *agglomeration effects* which are merely the indirect product of the juxtaposition of means of production or reproduction and are not linked, as is the preceding type of effect, to any particular material object. The production of this type of effect can be said to be in some sense collective: it is a social combination — conscious or not, deliberate or not — of individual urban agents (builders of blocks of flats, houses, shops, offices, factories, etc.).

Use value thus consists solely in the capacity of *urban space* to facilitate *interaction* between the different elements of the city.

We shall return to this second type of effect in our analysis of urban ground rent, where it will be shown that situation rent is a direct utilization of this use value for speculative purposes.

Let us return to urban effects of the first type, those produced by means of circulation and consumption.

These useful effects are certainly use values but in no sense are they material objects, products which could serve as physical supports of the value imparted by labour power. Marx showed that the creation of commodities, supports for the contradiction between value and use value, presupposed the 'alienation' of the product from the production process, the separation of the product in which the value created by labour power could be *crystallized*. Such is not the case for useful effects or 'services' as long as their use value is not crystallized in any material object.

With two exceptions: transport and the storage of commodities, in so far as these two activities imply, as Marx clearly showed, a *transformation of the use value* of the *commodities transported or stored*.[17] It is because the labour expended in transportation or storage *adds a use value to the product* (by transforming it from a potential commodity into a real commodity, actually available on the

[17] We refer here to Marx's basic texts: on the transport industry, see, *inter alia*, *Capital* II (Progress Publishers, Moscow, 1967), chapters I (esp. pp. 53–4) (§ 4) and 6 (pp. 152–5) (§ 3). On storage, see *ibid*., chapter 6, p. 139 (§ 2).

consumption market, and thus sold) that these two activities
constitute an extension of the process of production into the process
of circulation.

But these two exceptions prove the rule. These *'services'*, these
'useful effects', be they *public transport, housing, medical care or
educational activities, or banking or commercial activities*, are not
crystallized in any material object, nor do they add more value to
commodities produced in other sectors. Thus they do not create any
additional value and are totally unproductive (of surplus-value).

In what respects, then, can expenditure relating to means of
consumption and circulation be compared with that relating to means
of production and communication?

This question can only be answered correctly by *considering in
their totality all the various costs occasioned by the extended
reproduction of capital*: Marx in fact considers only the costs of
production (which include the costs of making machines), and the
indirect costs of production (i.e. the costs of production of means of
communication and storage, and also the costs of circulation in the
strict sense, banking and commercial activities) necessary to the
productive utilization of capital but which do not transmit or add any
value. To these latter costs we shall add the costs of consumption
referred to above. Now in the case of costs of circulation, as in the
case of consumption costs, the money advanced is not an *expenditure
of income*, but an (unproductive) *expenditure of capital*.

In other words the financing of a bank, *while it 'creates neither
product nor value'*[18] and cannot thus be treated as an investment —
i.e. as constant capital — does act 'as though one part of the product
were transformed into a *machine* which buys and sells the rest of the
product'.[19]

Thus in the cases of consumption and circulation costs the money
advanced is certainly a capital expenditure but, unlike constant
capital, it results from a deduction from the surplus-value already
produced. Hence the proposed concept, *'expenses capital'* (*capital de
frais*).[20] Now expenses capital acts on the organic composition of

[18] *Ibid.*, 136 (chapter 6, § 1), emphasis added.
[19] *Loc. cit.*, emphasis added.
[20] Economic analysis of the repercussions of the growth in social expenditure,
and in particular of urban expenditure, on the tendency for the rate of profit to
fall, refers to the general theory of devalorization and overaccumulation of
capital in the State monopolist capitalist period. We shall merely refer here to the
most important works on this subject: Paul Boccara, Capitalisme monopoliste
d'Etat, accumulation du capital et financement public de la production,

capital in the same way as constant capital: it *raises the organic composition by increasing the mass of accumulated social capital without itself being productively utilized*. But these two processes converge even more closely if one accepts the general over-accumulation-devalorization hypothesis.[21] We have already shown how capitalism's unceasing search for increased productivity in order to fight against the tendency for the rate of profit to fall is no longer accomplished today solely by raising the rate of surplus-value, but also by the socialization of the general conditions of production.

But these new weapons in the fight against the latter tendency are, like the old ones, double-edged: by increasing the mass of social capital not productively utilized, capitalism raises anew the organic composition of capital and brings about a new overaccumulation.

Moreover, all of productive capital does not act in the same way on the organic composition. The overaccumulation-devalorization hypothesis enables one to distinguish *different degrees of devalorization of capital* within the productive sphere. For example, railways and means of communication as a whole are precisely part of a sector which is particularly *devalorized* due to the excessively high organic composition — as Marx noted in the first half of the nineteenth century.

Thus the difference 'in kind' between the *constant capital* of means of communication and the *expenses capital* of collective means of consumption and means of social circulation is becoming blurred from the point of view of the *devalorization* of capital, the difference in kind is becoming a *difference of degree* between a *totally devalorized capital* producing zero extra value (expenses capital), and a very highly devalorized capital such as that invested in means of communication. One can thus speak of the urban general conditions of capitalist production as having a common economic function. The financing of collective means of consumption, like the financing of means of material and social circulation, increases the mass of capital which is devalorized in relation to that which is productively utilized at or above the average rate of profit.

While as a whole urban expenditure strengthens the tendency for

Economie et Politique 143–4 (International Conference, Choisy-le-Roi, 26–29 May 1966), and more recently, La crise du capitalisme monopoliste d'Etat et la lutte des travailleurs, *Economie et Politique* (special issue, March 1970). [Also in P. Boccara, *Etudes sur le Capitalisme Monopoliste d'Etat, sa Crise et son Issue* (Editions Sociales, Paris, 1974).]
[21] See p. 130, fn. 20.

the rate of profit to fall, from the point of view of its capacity to *collect* and *appropriate* surplus-value rather than its capacity to *create* it, it can be divided into two quite separate sectors. In other words, in so far as what counts for the individual capitalist agent is not the production of surplus-value but the *share of profit* he can appropriate, it matters little whether he obtains this profit from the manufacture of commodities or from the sale of legal or financial 'services'. Concretely, the *profitability* of a given economic sector will depend not on whether the sector is part of the process of creation of surplus-value or not, but on the *rate of profit* and speed of *rotation* of the capital invested.

It is this which explains the historic separation between the — highly profitable — circulation of capital sector (banking and commercial capital) and the collective means of consumption sector whose profitability is restricted to isolated fields close to the commercial sector. From the time of Haussman right up to the present day one can follow the opposition between the flourishing growth of financial institutions in the centres of the big cities and the Malthusianism shown by the capitalist class towards the development of collective means of consumption whose realization on a large scale is always the result of long class struggles, as we shall see below.

Malthusianism as regards working-class housing, elementary standards of public health, basic infrastructure for building land in France in the 1920s or the socio-cultural facilities of the '*grands ensembles*' [large developments of blocks of flats] developed in the post-war period, etc. In our view the explanation is to be sought not at the level of their 'unproductive' character but in their inadequacy from the point of view of the criteria of profit formation, and of monopolistic surplus profits.

Whereas the means of social circulation permit the formation of very high rates of profit, the very structure of the use values — collective, durable, indivisible[22] — of collective means of consumption makes this a sphere where the application of market criteria is difficult and when in spite of everything they are applied the result is the impairment of the collective character of the means concerned. . . . For example, when housing is sold through the market it becomes a commodity increasingly reserved for an affluent élite or

[22] This observation has been made by numerous economists, including non-Marxist economists. See J-F. Besson, *l'Intégration Urbaine* (P.U.F., Paris, 1970); Jean Rémy, *La Ville, Phénomène Economique* (Editions Ouvrières, Brussels, 1967).

else an indirect means of tapping surplus-value by means of the systems of bank credit to which workers are subject.

But there are many collective means of consumption which by their very nature are opposed to the imperatives of profit. Due to the slow speed of rotation of capital in these sectors, to the risky and discontinuous nature of the progression of demand for them, public transport, schools, research centres, parks . . . constitute so many domains foreign to capitalist *profitability*, while necessary to the overall reproduction of capitalist social formations.

Locus of both the reproduction of labour power, through means of consumption, and of capital through urban systems of metamorphosis of commodity capital, the capitalist city increasingly becomes — as the need for the socialization of the totality of general conditions of production becomes more marked — the manifestation of two contradictory necessities:

> that of reproduction of capital which demands ever more surplus labour;
> that of reproduction of labour power which demands, conversely, through the development of cooperation, always more free time, always less necessary labour, and finally the very suppression of the opposition — originated by capitalism — between constrained time and 'free' time, in order to meet the new exigencies of the scientific and technical revolution now commencing.

But the contradiction is not located solely within the economic field: it necessarily has repercussions on the mode of life itself in so far as the *market* elements of the city, by reducing social relations to an impersonal exchange of standardized values, subordinated to the sole standard of labour time, are opposed to the *non-market social relations* woven by the new collective means of consumption which give rise to the possibility of man no longer being a 'detail-worker . . . reduced to a mere fragment of a man' but a 'fully developed individual', source of initiative and collective creation.

2 Capitalist limits deriving from anarchic competition between the various agents who use or transform urban space

We have already noted the opposition between the — relatively rational — organization of cooperation within a production unit or a number of establishments controlled by the same capitalist group and the 'anarchy' manifested at the level of the *territorial* division of labour: '*Chance* and *caprice* have full play in *distributing* the producers and their *means of production* among the various branches of industry.'[23]

In so far as the development of an urban agglomeration depends closely, as we have already indicated, on its articulation with sources of employment, the mode of location of industrial firms and offices will have an important bearing on the development of cities. Now, it is increasingly apparent today that the locational criteria used by big capitalist firms are entering into contradiction with the *technological and social necessities* of any real territorial planning, i.e. of developed cooperation at the level of the nation as a whole.

A recent opinion poll[24] of a group of American and European firms, mostly large and from diverse branches of industry, showed that the main factor entering into their choice of location was the *situational advantage* conferred by the existence of good links with other countries, of facilities and services of all kinds (ports, airports, telecommunications links), in other words, the *full range of urban infrastructure* — thus *what Marx called the 'relative density' of the population.*

The city thus plays a fundamental economic role in the development of capitalism, but conversely urbanization is moulded, shaped by the needs of capitalist accumulation.

The same survey found that big capitalist firms continue to prefer Lombardy to the Mezzogiorno; in 1968 97.2 per cent of new jobs went to the centre and north of Italy and only 2.8 per cent to the south. In the 1951–63 period, the distribution of new jobs was as follows: 76 per cent to the centre and north, 24 per cent to the south.

The social division of labour under the effect of monopolistic accumulation thus engenders two contradictory spatial phenomena, both of which, however, result from the common search of all capitalist firms for a location enabling them to reduce indirect production costs as much as possible.

These phenomena are, on the one hand, the increasing underdevelopment of the regions least well-equipped in urban infrastructure (material means of circulation and collective means of consumption), and, on the other hand, the growing congestion of the gigantic 'megalopolises' in which the most varied and densest means of communication and collective means of consumption are already

---

[23] K. Marx, *Capital* I, 355 (chapter 14, § 4) emphasis added.
[24] The poll was carried out on behalf of the Olivetti Foundation and the Club Turanti, organizers of a 'Round Table' at Venice, 8–9 November 1969, attended by representatives of public and private industry and political leaders.

concentrated. Concentrations within which the same process of spatial differentiation between the best-equipped areas, which will become even better equipped — business districts, residential districts for the dominant classes — and the least well-equipped areas, will be reproduced, with a tendency for the gap between them to grow ever wider.

3 The role of ground rent in urban development. Land prices and urban segregation

While the anarchic growth of cities, their uneven development, is in large part due to the location strategies of firms, there is another type of urban agent which plays a particularly negative role: the land-owner. In *Capital*, Marx reduces the use value of land to two functions: that of *instrument of production* (mines, waterfalls, agricultural land) and that of *simple passive support* of means of production (factories), circulation (shops, banks) or consumption (housing, etc.):

> The soil itself serves as an instrument of production, which is not the case with a factory, or holds only to a limited extent, since it serves only as a *foundation*, as a *place* and *space* providing a *basis* of operations.[25]

Now, in our opinion, a third use value of land takes on a growing importance with the socialization of the general conditions of production: what we have described as its capacity for *concentration*, i.e. for *socially combining* the means of production and means of reproduction of a social formation.

A consequence of the private appropriation of land, the *fragmentation* of this use value — whose consumption, by definition, cannot be other than collective — is becoming an obstacle, within the capitalist mode of production, to the development of social productive forces. But in order to understand fully the present-day importance of ground rent it is indispensable to attempt to clarify the character of *present-day urban land-owners*.

For some Marxists the appropriation of urban ground rent is carried out increasingly by the *petite* and *moyenne bourgeoisie* which is thus benefiting from the fragmentation of the large landed estates over the last two hundred years. For them ground rent — the brake on or obstacle to economic growth and also to the free circulation of

[25] III (Progress Publishers, Moscow, 1971) 781 (chapter 46), emphases added.

capital — is thus identified with the survival of pre-monopolistic social strata (small land-owners) whose class interest is opposed to that of monopolistic development.

It may then be wondered how it happened that the founding of monopoly capitalism at the end of the nineteenth century was not followed by the *elimination* of this 'archaic' obstacle to monopolistic accumulation. Why the current phase of monopoly capitalism, State monopoly capitalism, marked by the systematic and generalized intervention of the State to facilitate monopolistic accumulation, has not led to the abolition of a ground rent which only benefited social strata in decline. A purely political explanation might be advanced: that the collectivization of land or the control of land prices by the collectivity was impossible because of the importance of these middle classes of small land-owners — necessary supports of the political hegemony of the dominant fractions of capitalism.

But such an argument, valid for a country like France, is less easy to understand in those developed capitalist countries in which monopolistic domination, though it is exercised without the support of such a mass of small land-owners, has in no way eliminated the private ownership of land. In reality, monopoly capitalism is characterized, in our opinion, not by an opposition between 'productive' monopolies and 'passive' small land-owners who speculate on an economic growth to which they have contributed nothing, but much rather by the *gradual and contradictory appropriation of ground rent by big monopoly groups*.

Lenin drew attention to this transformation in the function of ground rent:

> The monopoly of the banks merges here with the monopoly of ground rent and with monopoly of the means of communication, since the rise in the price of land and the possibility of selling it profitably in allotments, etc., is mainly dependent on good means of communication with the centre of the town; and these means of communication are in the hands of large companies which are connected, by means of the holding system and by the distribution of positions on the directorates, with the interested banks.[26]

In Lenin's time — in other words at the stage of simple monopoly capitalism — monopolistic appropriation of urban ground rent was

[26] V. I. Lenin, *Imperialism, the Highest Stage of Capitalism* (Foreign Languages Press, Peking, 1965) 65 (chapter 3).

manifested principally in the frantic speculation engaged in by private railway or tram 'companies', selling off plots of land located around tram and railway lines.

However, one may ask oneself whether the devalorization of the capital invested in railway and tram lines does not reduce considerably the land-owner's chances of recovering a portion of the surplus profits in this sector.

Furthermore, the merging of landed monopoly and financial monopoly eliminates the distinction founded by ground rent between the share of profit collected by the land-owner and that collected by the capitalist in the strict sense.

On the other hand, the hypothesis may be advanced that ground rent in the true sense has now become reconstituted through the letting — which has developed increasingly since the last war — of commercial premises to (financial or commercial) capitalists.

A very high rent may in fact result on the one hand from the separation between the property developer-land-owner and his capitalist tenant, and on the other hand from the low organic composition of capital in the whole of the sector concerned with the circulation of capital, which conditions the formation of surplus profits.

Thus the classical stage of capitalism, marked by the opposition between industrial capital and agricultural landed property, is succeeded by the monopoly stage marked by the merging of financial capital and ground rent. A merger which, far from eliminating the contradiction between capital and ground rent, may on the contrary develop it by linking it with the wider contradiction between the parasitic, speculative tendencies of capital and its tendency to increase the rate of surplus value by increased investment in production.

The monopolistic appropriation of urban ground rent — as well as being a factor strengthens the tendency of the rate of profit to fall — is above all a structural obstacle to all real urban planning; collectivization of the use of urban land in fact clashes much less with small private property, which the new arsenal of laws allows to be expropriated very 'efficiently', than with monopolist private property whose elimination presupposes the abolition of the capitalist mode of production itself.

In fact any serious historical study of property developers[27] shows the gradual shift from an urban ground rent fragmented among a

---

[27] See Christian Topalov, *Les Promoteurs Immobiliers* (Mouton, Paris, 1974).

multitude of small independent developers to a ground rent monopolized by the large international financial groups which dominate the land and property markets.[28]

Urban ground rent — the third limit inherent in the capitalist mode of production — thus leaves a permanent mark on urban development. In our view its principal spatial manifestation lies in the phenomenon of *segregation*, secreted by the mechanisms of formation of land prices. This can be characterized by three dominant tendencies:

(1) An opposition between the centre, where land prices are highest, and the periphery. In our opinion this 'situation rent' is explained by the key role of agglomeration effects;

(2) A growing separation between areas and housing reserved for the most affluent social strata and working-class housing areas;

(3) A generalized dispersal of 'urban functions', scattered into areas which are geographically separate and increasingly specialized in function: office districts, industrial zones, residential areas, etc. This is the tendency which urban policy has systematized and rationalized under the name of 'zoning'.

The link between this third phenomenon and ground rent lies essentially, at least this is our hypothesis, in the mechanism of social selection constituted by the growing divergence between land prices at the periphery and in the centre, the centre being increasingly reserved for the headquarters of international firms, the only ones able to appropriate this situational advantage.[29]

III The role of class struggle and the State in urban development: elements for an analysis of the urban policies of capitalist states

The hypothesis we have just elaborated of a triple capitalist limit impeding the socialization of urban development would seem to run counter to a number of undisputed facts.

[28] Among the multitude of studies describing this process, the work by E. P. Eichler and M. Kaplan, *The Community Builders* (University of California Press, Berkeley, 1967), may be mentioned: this work shows clearly the growing grip of big American firms on the property market, at the various stages of construction and marketing.
[29] See N. P. Gist and S. F. Fava, *Urban Society* (Cromwell, New York, 1964) 221, on the extension of the central business district. See also M. Portefait, *Etude de la Cité Financière de Paris* (B.E.R.U., Paris, 1968), and the study by Madame Demorgon of l'Atelier Parisien d'Urbanisme (A.P.U.R.): *l'Implantation des Bureaux Neufs à Paris (1962–1968)*.

How is it that the capitalist mode of production has been able to 'engender' collective means of consumption such as our educational system or health system, even despite all their current shortcomings?

How has it been able to engender the building of hundreds of thousands of working-class dwellings in France in the years 1954–60 etc.? Certainly, one could invoke the economic imperative of the necessity of an increase in the productivity of labour; we have shown in fact how capitalist accumulation *necessitated* the socialization of the general conditions of production. But we have not explained how, *concretely*, the laws of free competition and the search for profit could *by themselves* engender the financing of unprofitable collective facilities.

In fact they cannot; and we shall attempt to show that the reproduction of capitalist relations of production necessitates, at *every* stage of development of this mode of production, the economic intervention of a social agent, separate from individual capitalist agents, namely the State.

Too often, Marxist analyses of the State are restricted to an emphasis on its repressive function in the service of the dominant class — which is only a half-truth. A half-truth in so far as the bourgeois State has a dual function:

(1) to maintain the *cohesion* of the social formation as a whole;
(2) to directly enforce the domination of the bourgeoisie.[30]

Now the first function implies the second in so far as the domination of the capitalist class presupposes the existence of an *agency independent of society* capable of 'regulating' or 'normalizing' the class struggle.

But the exact meaning of this function of assuring cohesion also seems to us to require clarification. In our view from the very beginning of capitalism the scope of this function has not been purely *legal* but also *economic*.

Thus far from being reducible to ideological action or even to social measures permitting the 'harmonious' reproduction of class relations, the State's cohesive function is at the same time an intervention by the State on the economic base.

Thus in the capitalist mode of production, the building of roads — necessary to the reproduction of the economic system as a whole, but

[30] F. Engels, Ludwig Feuerbach, in K. Marx and F. Engels, *Basic Writings on Politics and Philosophy*, ed. L. S. Feuer (Fontana, London, 1969) 277 (§ 4).

scarcely profitable for a newly-born capitalism restricted to the immediate exploitation of productive labour — is the task of the *political* agent which is responsible not only for ideological cohesion but also for the *economic reproduction* of the relations of production, in other words: the State.[31] Certainly, Marx shows that:

> The highest development of capital exists when the general conditions of the process of social production are not paid out of *deductions from the social revenue*, the State's taxes . . . but rather out of *capital as capital*.[32]

Does this mean that at its highest stage of development capitalism *replaces* State intervention by the intervention of capital — in the form of the joint-stock company? The actual conditions of 'private' financing of the general conditions of production in the *most developed* capitalist countries show that this is not the case: the American railways are 80 per cent subsidized by public money and the private management of motorways [e.g. in France] similarly presupposes a constant intervention of public capital. Thus far from being peculiar to a youthful stage of capitalism or to precapitalist formations, the *economic intervention of State power* is a constant and growing necessity for the extended reproduction of the capitalist mode of production.

However, to limit oneself to this analysis of the State would be to run the risk of falling into an economism or functionalism foreign to historical and dialectical materialism.

As well as being a political organization in the service of the bourgeoisie, an agent for the propagation of the dominant ideology, the capitalist State is *also* the condensed reflection of the class struggle — which leads it to develop the 'progressive' face of capitalism . . . while at the same time accentuating the contradiction between the socialization of productive forces and their private social envelope.

This third function of the State apparatus is in our view the most difficult to grasp, since it demands the perfecting of a dialectical method and not a recourse to mechanistic analyses, the legacy of the positivist and idealist tradition of the social sciences.

How, in other words, can it be shown simultaneously:
that State intervention enables the capitalist system to resolve the

[31] See K. Marx, *Grundrisse*, 526.
[32] *Ibid.*, 532.

immediate contradictions that no individual capitalist agent either can or wants to resolve?

that this intervention is not that of an 'autonomous instance' functioning solely as a 'safety valve' designed to prevent the explosion of the social formation? Whereas the mechanistic metaphor of safety valve suggests the smooth running of a well-regulated machine, for Marx, State intervention was simply the reflection of mass struggles and worker pressure obliging the State to limit the 'spontaneous tendencies' of capitalist accumulation.

that these political reforms, far from resolving capitalist contradictions, on the contrary carry them to a still higher level?

We shall attempt to articulate dialectically these three contradictory aspects of State intervention in relation to a specific example studied by Marx: the extension of the reproduction of labour power by means of factory legislation and the first rudiments of primary education.

We shall then suggest a generalization of the results of this analysis by examining the way in which the different forms of urban life have been engendered by class struggles and their pressure on the policies of capitalist states. As Marx says:

> The bourgeoisie, which by creating technical and agricultural schools for its sons was however only obeying the most deep-seated tendencies of modern production, gave to the proletariat only the shadow of vocational training.[33]
> Though the Factory Act, *that first and meagre concession wrung from capital*, is limited to combining elementary education with work in the factory, there can be no doubt that when the working-class comes into *power* as inevitably it must, technical instruction, both theoretical and practical, will take its proper place in the working-class schools. There is also no doubt that such *revolutionary ferments*, the final result of which is the abolition of the old division of labour, are *diametrically opposed to the capitalistic form of production, and to the economic status of the labourer corresponding to that form.* But the *historical development of the antagonisms, immanent* in a given form of

[33] K. Marx, *Capital* I. [The above quotation is a translation of a passage in the French edition (Editions Sociales, t. 2, 166). The corresponding passage in the English edition is substantially different (I, 488).]

production, is the only way in which that form of production can be *dissolved* and a *new form established.*[34]

In our opinion this model of dialectical analysis shows clearly how all the contradictory aspects of the State's function can be grasped simultaneously.

(1) Factory legislation enables capitalism to 'regulate' the reproduction of its relations of production: the State thereby intervenes both as a social agent separate from individual capitalist agents, exercising its power of coercion over them, a power which in the last resort allows the maintenance of their class domination.

(2) State policy is merely the reflection of class struggles. Factory legislation is not granted to the popular masses, it is a *'first and meagre concession wrung from capital'*, in the same way that the establishment of a normal working day is the 'result of centuries of struggle between capitalist and labourer'. It is particularly interesting to find Marx emphasizing the fact that this law was enacted by an ultra-reactionary parliament, 'the parliament of the ruling classes', which, however, had a progressive role by partially relieving the misery of English workers and opening the doors of education to them for the first time. According to Marx, the English legislation of 1867 shows concretely the 'necessity *imposed* on the parliament of the ruling classes' of adopting drastic measures against the 'excesses' of capitalist exploitation.[35]

(3) These concessions wrung from capital in no way resolve the 'antagonisms immanent' in the capitalist mode of production: it is the 'revolutionary ferments' which develop the contradiction between capital and labour and hasten the arrival of the dissolution of the mode of production and the establishment of a new mode.

It is these complex dialectical relations linking the State apparatus to the economic infrastructure and to the class struggle that we believe can be rediscovered through the historical study of the *urban policies* of the major developed capitalist countries. Within the scope of this article we can merely give a few indications of the triple function of the capitalist State in urban development. To go further than this would require a rigorous application of Marxist periodization (theory of stages, phases and periods of historical development) to the wealth and variety of urban materials.

We shall limit ourselves here to noting the common characteristics of the urban policies of the developed capitalist States.

[34] *Capital* I, 488 (chapter 15, § 9), emphases added.
[35] *Ibid.*, 494 (chapter 15, § 9), emphasis added.

(1) The intervention of the capitalist State has permitted the consolidation in the short term of the anarchic processes undermining urban development. On the three crisis points for capitalist urbanization: the financing of devalorized urban facilities, the coordination of the various agents of urbanization and finally the contradiction between the collective use value of land and its fragmentation by ground rent, on these three points of rupture, State intervention has enabled a short-term resolution of problems which for individual capitalist agents were insoluble.

The public financing of unprofitable means of communication and collective means of consumption has enabled capitalism to promote simultaneously — despite the disproportion between the sums involved — the development of all the *general conditions* of production: both means of consumption and means of circulation.

Second intervention: urban planning in the narrow sense, i.e. the coordination by the State of the occupation and use of urban land, while having had very uneven results, has however enabled immediate difficulties to be resolved. Thus the 1850—60 laws on public health and sanitation required local authorities to exercise a certain degree of control over the sanitary conditions of working-class housing.[36] The laws governing subsidized housing passed under the Third and especially the Fourth Republic led to the construction of hundreds of thousands of dwellings which were incomparably more comfortable than the original dwellings of many families with modest incomes. Similarly, one could quote numerous examples of the construction of roads, water supplies, schools and transport facilities . . . resulting from the urban policy followed by the Conseil Général de la Seine during the inter-war period.[37]

The financial, coercive[38] intervention of the State enables the most obvious defects of capitalist competition and ground rent to be eliminated.

Third intervention: attempts at land collectivization, while they have not succeeded in eliminating the segregative mechanisms of ground rent, have enabled — thanks to municipal land banks (Germany, Hungary, Scandinavia) or different forms of taxation of

[36] See Roger H. Guerrand, *Les Origines du Logement Social en France* (Editions Ouvrières, Paris, 1966).
[37] See Alain Cottereau, Les débuts de la planification urbaine dans l'agglomération parisienne, *Sociologie du Travail* 4 (1970) 362—92.
[38] We refer here to the effectiveness of planning regulations, which varies, it is true, from one country to another: in Holland and Scandinavia they are more effective than in France, for example.

profits from land — limited planning experiments to succeed, as in the case of the Scandinavian new towns.[39]

(2) State intervention is neither a spontaneous mechanism set off automatically by the mode of production nor exclusively the effect of action by the dominant classes.

The second of these points may appear open to debate in so far as certain planning laws do not seem to be direct consequences of the class struggle, but simply consequences of the 'panic' of the dominant classes themselves threatened by the 'decay' of the cities.[40]

But a more thorough historical study shows that behind the apparent non-intervention of the working class, the bourgeoisie's very 'fear' of a possible popular uprising, its general struggle against the development of a revolutionary labour movement, led it to take political measures which cannot be separated from this context.[41]

While we possess no undisputed documents concerning the public health laws promulgated at a time when the labour movement was scarcely formed, the same is not true, for example, in the case of the legislative measures taken by the French government in favour of the 'mal lotis' ['the badly off'] in the 1920s. In the face of the growing discontent of the 'mal lotis' — expressed for example in the constitution of protest organizations such as the Federation des Travailleurs Mal Lotis, strongly influenced by the French Communist Party[42] and which increased the support for this party[43] at the legislative elections — the French State was led to act 'under the pressure of the facts and the parties involved',[44] in order to try to halt the Communist advance.

(3) As partial resolutions of immediate difficulties, capitalist urban policies simply carry the contradiction between the necessities or urban socialization and the necessities of capitalist accumulation to a higher degree. Far from suppressing the class struggle, economic and legal intervention by the State apparatus in the urban domain simply extends its field of application.

[39] See Pierre Merlin, *New Towns* (Methuen, London, 1971).
[40] See in particular K. Marx, *Capital* I, 658 (chapter 25, § 5b), and R. H. Guerrand, *op. cit., passim.*
[41] See R. H. Guerrand, *op. cit.*; M. G. Raymond, *La Politique Pavillonaire* (Centre de Recherche d'Urbanisme, Paris, 1966).
[42] Jean Bastié, *La Croissance de la Banlieue Parisienne* (P.U.F., Paris, 1964) 283.
[43] *Ibid.*, 277.
[44] *Ibid.*, 278.

Limited in Marx's time to the problems of housing and nourishment,[45] the reproduction of labour power refers nowadays to a complex set of collective means of consumption and an environment which are the historical product of class struggles. But the growing socialization of conditions of urban life today is increasingly entering into contradiction with its capitalist limit:[46] the lack of collective means of consumption, and urban segregation, which split up the worker into socially and geographically separate functions (work, leisure, culture . . .).

State intervention, far from lessening this contradiction, exacerbates it; thus it may be said that the *political reproduction* of urban social relations is in the long run *an extended reproduction of the urban conflict between the individual* fragmented by zoning laws, worn out by more and more commuting, deprived of all access to cultural facilities *and the defenders of urban segregation*.

Marx showed, in connexion with urban renewal policy in England in the 1860s, how the 'improvement' of city-centres, far from benefiting the mass of the population, simply led to greater segregation between the richest — the beneficiaries of renewal — and the poorest, the majority of the population forced to migrate to the already over-crowded and under-equipped periphery.[47]

Certainly since 1860 class struggles have forced the State into a massive programme of building working-class houses whose standard of comfort today is incomparably better than that in 1860. But the gap between the new historic needs of our age and their satisfaction has not diminished. Quite apart from the persistence of shanty towns in the major Western metropolises, the tendency for the popular masses to be driven out into the *least well-equipped* areas of the agglomeration has hardly weakened,[48] and it may be said that on the

---

[45] K. Marx, *Capital* I, 654 (chapter 25, § 5b).
[46] Thus the ideological and political character of the Sarraut law appears clearly in the statement by Senator Chastenet, spokesman for the right-wing parties, to the Senate on 9 March 1928: 'Let us fight against the communists by turning them into home-owners.' Quoted by J. Bastié, *op. cit.*, 278. See also M. G. Raymond, *La Politique Pavillonaire*.
[47] *Capital* I, 657 (chapter 25, § 5b).
[48] For a clear demonstration of the segregative effect of renewal policy in Paris, see Groupe de Sociologie Urbaine de Nanterre, Paris, 1970: Reconquête urbaine et rénovation-déportation, *Sociologie du Travail* 4 (1970) 488—514. For the United States, see M. Castells, La rénovation urbaine aux Etats-Unis, *Espaces et Sociétés* 1 (1970) 107—35.

contrary housing policy has been a major factor in the flight of the poorest citizens to the outer suburbs.[49]

We are well aware, at the conclusion of this article, of not having presented a real scientific explanation of present-day urban phenomena; at most we have attempted to 'suggest' the scientific fecundity of Marxist concepts when confronted with the various aspects of urban reality.

In our view to go further than this would require a systematic combination of regional or national monographs and international comparisons, in particular between capitalist and socialist countries.

The aim of this article has been simply to contribute to the clarification of a number of ideas which in our view should serve as the theoretical base for empirical studies both in urban economics and in urban sociology.

[49] See Jean Gottman, *Megalopolis* (Twentieth Century Fund, New York, 1961; M.I.T. Press, Cambridge (Mass.), 1967).

6 Manuel Castells

Theoretical propositions for an experimental study of urban social movements*†

Traditionally work in urban sociology has been located within the problematic of social integration, as is to be expected given the nature of the demand to which it is a response, a demand closely linked to a reformist paternalism seeking to wipe away the misdeeds of capitalist industrialization in the field of collective consumption.

Now in advanced capitalism urban problems are increasingly the subject of political debate and are the focal point for new forms of class struggle. The analytical tools forged by urban sociology are thus not only instruments of accommodation to the system as they always have been, but, as research tools, are completely incapable of accounting for the essential characteristics of the problems posed by social practice.

New theoretical formulations are necessary in order to explain the growing importance of 'urban problems' in the management of society, to specify their scope and to bring out the social mechanisms underlying them. Our aim then is to contribute towards laying the foundations for a sociological analysis of urban politics.

The term urban politics refers to three specific theoretical fields: the political (*le politique*), politics (*la politique*) and the urban.

*[Translated with permission of the author from M. Castells, Propositions théoriques pour une recherche experimentale sur les mouvements sociaux urbains (Unpublished paper presented at the Seventh World Congress of Sociology, Varna, 1970; a Spanish translation has been published in *Revista Mexicana de Sociologia* 34 (1972) 1–26).]
†This text seeks to develop a number of conceptual tools for the analysis of urban social movements. It takes as read a previous critique of the existing planning and sociological literature as well as a number of theoretical assumptions which we shall attempt to develop further here but which will not be fully spelt out. The relevant works and references are cited in my articles Théorie et idéologie en sociologie urbaine, *Sociologie et Sociétés* 1 (1969) 171–90 [chapter 3 in this volume], and Vers une théorie sociologique de la planification urbaine, *Sociologie du Travail* 4 (1969) 413–43.

The political refers to the structures by which a society excercises control over the different instances which constitute it, *thereby* assuring the domination of a particular social class.

Politics refers to the system of *power* relations. The theoretical location of the concept of power is that of class relations. By power we mean the capacity of one social class to realize its specific objective interests at the expense of others. By objective interests we mean the predominance of the structural elements which, in combination, define a class, over the other elements which are in a contradictory relation with them.

The term *urban*, once freed from the ideological connotation of so-called '*urban culture*', or '*urbanism*', refers in principle to two sets of problems:

those relating to the social organization of space,

those relating to the processes of collective consumption
(consumption = reproduction of labour power)

But in fact the organization of space as such belongs to the category of what may be termed *regional* problems, since it would be inconceivable to treat the urban network except in its entirety. Thus the term *urban* has a more specific referent, namely, the territorial limits which define the 'city'. And, in the last analysis, the 'city' is a *residential unit of labour power.* An agglomeration cannot be defined as a productive unit, for this term refers to firms, sections of industry and trusts, but only as a *unit of collective consumption* corresponding more or less to the daily organization of a section of labour power (the limits of an agglomeration, for example, are defined by the limits of commuting).

Within the boundaries of this unit may be found both other elements (production, exchange, management) and sub-units (districts, neighbourhoods), but the basis of the boundaries must not be forgotten since it specifies the 'city' in relation to consumption processes.

Urban problems then are problems relating to collective consumption, defined within a consumption unit (the agglomeration), and problems relating to the organization and functioning of this unit in so far as changes in the unit also have effects on the consumption processes in question.

The role of the agglomeration as a consumption unit is the same as the role of the firm as a production unit.

These clarifications enable us to proceed to define the object of our enquiry.

Though the field of experience that concerns us possesses its own unity, namely the articulation of *power* and the *urban*, it may be grasped from two different points of view according to whether one is interested in *structures* or in *practices*, or, to put it more clearly, according to whether the theoretical object is to be the analysis of changes in the configuration of the system (social formation) or the processes by which it is transformed, in other words, social relations in so far as they are a direct or refracted expression of social classes. Although a distinction between the two perspectives is essential when it comes to actually carrying out an investigation, we shall see that, at the end of the day, whichever approach is taken as the starting point, one ends up by having analyzed the process as a whole, since structures are only articulated practices and practices only relations between relations defined by certain combinations of structural elements.

The study of urban politics can thus be broken down into two analytical fields, fields which in reality are indissolubly linked: urban planning, in its various forms, and urban social movements.

We shall be concerned here with the elaboration of analytical tools for research within the second of these fields. But first of all we must clarify what we mean by urban social movements. To do this we must introduce a theoretical framework based on a Marxist perspective whose sole justification is its fruitfulness in concrete research.

I Social structure, urban system and social movements
Every concrete piece of sociological analysis makes use of a set of theoretical concepts. We shall define and elaborate briefly the basis of the set of concepts used here before going on to specify it in relation to our particular problematic.

(1) We shall take as our point of departure, at a very general level, the set of concepts developed by Louis Althusser and the research workers at the École Normale Superieure from a reading of *Capital*. This analytical framework can be sketched in briefly as follows. The central concept is that of mode of production. By mode of production is meant not the economic but a specific form of articulation of the fundamental elements (instances) of a social structure, namely the economic, political-legal, ideological and possibly other 'systems'. In every mode of production one system, which varies in identity, is dominant, and the place of this system in the structure characterizes the mode of production in question. In every mode of production one system is determinant in the last

instance. This system is invariant; it is always the economic. It is the type of economic system (i.e. the particular structuring of its elements) which explains which system is dominant in each mode of production and thus the particular configuration of the various systems (matrix of the mode of production). A particular historical society (social formation) is the particular mix of several modes of production, one of which is dominant.

Each system is made up of interrelated elements. The way in which these structural elements are articulated in certain types of relation defines the state of the system, itself dependent on the general matrix of the mode of production. In the case of the economic system, which is crucial, these elements are three in number: labour power, means of production (object and means of labour) and 'non-worker'. The labour process is the intervention of labour power on the means of production in order to realize the product (which itself can be broken down into the (re)production of labour power and the (re)production of the means of production). In this process two relations appear between the three elements: (a) a relation of ownership (not to be confused with legal ownership which belongs to the political-legal system),[1] and (b) a relation of 'real appropriation', concerning the control of the technical process of work. The places of the political and ideological systems are not clearly defined; however, they can be deduced from the role played by these two systems in the structure as a whole, a role of regulation-domination in the case of the political system and a role of 'recognition-communication-legitimation' in the case of the ideological system.

The characteristics of the capitalist mode of production, the only one to have been studied scientifically, at least in its economic region, are as follows: (a) the ownership and 'appropriation' relations are homologous: the non-worker is owner of labour power and of the means of production and, at the same time, 'controller' of the technical process of production and (b) the economic system is not only determinant but dominant.

There is a crucial distinction between structure and practices. Practices are the relations among different elements and different structures. Agents, whose most obvious expression is in social classes, are only the supports of these structural relations. The relations between the social classes of a particular society are the effect on social relations of the complex combination of modes of production articulated within it. Finally, power relations, which are of particular

[1] [See p. 23, n. 29.]

importance in our analysis, are relations between social classes, i.e. relations between relations, and governed by the particular form of articulation of a society.

With this framework as our starting-point we can now proceed to the analysis of concrete situations by demonstrating the structural determination both of the 'social problems' or stakes emerging in social practice and of the relations between actors produced by these stakes. Our aim is not to place events back within a context but to show the realization of a structural law or set of laws within a social process. This operation is equivalent to a demonstration or proof of the law.

(2) Every social structure is in a constant state of change. Each new situation brings about a tendency for the system to readjust (or regulate) itself by means of a series of practices carried out by the actors. Since the system is not harmonious but contains contradictions, the new situation resulting will depend on the interaction between structural arrangements tending to conserve the state of the system and the contradictory relations established between the actors, or supports, differentially located in the places of the system (class relations).

The term *social movement* may now be defined as an organization of the system of actors (conjuncture of class relations) leading to the production of a qualitatively new effect on the social structure (pertinent effect). The term 'qualitatively new effect' may refer to either of two basic situations:

at the level of *structures*: a change in the structural law of the dominant system (which in the capitalist mode of production is the economic as far as the ownership relation is concerned).
at the level of *practices*: a change in the balance of forces in a direction counter to institutionalized social domination, the most characteristic index of which is a substantial change in the system of authority (i.e. in the political-legal apparatus) or in the organization of counter-domination (strengthening of class organizations).

(3) Every social stake has its more or less immediate source in a contradiction or dislocation between the elements of one system, between elements belonging to different systems, between these systems taken as wholes, or finally between structures or forms belonging to different modes of production articulated within the same social formation.

In order to identify this source a first technique is to code the real problems being dealt with by urban policy in terms of the concepts outlined above. This procedure has two advantages: previously discovered laws of the mode of production in question can be applied to the problems concerned; and the problems can be used to discover new laws which can in turn be transposed to other domains of reality (social forms) in which the same structures are realized in a different way.

Thus, *for example*, at each level of the social structure manifestations of so-called urban or regional problems may be found:

Contradictions internal to the *economic* system

	Problem
• Contradiction between the ownership relation and the real appropriation relation (each individual firm profits by pushing towards greater concentration whereas organized decentralization would bring the greatest overall technical advantages)	Regional imbalance and excessive industrial and urban concentration
• Contradiction between labour power/non-worker (ownership relation) means of production/non-worker (ownership relation)	Housing crisis Obsolescence of industrial plant and infrastructure
• Contradiction between means of production/non-worker (real appropriation relation) labour power/non-worker (real appropriation relation)	Mistake in planning of industrial areas Lack of skilled labour available locally
Between the *economic* and the *political*	Boundaries of administrative areas do not correspond with limits of agglomeration as an economic unit

Between the *economic* and the *legal*	Easy availability of land is checked by private and fragmented ownership of land
Between the *economic* and the *ideological*	"Alienation" among inhabitants of large blocks of flats
Within the *political* (dominators/dominated)	On local politics: State/local authority/citizen
Within the *legal*	Owner/tenants
Within the *ideological*	Ideology of urban life (modernity)/community ideology of 'belonging' to the city
Between forms belonging to two modes of production	Traffic congestion: contradiction between the city (feudal mode of production) and the car (capitalist mode of production)

(4) However, the framework as presented so far is too general and requires a whole series of specifications in order to be of use in concrete research.

Having stated that the object of research is 'the urban' as a unit of collective consumption, it is necessary to show how the social structure is articulated and how the system of actor-supports is organized within such a unit.

This may be done by introducing the two concepts of urban system and system of urban actors.

By *urban system* we mean the particular way in which the elements of the economic system are articulated within a unit of collective consumption. (The fact that we are concerned only with the elements of the economic system follows from the definition of the urban as having an economic referent: the territorial area of a sub-unit of labour power.)

The *urban system* (or social structure on which social processes in units of collective consumption are based) is defined by the set of relations between the two fundamental elements of the economic system and the two elements which derive from them:

Element P (production): specific means of production

Element C (consumption): specific labour power

(the element non-worker appears as a necessary effect of the
economic system in *reproduction*, and can be divided into three
products:

- reproduction of the means of production
- reproduction of labour power
- appropriation of the product by the non-worker:
  - social stratification at the level of *social organization*
  (system of distribution)
  - functioning of *institutions*
  - at the level of structures, this may also return to the
  reproduction of the means of production and/or of labour
  power.)

Element E (exchange) between P and C, within P and within C.

Element M (management) or regulation of the relations between P,
C, E according to structural laws. M represents the articulation
with the political system, but is in no way exhaustive of relations
with the latter system.

Examples of concrete expressions of these elements:

P (production): the set of activities producing goods, services and
information, e.g. *industry, offices.*

C (consumption): the set of activities concerning the (individual
and collective) social appropriation of the product, e.g. *housing,
collective facilities.*

E (exchange): the exchanges produced between P and C, within P
and within C, e.g. *transport and shopping facilities.*

M (management): the process of regulation of relations between
P, C and E, e.g. *local government, urban planning.*

Every 'urban problem' is structurally defined by its place in a
conjuncture of a given urban system, and this determines both its
social significance and how it is dealt with in social practice. But it
is not defined solely by its place in the urban system but
simultaneously by:

its place in the urban system

its place in the general social structure, in the systems and
elements other than those present in the urban system, and
especially, in the ideological and the political-legal other than at a
local level.

its place in *social organization* (i.e. in historically given social
forms resulting from the particular way in which structures and
practices are articulated on a domain of the real) and especially
how it is dealt with by:
- the stratification system (distribution)
- the organizational system (system of means)
- the material forms specific to the problem (ecological forms in
the case of urban problems)

The links between these different systems and between the
different problems thus treated cannot be established by a structural
connexion, but only by the intermediary of actor-supports, those
men-who-make-their-history-in-determined-social-conditions. These
actors, in so far as they exist not in themselves but through the
elements they convey, must also be defined in a manner specific to
the urban system but which takes into account the places they occupy
in other instances of the social structure. Thus we must define a
system of urban actors by the differential appropriation of places in
each element of the urban system, and articulate it with:

(1)   the places defined in other instances
(2)   social practices bearing on specific domains separate from
      'urban problems' and which must be treated by the same
      decoding procedure. In the framework of an 'urban analysis',
      however, they must be regarded as constant and taken into
      consideration only in so far as they produce effects on the
      problem being considered.

We can now define an *urban social movement* as the system of
practices resulting from the articulation of a conjuncture of the
system of urban actors and other social practices, such that its
development tends objectively towards the structural transformation
of the urban system or towards a substantial change in the balance
of forces within the political system as a whole.

A simplified picture of all these relations is given in Table 1.

It may be noted that 'social movements' and 'urban politics'
are approached by means of the same concepts, and that the
structural study of politics necessarily involves passing through the
field of practices. But the difference of emphasis is not without
practical effects in so far as one may seek a detailed understanding of
the mechanism by which an urban social movement emerges without a
thorough study of all its structural implications.

TABLE 1

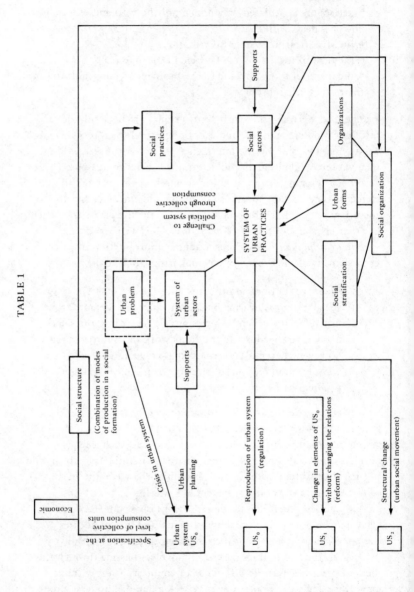

156

We are still at too high a level of generality. In order to get closer to the concrete situations research has to decipher we must break down the urban system and hence the system of urban actors, into their component elements, without however shifting theoretical framework.

II The internal structure of the elements of the urban system

To state that the consumption element specifies the reproduction of labour power or the production element the reproduction of the means of production at the level of the urban unit, is to refer to a problematic which is much too general to be translated into explanatory propositions. It is thus necessary to break these elements down into sub-elements.

Internal analysis of the various elements of the urban system, if it is to be more than intuitive, must be carried out in terms of a single principle. It must not introduce elements which have not been previously theoretically defined. We shall thus state that each element can be broken down into sub-elements defined by the refraction on it of the other elements (including itself) and/or of the other systems of the social structure. Things will become clearer when we apply this principle and give concrete examples in each case (remember that the examples are only indicative since concepts never coincide completely with reality).

1 Consumption

The consumption element expresses, at the level of the urban unit, *the process of reproduction of labour power*. We shall thus distinguish between the simple and the extended reproduction of labour power, and, within extended reproduction, between the refraction of the three systems, economic, political-legal and ideological.

Simple reproduction of labour power	C_1	Housing and basic services (sewerage, street lighting, roads, etc.)
Extended reproduction of labour power		
extension within the economic system (biological reproduction)	C_2	Parks, pollution, noise, etc. (environment)

extension on the institutional C_3 Educational facilities
(political-legal) system
(acquisition of skills and
socialization)
extension on the ideological C_4 Socio-cultural facilities
system

2 Production

A fundamental distinction must be made between the means of labour
and the object of labour (particularly raw materials), on the one hand,
and the orientation of production to the organizational system as such
or as a productive organization, on the other.

			Example
Elements internal to	means of labour	P_1	Factories
the labour process	object of labour	P_2	Raw materials
Relationship between the labour process and the economic system		P_3	Industrial environment (technical environment)
Relationship between the labour process and other systems, and with social organization		P_4	Management, information (offices)

3 Exchange

By definition, the element *exchange* can be broken down into as
many sub-elements as there are possible transfers within or between
the elements and systems of the social structure in relation to a given
urban unit:

Transfer	*Sub-elements*	*Example*
Production → Consumption	E_1	Commerce and distribution
Consumption → Production	E_2	Commuting (urban transport facilities)
Production → Production	E_3	{ Freight transport { Ordering and management
Consumption → Consumption	E_4	{ Personal journeys { Residential mobility
Consumption → Ideological	E_5	Diffusion of information, shows, etc.

Production → Ideological E_6 Public buildings
Consumption → Political E_7 Decision centres
Production → Political E_8 Business centres

4 Management

The management element articulates the urban system to the political system and regulates the relationships between the elements. It is thus defined by its position in two dichotomies: global/local (representing the political system as a whole, or linked to local conditions), and specific/general (bearing either on one element of the system or on the whole). There are thus four possible sub-elements:

	Local	Global
Specific (bearing on one element)	M_1 urban agency	M_3 planning body
General (bearing on the relationships between elements	M_2 local authority	M_4 a delegation of central authority ('prefect')

5 Sub-elements and system of places

By breaking down each element into sub-elements in this way, one is better able to tackle concrete situations in so far as they enable a much more specific analysis to be undertaken. But having identified the *location* of a contradiction, it is still necessary for the latter to be expressed socially through the differential appropriation of the elements by the actors. Thus within each sub-element one must define the places among which the actors will be distributed according to their position in the social structure. It is these differences in the places occupied by the actors which account for the existence of contradictory social practices and permit transformations in the urban system. The latter has therefore not only to be broken down into sub-elements but also *differentiated* by specifying the *levels* and roles within each sub-element.

Thus, for example, within element C_1 (housing)

levels   luxury dwellings
         public housing $(+, -)$
         slums, etc.

roles   lodger
         tenant
         co-owner
         owner

or, within P3 (industrial area)

> *levels*   well equipped
>   poorly equipped
>
> *roles*   articulation of industry to:
>   ● natural environment (water, space)
>   ● communications (transport network)
>   ● technical environment (industrial interdependences)

The relationships maintained by the different sub-elements of the urban system, their roles and levels, among themselves and with the social structure, define the conjuncture. The insertion of actor-supports in the structural frame thus constituted defines the urban system in relation to social practices, the only significant realities.

III Articulation of the urban system to the general social structure

The urban system is not external to the social structure: it specifies it, forms part of it. But in every concrete practice it is necessary to take into account its orientation to other levels than those specified in the urban system. This articulation takes place through the necessary insertion of urban actors in the system of economic, political and ideological places of the social structure, as well as in the different relations between these places which define the systems from an internal point of view.

Concretely, urban actors will take values (which may be zero in the case of absence, e.g. actors not defined in the productive system: office-workers) in the three systems:

Places	*Relations defined between the places*
Economic[2]	
Non-worker	Ownership relation
Labour power	Real appropriation relation
Political-legal	
Authority	Regulation—integration
	(structures) (practices)
Private	Maintenance of order—domination
	(structures) (practices)

---

[2] The place Means of production is redundant with the P/C distinction at the level of the urban system.

Ideological
Diffusion	Communication — recognition
Reception	(practices)
Transmission	Legitimation (structures)

The ideological must surely be differentiated into the ideological systems belonging to the various modes of production intertwined in a given social formation, specified in relation to urban problems;

Feudal mode of production: urban community
Liberal capitalist mode of production: urban modernity
Technocratic capitalist mode of production: New Towns
Socialist mode of production: collective facilities

IV Articulation of the urban system to social organization

In every historically given society, structurally determined processes are inserted in the crystallized social forms which give each moment its specificity. 'Urban' practices derive from the insertion of the urban system articulated to the general social structure into these social forms, i.e. from this three-fold determination of actor-supports and of the field of practices thus constituted.

The term social organization conjures up too many domains and refers to too many forms for us to be able to avoid selecting certain aspects which are particularly relevant to the problem being considered here.

Three dimensions may be considered as fundamental: *ecological forms* (or forms related to the organization of space), *social stratification* (distribution of the product among the supports) and the *organizational system* (formal arrangement of systems of specific means).

Places in *ecological forms*

	concentration	dispersion
centrality	city-centre I	II exchangers
periphery	New III Towns	IV suburbs

Multifunctionality/Unifunctionality

		P		C		E
I	1	5	:	9	:	13
II	2	6	:	10	:	14
III	3	7	:	11	:	15
IV	4	8	:	12	:	16

Places in the *stratification system* (dimensions following Max Weber)

Levels	'Class' (income)	Status (education)	'Party' (degree of involvement in hierarchy of institutional authority)
+	+	+	+
=	=	=	=
−	−	−	−

Finally, the problem of *organization*, which is truly central to our research. While theoretically organization can be defined as a social form, any detailed discussion of it must be preceded by a clarification of the articulation of practices in the system of actors *since it is in relation to the fusion, separation, and transformation of these bundles of practices that organization plays an essential role.* We shall thus try to state precisely this role after having first sketched in a general picture of the structural determination of actors and their practices.

V The structural determination of urban practices

By urban practices we mean those social practices related to the internal organization of collective consumption units or which, while directed towards general problems of collective consumption, take urban units as their field of action.

Urban practices form a system. But they have no significance in themselves. Their only significance is that of the structural elements which they combine. These combinations are realized by means of actors, through the determination and multidimensional memberships of these actor-supports. *The field of urban practices is a system in which given combinations of structural elements are themselves combined.* It simultaneously realizes and manifests the structural laws governing the organization of the system and its transformation.

The complete set of possible determinations is summarized in Table 2. Despite its complexity it represents only one possible framework since any social process can be understood in varying degrees of detail. In effect one could either relate practices, structural effects and situations together with a simple classification in which several fundamental elements are combined, or, conversely, analyze a particular process occurring between the sub-elements. To each object of research there corresponds an extension, contraction, or particular arrangement of the field of practices and, hence, a redefinition of the system of actor-supports. In brief, everything depends on the 'problem' being considered. Reference is to places and not individuals.

What is the real contribution of this Table?

From the point of view of *structures* (the study of 'urban politics'), it enables the inputs and outputs of each problem considered to be studied, or, to put it more clearly, given a situation of dislocation or contradiction in one of the processes, it enables the consequences for the system to be seen.

From the point of view of *practices*, the Table enables one both to uncover the processes of formation of certain practices (by examining the structural combinations on which they are based) and to define them by their effects and not by their subjectivity. Now at last subjectivity itself is clarified and seen to play a certain role in the social structure. Meaning only has meaning outside of itself. But this 'outside' can only be the production of a socially identifiable effect, and hence must be part of a pre-defined framework.

For any urban practice one can thus:

(1) Define the structural combination (revealed by the characteristics of the actors) which has produced it.

(2) Give it a name (or fit it into a typology)by analyzing its *horizon* (the structural consequences predictable given the logic of its development)

   For example: Reproduction of the urban system (regulation)

   Change in one element of the system (reform)

   Reproduction of another structural instance through the urban system (maintenance of order)

   Transformation of the structural law of the urban system (urban social movement)

   Challenge to the political system (social movement with an urban base)

   No effect, apart from the practice itself (demagogic movement)

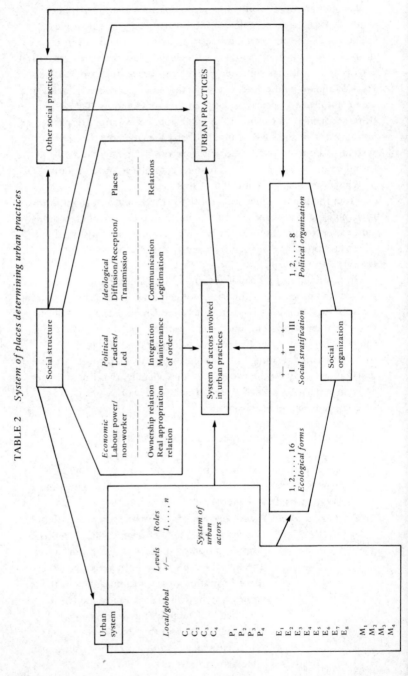

TABLE 2 *System of places determining urban practices*

(3) Establish the natural history of each of these practices, which involves characterizing the articulated set of opposed practices and seeing to what extent their initial structural charges and differential horizons cause them to become dominant, subordinate, or to disappear. The study of an urban social movement (defined by its determinants and horizon) thus becomes the study of this set of contradictory practices realizing general laws but always remaining unique because conjunctural.

However, while the Table may facilitate systematization (and hence the accumulation and inter-relating of research results, beyond their empirical diversity) it does not in itself provide any guarantee of greater explanatory capacity, in particular since no hypotheses have yet been elaborated.

The only possible solution to this deficiency is concrete research. However, one can have a certain amount of confidence in the analytical power of Marxist concepts whose use up till now has increased the legibility of the social frame *on condition that they have been sufficiently specified in relation to the object in question.* As far as urban problems are concerned, this translation remains to be done.

To put forward hypotheses concerning all the possible combinations in the Table would be both excessively complicated and largely superfluous. In fact, the aim is not to exhaust all possible situations, but to make use of these concepts to carve up reality in order both to test general laws which are already known and to discover new relationships which display the same logic in differentiated form.

For this reason we shall say that there are no hypotheses related to the Table but only *limits* and *operating rules.* We shall attempt to be a little more precise as far as our specific object, urban social movements, is concerned.

As for the general framework, let us remember that we are focussing on a society where the capitalist mode of production is dominant. To say that is not to say everything (since, for example, at the very least one must identify the period and conjuncture) but it does establish certain limits.

In fact the urban system is a system with a dominant element, in this case the production element (P). And besides, the ownership relation cannot be fundamentally changed (at the level of the productive system, even if it is at the legal level).

For example, if we consider the system's determinations on urban planning in the capitalist mode of production we know that there is a dislocation between the particularistic control of labour power and the means of production and the collective character of the (re)production of these two elements. More specifically, at the level of reproduction of the means of production there is a contradiction between the higher profit obtainable by a firm by locating in an already established industrial area in a large agglomeration, and the dysfunctions resulting from the widespread adoption of such behaviour; similarly, there is a contradiction between this same profit-based strategy and the under-development of certain regions, which results in the non-use of available resources. Concerning the reproduction of labour power, there is a contradiction between the need to concentrate this power in industrial metropolises (both as a labour supply and a market), and the inability of capitals to provide an adequate supply of housing and facilities due to the lack of profitability, itself an effect of the income stratification resulting from the system.

If one accepts the idea of the political system as regulating the system (concrete social formation) as a whole, *according to the structural laws on which it is based*, then urban planning is its intervention on a given reality in order to counteract the dislocations expressed. Thus, in terms of the elements of the urban system:

dislocation in element P (re)production → (M → P)
dislocation in element C (re)production → (M → C)

However, these elements exist not in isolation but always in relation to one another. Thus an intervention cannot bear on the element itself, but only on the relation which defines it. At the level of the economic system of a mode of production we know there are two relations: ownership (control) and real appropriation (technical direction).

Besides, not every conceivable intervention by M is possible, because it must take place within the *limits* of the capitalist mode of production, otherwise the system would be *shaken* rather than regulated.

What are these limits? (1) In general, there must be no change in the ownership relation. (2) There must be no *direct* intervention by M on P. Some further remarks are necessary on this point: (a) there may be intervention by M on certain aspects of the technical process of work at the level of P, in the overall interest (e.g. zoning); (b) there may be indirect intervention by M on P (e.g. fiscal or financial incentives) in the form of a bonus for what may be called 'system patriotism'; (c) there may be direct intervention by M on C. However, such intervention has four characteristics: it always comes after the social expression of the dislocation, it is supplementary to direct intervention by P on C, its *form* reflects the effect of the ideological on the economic, and *in particular* it depends directly on the state of politics, that is to say, the social pressure exercised by labour power; (d) when the dislocation to be dealt with is based on a state of P, the intervention by M on P tends to take place by means of interventions on the other elements of the system, and especially on E.

In general, two contradictions are fundamental: that between labour power and non-worker, and that between ownership relation and real appropriation relation (productive forces). The urban problematic oscillates around two essential poles: element C (consumption) at the level of the ownership relation, and element P at the level of the real appropriation relation. Thus every dislocation of the system favouring consumption, at the level of the ownership relation, carries the risk of transcending it. Conversely, every dislocation deriving from an emphasis on P, at the level of the real appropriation relation, carries the risk of disequilibriating it through the hyperdetermination of element P affecting labour power.

Contradictions will be all the more intense

when they concern the economic system,
when they concern the ownership relation (relations of production),
and when they challenge the dominance of element P (organization of productive forces).

Every fundamental contradiction which is not regulated by the system results in an overdetermined contradiction within the political system.

Finally, contradictions become organized among the places of the different systems according to a content defined by the relation(s) which characterize the function of the system in the social structure (e.g. for the political system, the regulation-domination relation function defines the places 'leaders-managers of the system as a whole' and 'led concerned with their individual interests'; these places, occupied by different supports, define oppositions (contradictory situations) which are all the more intense in that they are overdetermined by more general oppositions (ideological-political) or oppositions more closely connected to the dominant system (economic)).

In fact, the rules of functioning of the urban system are easy to determine since they are simply specifications of the general rules of the mode of production. The picture becomes more complicated when one has to reproduce the logic at the level of the sub-elements, and, in particular, when one has to consider not only the functioning (reproduction) or the system, but also its transformation. In these cases it is necessary to study the linkages between contradictions, or, in other words, the transition from a partial dislocation to the condensation of oppositions in a principal contradiction which, embodied in the confrontation of social practices, leads to the emergence of new structural rules which are impossible to deduce from the mechanisms of functioning and extended reproduction alone.

The experimental study of these transformations involves the analysis of the social movements which are at their base.

VI Hypotheses for the study of urban social movements

Having thus given a precise definition of our object, we can now formulate some general orientations concerning the analysis of urban social movements, i.e. of that state of urban practices which leads towards the structural transformations indicated above.

What are the conditions and processes of formation of these social movements?

A social movement springs from the conjunction of: (1) a particular type of structural combination, which cumulates several contradictions, and (2) a particular type of organization. Every social movement provokes a social counter-movement by the system which can simply be seen as the expression of an intervention of the political system (integration-repression).

(1) *The accumulation of contradictions* occurs through the appropriation by actors of contradictory places within the same element of the urban system, social structure or social organization, or of different elements within the same relation (e.g. the role of tenant or owner within the consumption element C_1 (housing), or labour power/non-worker within the ownership relation, or labour power/means of production (C/P) within the real appropriation relation).

The following rules may thus be given:

The greater the number of accumulated contradictions, the greater the mobilizing potential of the social charge.

The greater the extent to which the contradictions are concentrated in the economic system (or its specification, the urban system) or are derived from contradictions in that system, the more important they will be. Conversely, the greater the extent to which contradictions are purely political or purely ideological, the more they will be liable to integration through system regulation.

The more fragmented the treatment of contradictions, the slighter the chances of confrontation and mobilization.

Direct confrontation between practices based on structural combinations whose opposition derives from a fundamental contradiction can only be resolved by system regulation or by articulation with another contradiction. Thus every contradiction which is unresolved but remains posed between complementary and opposed elements issues into another contradiction. The linkage between contradictions (*revealed by changes in the system of actors*) issues into the location of condensations of contradictions of the system: *the political system.*

When there is a lack of correspondence between the elements appropriated by the actors present, contradictions can only be expressed through the articulation of these isolated elements within other fields of social practice.

The articulation of other practices with urban practices produces an increase in the contradiction when they are defined on fundamental contradictions and a decrease when they are not.

The intervention of ideology has a particular importance at the level of *forms* of expression of the movement; the intervention of the political, at the level of their historically given *content*; and the intervention of the economic, at the level of their dynamic (structural horizon).

(2)   The role of *organizations* (systems of means specific to a goal) is basic because, while the actor-supports permit the constitution of combinations between structural elements, it is the organization which is the location for their fusion or articulation with other social practices. In the absence of an organization, urban contradictions are expressed either in refracted form, through other practices, or in 'wild' form, as pure contradictions lacking any structural horizon.

The genesis of an organization does not form part of the analysis of social movements, for only its effects are important. An organization is a crystallization of social practices and its characteristics will determine the effects it has on particular structural combinations expressed in the system of actors.

An organization can be defined structurally as an intervention of a particular structural combination (expressed by a *membership horizon*: the sum of the combinations of the actors at its base) on another and different structural combination of which it forms part: the *reference horizon* (the sum of the combinations of actors which constitute it if the objectives of the organization are realized).

The role of organizations in the formation of a social movement is to *link* the different contradictions present in the structural combinations with which it is concerned. The role of an organization seeking to destroy the social movement is to *unlink* those contradictions which are already linked.

On the other hand, an organization may either develop from the system of urban actors or be imported from other practices. *Fundamental hypothesis*: if an organization develops simply from the interrelation of elements contained in some part of the system of urban actors, it cannot result in a qualitative change in orientation and its role is simply to consolidate a fragmented action determined by the different places. This is the zero level of organization (coordination of spontaneity) and cannot give rise to a social movement. Thus the creation of a social movement necessarily requires the union of a series of intense contradictions which can only be achieved by an organization imported from *other practices*. A purely 'urban' organization can at most be an instrument of *reform* (see our typology of urban practices).

In all cases other than the latter, the organization, while intervening on the system of urban actors, has an external origin and must correspond to one of the categories below (depending on its objectives, defined outside the urban system):

1. Instrument of domination
   and integration   Instrument of
   (transmission belt) ←————————————→   contestation
2. Economic contestation
3. Ideological contestation
4. Political contestation
5. 2 + 3
6. 2 + 4
7. 3 + 4
8. 2 + 3 + 4

The organization is not the *deus ex machina* of a social movement. Its explanation lies outside a specific analysis of the urban (in so far as it is the crystallization of other practices). But it is perfectly possible to analyze a new organization, specific to the urban social movement, as a fusion of the characteristics of the 'imported' organization and the structural combinations present in the system of actors. A social movement will emerge in so far as the practice and discourse of the organization link the contradictions supported by the actors, without either unlinking them in a fragmented fashion (reformist ideology) or fusing them together in a single totalizing opposition (revolutionist utopia).

An urban social movement emerges when there is a correspondence between the fundamental structural contradictions of the urban system and a correct line within an organization formed from the crystallization of other practices.

VII The execution of research

While it would be entirely arbitrary to start considering methodological problems without first delimiting an empirical object, we can at least indicate a *style of work* in order to begin to provide a link between the theoretical concerns of this article and the research results we are ultimately seeking to arrive at.

We are already in a position to state what should be the starting-point in studies of urban social movements. Or, to be more precise, that the usual starting-point, *organizations*, is the *wrong* one. Rather, one must start by identifying contradictions ('problems') or drawing attention to mobilizations specific to these problems. One must then go on to:

Identify the stake(s) and code them in structural terms.
Identify the social groups intervening in relation to each stake and code them *using the same concepts*, in varying degrees of detail, as in Table 2.
Characterize the organizations and determine how they are articulated to the system of actors.

The next step is to proceed to a concrete analysis of the situation which at the same time will amount to the demonstration of a law, in so far as the situation realizes this law by being made intelligible through the interrelating of the real elements subjected to our theoretical coding.

In order to overcome the classical problems in quantitative research arising from the application of the experimental method to a non-experimental situation, we shall make the assumption of field closure, and treat as constant all elements not included in a particular analysis. It will then be necessary to find procedures for qualitative research equivalent to the control procedures used in quantitative research.

The most adequate experimental verification technique appears to be the *simulation model*, which might operate as follows:

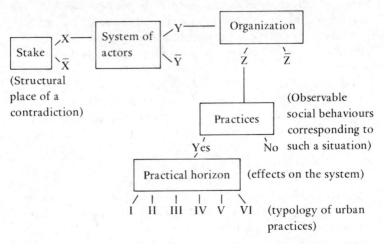

Clearly this diagram could be made as complex or as simple as one wished:

By breaking down each element into sub-elements.
By changing the order of verification (the model could be set out starting from a type of practice, for example).
By combining stakes together.

But whatever the circumstances two fundamental operating rules apply:

(1) Verification is achieved by using the dichotomy presence/absence and through the determination of each chain by a single combination of elements.

(2) The control procedure (analogous to the partial correlation coefficient) consists in treating the differential organization of practices in terms of distinctions deriving from the system of actors. For example, one could divide up the category of actors belonging to a low level within the tenant role in C_1 (housing) by adding a further criterion, refraction of the social structure at the level of the economic system (office-workers, manual workers), and then comparing the behaviour of the two sub-categories in relation to the practice concerned (e.g. a rent strike).

Since we are dealing with non-experimental situations and with practices and not questionnaire responses, it will usually prove difficult to obtain a complete set of controls. But at least we shall have available a number of systems of practices corresponding to different clusterings of the same actors and to the treatment of a variety of problems. These varied situations will provide us with elements of comparison, and hence explanation, since we shall be very close to the type of research situation familiar to the sociologist.

Accepting that very considerable technical problems remain to be resolved, the way is nevertheless open for their formulation and, hence, resolution. A way which seems to us, both on the theoretical level and on the methodological level, as fruitful as it is unexplored.

José Olives

7

The struggle against urban renewal in the 'Cité d'Aliarte' (Paris)*†

The 'Cité d'Aliarte' in Paris in which we have attempted to analyze the process of emergence of urban social movements is a very mixed area, both ecologically and socially. Stone-built buildings are found side by side with crumbling slums, and bourgeois dwellings and parks adjacent to the hostels and cheap hotels in which African immigrants are housed, crowded together in wretched sanitary conditions.

Adjoining the residential areas one finds a few large industrial establishments, but most of all a profusion of small industrial firms and small shops, scattered throughout the area. The abundance of small cafés and shops catering for everyday needs is an index of the large, French and immigrant, working-class population to be found in the neighbourhood, rooted there by advancing years and low incomes, and by the high degree of segregation to which it is subject in a hostile urban environment.

A *lycée* and two hospitals provide important reference points within the area. The role of the Apollo *lycée*, as we shall see below, was distinguished by the active participation of its students in political agitation and in the launching of urban social movements in the area.

The ease with which the Cité d'Aliarte can be reached — it is a rapidly expanding railway terminus for both provincial and suburban lines — constitutes an initial basis for an 'urban reconquest operation'.[1]

The process of urban renewal observed in the Cité during the period covered by the present study, started in 1956 in two different

---

*[Translated with permission of Editions Anthropos, Paris, from J. Olives, La lutte contre la rénovation urbaine dans le quartier de 'La Cité d'Aliarte' (Paris) *Espaces et Sociétés* 6–7 (1972) 9–27.]

†[The study was carried out from the Centre d'Etude des Mouvements Sociaux, École Pratique des Hautes Etudes, Paris. Only the names of the neighbourhood and the streets have been changed.]

[1] [For an analysis of urban renewal in terms of 'urban reconquest', see Groupe de Sociologie Urbaine de Nanterre, Paris 1970: reconquête urbaine et rénovation-déportation, *Sociologie du Travail* 4 (1970) 488–514.]

parts of the area under the charge of the Office Public des H.L.M. (O.P.H.L.M.).[2] It was continued in the area surrounding the station from 1957 onwards, and in three much larger areas from 1962. The four latter operations were executed by a semi-public urban renewal agency. It was as this large-scale operation developed (an offensive by the French monopolistic bourgeoisie seeking to recover the Paris agglomeration for the middle classes) that urban stakes emerged; sufficiently large — viz. the eviction of tenants from the buildings to be renewed — to trigger off urban contestation actions additional to the struggle for more and better housing which had been pursued in fragmented fashion till that time.

Undoubtedly this would not have been possible without the favourable conjuncture of political crisis — May 1968 — which led to the appearance throughout Paris of organizations acting at the neighbourhood level. Since then, the urban has increasingly become a political stake for the bourgeoisie and for popular struggles.

It was the very active political group in the Apollo *lycée*, created in June 1969, which was at the origin of the various committees engaged in the different aspects of the struggle in the Cité d'Aliarte, and which was thus the source of the earliest forms of organization in the struggle against urban renewal.

Our purpose here is not to trace the history of the urban political and protest movement in the Cité d'Aliarte, but to analyze at a semi-theoretical, semi-descriptive level the relation between the various component elements of each type of action capable of giving birth to an urban social movement. Having established the ecological and historical coordinates within which the eighteen actions we recorded developed (and which are summarized in the Appendix) we shall now move directly to a consideration of these actions.

Urban protest movements
Since our aim is to identify the conditions under which urban social movements emerge and not to give a systematic description of the development of particular struggles, we shall try to draw up, in so far as this is possible, a general outline of the main elements of the various actions and of the interrelations between these elements, relating them to the type of effect produced on the urban system

[2] [A public sector agency responsible for the construction programme of H.L.M. (*habitation(s) à loyer modéré*); the latter is subsidized housing and corresponds roughly to council housing in Great Britain, but consists mainly of blocks of flats rather than houses.]

(structures) and within the political field of class struggle (social relations). In order not to overburden the text we shall use the reference number of each action summarized in the Appendix each time we can do without a detailed description of the facts. Neither the material available, nor the theoretical analytical instruments at our disposal, enable us here to establish systematically correlations between variables. For the time being we must restrict ourselves to underlining the relations which appear to us to be relevant, and to putting forward hypotheses.

Every protest movement springs from the perception of a *stake* (expressing a contradiction at the level of structures) by a *social force*. This is only possible — judging by the cases studied in the Cité d'Aliarte — when there is a minimum degree of organization of the *social base*. It is not sufficient for the stake to be large and defined on a social base: this was the case for example in the actions carried out concerning the hotels in rue d'Ilèse, and at 77 rue d'Aulis (Nos 15 and 16) where the eviction of immigrant workers by the renewal agency could not be stopped due to the lack of organization (fragmented response within the base and belated intervention by political groups).

On the other hand, neither does the presence of an organization lacking a social base result in an urban or political effect. This could be observed in the Cité from two quite different types of action:

(1) *Action which is short-lived and carried out by a small group* (Nos 11 and 13): for example, the distribution of free *métro* tickets by members of a group advocating free travel, or protests against fare increases.

(2) *Contestation which is political but predominantly ideological*: i.e. which attempts to link all the contradictions of the system into a global opposition, or else tries to put forward a critical utopia in opposition to the everyday life imposed by bourgeois society. Contrary to the *métro*-work-bed (*métro-boulot-dodo*) culture, an immediate and experimental attempt is made to establish a 'new way of living'. As is shown by the experience at the Maison des Danaens (No. 2), this kind of action only results in a highly debatable sensitization of the youngest age-groups. . . . The Maison des Danaens was founded at 69 rue d'Argolide, following the success of a resistance action against eviction in the same street (No. 1) by students from the Apollo *lycée* and local militants grouped together within a local political organization who took over an unoccupied café situated opposite the immigrant workers' hostel. The aim was to gather together young French and immigrant workers in a place where they would be able to 'come and amuse themselves without having to

buy drinks, talk freely, discuss, struggle together against the dog's life imposed on [them] ; a place of a sort that no longer exists in France'. Festivals were organized, general meetings held, and a legal and medical advice centre established. Literacy courses were started, meetings with doctors organized and a women's liberation group created.

Besides the demand for cultural and leisure facilities there was opposition to the renewal programme of the City of Paris which would benefit a semi-public renewal agency. The City of Paris and the renewal agencies reacted by violent repression, demolishing the old café in a few hours, with police help.

This repression gave rise to a number of reactions, newspaper articles and speeches in the streets of the Cité, but the urban or political effects, as understood here, were nil.

However, among actions which failed due to the lack of a social base one should distinguish between those where the *stake* was *small* (as in the case just described, and in so far as the stake there was defined primarily at the ideological level), and those where the *stake* was *sufficiently large* (as in the case of the protests against fare increases, and the demands for free transport) but which clearly require a higher level of development of the struggle in so far as the stake could only be grasped by an organization based on a wider area (the Paris agglomeration as a whole). If in the former case the stake corresponds to secondary contradictions at the level of the urban system, in the latter, the contradictions turn out to be fundamental, but dislocated in relation to the state of development of the class struggle.

Urban and political effects will occur neither without organization, nor without a social base (apart from effects such as pure and simple suppression and, at the ideological level, the dubious fruits of exemplary action).

Moreover, the presence of an organization is not sufficient by itself for an action to result in tangible effects. In the case of a *purely protest organization* (like for example the locally-based organization carrying out welfare work among immigrants), any *legal action* it undertakes (petitions, requests, etc.) can never lead to effective results, in so far as it fails to mobilize people against possible repression. Thus, when repression does not follow, this type of action may have an urban effect, as was the case at 18 rue de Thespie (No. 8), but when repression does follow the action fails — as was shown very clearly at 212 rue de Graïa (No. 9).

A third variable must thus be introduced: the *type of action*, which

depends to a large extent on the *type of organization*, but whose role
is decisive when the organization is solely of the protest type. The
case of the struggle for better housing conditions in the H.L.M.de
Ténédos (No. 3) shows very clearly how an action carried out by a
protest association can only have an effect, when faced with
repression, if the type of action succeeds in mobilizing the social base.

In fact, in the H.L.M. in question, the residents formed an
association to demand better housing conditions, and, in particular, to
insist on the provision of all the facilities which had been planned but
not provided once the construction of the buildings set aside for them
had been completed, viz. sanitary and fire safety equipment, basic
welfare facilities (crèches, etc.). The action started with legal protest
measures: approaches to local councillors, petitions, the sending of
letters signed by hundreds of neighbours, etc. The residents went out
onto the street, put up a streamer explaining the object of their
demands, and slowed down the traffic by throwing rubbish into the
street. In the face of this mobilization the police dared not intervene.
Next, a deputation of neighbours was received by the O.P.H.L.M.
sub-office and the latter soon undertook to remove the rubbish and to
commence the construction of footpaths for pedestrians. A
representative of the Office made a visit to check the fire safety
equipment. Works started, and until their completion the residents
were exempted from the rent increases which had come into effect
twelve months before.

Given the presence of organization-type of action and social base,
it appears that it is the size of the stake which is decisive — in all the
cases studied — in determining whether urban or political effects are
obtained or not.

It still remains to be seen to what extent the size of the stake is
determined by the real intensity of the contradiction, and to what
extent by the political conjuncture (balance of forces in the class
struggle at a particular time and place). The relative importance of
each of these two determinations cannot be resolved by empirical
observation. In fact urban effects were produced almost exclusively in
actions triggered off by attempts to evict immigrant workers from
their hostels or hotels because of the demands of the renewal
programme. Obviously in such cases the stake is very large, but the
case of the H.L.M. de Ténédos, where an exemplary success resulted,
shows that a much smaller stake can also result in an urban effect.

In the present political conjuncture where no organization is
capable of satisfactorily linking (or even simply grasping the

specificity of) the contradictions of the system at the urban level (a situation reflected in the limited number of organizations involved in the class struggle at the level of collective consumption), stakes became large in so far as they can be perceived with a minimum of organization — and hence integrated with a very low level of class formation (coordination of spontaneity) — and not because of the real intensity of contradictions within the structure (urban system).

This is perhaps the reason for the fact that all the actions which led to any urban and/or political effect in the Cité d'Aliarte were more or less of the same type (with the exception of the case already described of the H.L.M. de Ténédos). They were linked to the fight against evictions triggered off by the renewal programme or centred on the hostels and hotels inhabited by African immigrant workers. The size of the stake and the homogeneity of the social base facilitated mobilization against the opponent (i.e. against the semi-public urban renewal agency, or private developers, supported by local representatives of State power and its repressive apparatus) and the politicization of the struggle (as against the fragmentation characteristic of actions involving French workers or higher strata of the population).

The political effect of each of the actions which took place during the two-year period was cumulative and achieved its greatest victory from the start of this year[1972] when evictions were halted throughout the Cité d'Aliarte. And though they were due to start again on 1 March they did not do so. The capitalization of minor victories in the planning sphere at the political level was possible here probably because of the homogeneous character of the population affected by the stakes (African immigrants), which on the one hand enabled a number of different urban demands to be linked, and on the other enabled these demands to be linked to the wider class struggle waged by immigrant workers against their exploitation by the monopolist subject. Revolutionary political action in the Cité d'Aliarte thus took place on two fronts: a struggle against the superexploitation of immigrants in the work-place and a struggle against the ecological, social, and cultural segregation to which immigrants are subject at the level of reproduction of labour power.

It is probably these very particular urban circumstances that account for the sole example of successful urban protest on a wide scale in the Paris agglomeration. This case was precisely one where a struggle originating at the level of collective consumption extended outside this sphere (which is indispensable to avoid the trap of

reformism or the dissolution of a movement through its paternalist
integration into the system) to weld itself to class political struggle on
other fronts.

We shall now examine in detail the particular mechanisms of some
of the individual actions which led to this result in order to gain a
better understanding of them. Among the seven actions which had an
urban effect (and in which organization, mobilization, a social base
and a 'large' stake were thus present), only two had to face severe
police repression. The dynamic of their development shows in both
cases that:

(1) as in all other actions resulting in an effect, *legal measures were
always accompanied by a high degree of mobilization of the social
force;*
(2) *these were the only cases where a political effect resulted*
(sensitization of other strata of the population of the Cité,
strengthening of the organization, establishment of political groups
acting in the area);
(3) *the political effect was a consequence of the partial victories at
the level of urban effects, and had a retroactive influence on the
development of the action.*

In brief, it can be seen that *repression could only be met
effectively in these two cases — where not only the social base but a
large proportion of local residents were mobilized, or at least
sensitized to the stake.*

The two actions in which evictions were resisted took place almost
simultaneously, and as can be seen in the Appendix (Nos 1 and 4); in
both cases, the stake, base, opponent and demands were very similar.
Because of their exemplary character, however, we shall give a
detailed analysis of both.

At 38 rue de Pylor (No. 4), the owner of the property (a hotel),
under the pressure of a private property development company, tried
to evict the forty-nine (mainly immigrant) workers living there. The
latter riposted by a rent strike which lasted one year and which was
made possible by the support of the workers in the Cité d'Aliarte who
secured the retreat of both police and speculators in face of the
strikers. Continuing mobilization enabled a promise to be extracted
from the developer that the forty-nine tenants would be rehoused, but
this proved to be a manoeuvre to stop the strike since rehousing was
only provided for three days.

The residents of the building, supported by militants belonging to the protest and political organizations participating in the action, answered by occupying the building until acceptable alternative housing was provided (i.e. close to the work-place, and at a similar rent). Threats of eviction were renewed, this time accompanied by the destruction of six rooms and a number of walls. Staircases were smashed, water and electricity supplies cut off and sanitary installations put out of action. The level of mobilization of the social force present enabled a further increase in organized resistance to the repression to take place. Petitions were sent through the intermediary of a protest and welfare association concerned with immigrants, with the support of a lawyer. The deliberate damage to the building was stopped and this victory allowed the support of the residents of the neighbourhood to be rallied to the struggle by the residents of the hotel, which led to a further increase in the combativeness of the squatters (when the developer visited the building he was almost lynched). A bailiff was called to verify the irregularity of the deliberate damage done and as a result ordered the repair of the lavatories and windows, and the making good of the damage to the structure. In addition evictions were placed back within 'the hands of the law'.

This legal victory led to a strengthening of the organization and an increased level of mobilization. Workers and militants participated as volunteers in the repair of the building. Information meetings were held. Despite a police prohibition, two films were shown ('les Zupiens' and 'Etranges Etrangers') on action by tenants' organizations against unauthorized eviction. The continued residence of the tenants in the hostel representing a manifest success in achieving the original demand, a political effect very clearly followed from this: the constitution of a local action group comprising militants belonging to various revolutionary organizations from outside the neighbourhood and who had taken part in the action. This local political group was subsequently responsible for numerous initiatives in the popular struggle in the Cité d'Aliarte.

At 69 rue d'Argolide (No. 1), in similar circumstances, the semi-public urban renewal agency demanded that the owner of the building — which it had just purchased — evacuate it; failing which he would be charged Fr.2000 per day. The building was deliberately damaged in the same way as in the previous case, but this time 17 workers were evicted on the pretext that their papers were not in order. The social force present (see Appendix) reacted by the unauthorized 'rehousing' of fourteen Algerian workers [to take their place] and simultaneously informed local residents by means of leaflets and posters, sensitizing them to the problem.

Police repression (identity checks among the residents, tearing down of posters from doors) took place one night a week. From this point on, dozens of people decided to guard the premises every night until 10 p.m., which led to the ending of police intervention.

A written question was sent to the Prefect of Paris and a deputation led to the Health Department of the Prefecture. Two days later it was decided to change to direct action: the door of the electricity meter was broken open and the electricity supply to the hostel reconnected. Water was restored by tapping a pipe in the house next door. Subsequently the electricity supply was re-established by the renewal agency and letters again delivered. The unauthorized restoration of sanitary conditions met with sabotage and slander from a 'working-class' organization which considered that it would lead to the blocking of the legal action undertaken.

At the end of the meetings of the various political, trade union, immigrant worker and residents' groups in the Cité d'Aliarte, speeches were made, vast quantities of leaflets distributed, and door-to-door visits made in order to keep the population informed. Also a new petition was sent to the Town Hall, this time accompanied by a large deputation. An information meeting on the evictions, announced for the same day, is prohibited by police headquarters which sends fifty armed policemen with dogs. As was shown in the previous case, when mobilization is high, repression brings about a positive reaction. This time the street is occupied and the people decide to go *en masse* to see the local councillor who presides over the semi-public agency responsible for renewal operations in the Cité d'Aliarte.

At the urban level, the effect of this mobilization is made manifest by the immediate repair of all the installations in the hostel at the expense of the semi-public renewal agency and in the *de facto* continued residence of the tenants; and, at the political level, by the withdrawal of the police and the consolidation of the position of the local political group in the Cité d'Aliarte created as an effect of the victory at 38 rue de Pylor described above. This two-fold effect has a retroactive effect on the organization and mobilization of the social base (those responsible for the deliberate damage join the immigrants in repairing the smashed floorboards and painting the walls).

To sum up this analysis of the two actions in the Cité d'Aliarte which had effects, it is apparent that the demands which were met, in this conjuncture, were always of two types:

(1) demands seeking to preserve the status quo (restoration of changed housing and sanitary conditions, continued residence of tenants in the hostel, etc.)

(2) demands seeking to obtain 'adequate rehousing'. In this case, given the ambiguous nature of the demand, it is difficult to know precisely to what extent it has been met.

None of the other specific demands (such as rent reductions, lower fares, etc.), nor the global demands which accompanied some of the actions was satisfied. Their political and ideological relevance apart, it is obvious that the latter were out of step with the level of development of the struggles in progress (balance of forces) and the state of development of working-class mass organizations (in this case, tenants' committees, for example). Thus neither the most radical challenges to the system (struggle against imperialism, critique of everyday life) nor those reforms capable of being completely integrated (alternatives to the renewal programme for the City of Paris) seem to have had effects on urban contestation in the strict sense. Their role is purely ideological and part of an electoralist strategy which sees the urban as a political stake in the battle for municipal representation.

By focussing our attention on the global demands expressed concerning the renewal programme it is possible to distinguish two types of plan presented as alternatives to bourgeois urban renewal. The first, presented by a traditional working-class organization, is entitled 'Renewal of our City' and comprises the following points:

Constuction of H.L.M. and housing within the means of old people.
Preservation of existing commercial and industrial enterprises.
Improvement and renewal of housing conditions.
Better shopping and transport facilities (public transport, car parks).
Rehousing in the same neighbourhood, and a removal and reinstallment allowance for tenants, co-owners, shopkeepers, retailers, craftsmen and artists forced to leave their premises.
New schools; modernization of existing schools.
Provision for social and welfare facilities (crèches, municipal nurseries, clubs, restaurants for old people, cultural centres, youth clubs, sports facilities, parks).

The second type of alternative programme is that put forward in turns by the various national organizations with local branches, and by the local political organization. It is much more schematic and most of the points included are spelt out better in the previous type of programme. The only difference between the two lies in the fact that this second type completely ignores immigrant workers (since they do not even fall within the category of 'tenants') and is clearly designed to appeal to the *petite bourgeoisie* and French workers whereas the first type demands in addition to 'social renewal':

(1) the equality of all workers in this field,
(2) the temporary occupation of empty dwellings.

Rather than explaining the mechanism of the actions, these global demands enable us to specify the mode of intervention of the two types of political organization working at the urban level in the Cité. These consist, on the one hand, of *legal-reformist action* (primarily as part of an electoralist strategy) *with its demobilizing and fragmenting effect* (separation of immigrant workers and Frenchmen within the base) on the part of an organization serving bourgeois policies to the working class; and, on the other, of *political and ideological protest action seeking to mobilize the social base* (immigrants) and to rally other social strata to their struggle.

If we now return to the distinction made earlier between the two types of urban effect, namely, stopping evictions and securing adequate rehousing, it is apparent that the former is always brought about in cases where there has been a high level of mobilization and where protest action has been accompanied by overtly political action. As regards the second type of effect, even if the fact of securing rehousing might lead one to believe that this type of action was more successful, we are inclined to believe the contrary to be true in that either no mobilization of the social force took place (No. 8) or else it was too weak (No. 7) to impose as a pre-condition of 'adequate' rehousing that tenants should be able to remain in the hostel. We are thus led to think that only continued residence after attempts at eviction is a solidly-based urban effect, in so far as it is the very evidence of a victory imposed by force and hence capable of being capitalized on by political struggle. There is no doubt that it is to action accompanied by this type of effect that the stopping of eviction throughout the Cité d'Aliarte is due.

Turning now to the schema put forward by Castells[3] for the

---

[3] M. Castells, Planification urbaine et mouvements sociaux: le cas de la rénovation urbaine à Paris, C.N.R.S. Colloquium, Toulouse, 1–4 June 1971, 35. [See M. Castells, *La Question Urbaine* (Maspero, Paris, 1972) 423 (lower diagram).]

analysis of the dynamics of protest movements against urban renewal
(Figure 1), we see that it remains valid (even for action other than
resistance to eviction) in general outline for the cases analyzed, if we
make one slight modification.

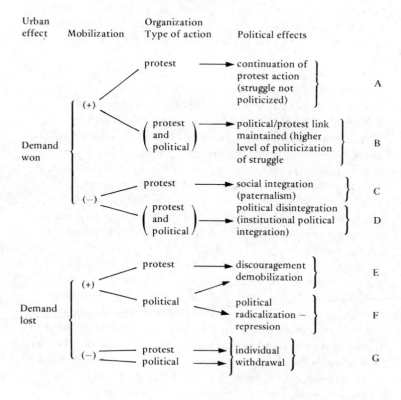

Figure 1

Result B (in Figure 1) is the one which occurs most frequently
among successful actions and its prevalence throughout the Cité
d'Aliarte explains the current success of the movement against
evictions. Result A is perfectly illustrated by the first case described in
detail, the H.L.M. de Ténédos (No. 3). Results C and D are
exemplified respectively by the actions which led only to the
'adequate' rehousing of tenants in the hostels at 18 rue de Thespie
(No. 8) and 87 rue d'Eléone (No. 7).

In analyzing unsuccessful actions we are tempted to introduce a
modification into the original schema. Mobilization in support of
political action, as in the case of 10 rue d'Aponte (No. 10), may bring

about the demobilization and division of social forces (result E) as may purely protest action (exemplified in the struggles in the Cité d'Aliarte by the action at 212 rue de Graïa (No. 9)). This is not to deny that mobilization in support of political action may not also lead to result F, as the movement concerning the Maison des Danaens described in detail above (No. 2) would seem to prove. As for result G, examples may be found in actions No. 11, 12, 13 and 14 shown in the Appendix.

After examining the different types of urban contestation produced in the Cité d'Aliarte, while we cannot claim to be putting forward a solidly-based explanation for the formation of urban social movements or for their momentary success in the area vis-à-vis the urban renewal programme, we would like to emphasize the three facts which, in our view, probably account for the state of progress of contestation in the Cité d'Aliarte, compared with that in most other parts of Paris. Namely, the existence of a *lower-class social base*, which makes possible the *establishment of revolutionary political organizations* (facilitating mobilization and avoiding the separation of the struggles encouraged by the various protest organizations) with *strong local support.*

Obviously a large question-mark hangs over the future of urban popular struggles in the Cité d'Aliarte.

In the case of urban renewal the stake is very large; in all the 'successful' cases the demands made throw the programme into question and cannot thus be satisfied without a substantial change in the urban system (or in the urban policy of the bourgeoisie). For the time being the balance of forces merely enables the long-term plans of the bourgeoisie to be delayed (halt to the 'reconquest of the urban centre' offensive). Even in the most 'successful' actions, the stopping of evictions throughout the Cité and the halting of the renewal programme there, the result of the political confrontation diverged from the demands made. But this dislocation between stakes which challenge the basic interests of the urban system and the demands of the popular struggle is not, at the present time, having a demobilizing effect (though one cannot foresee today the outcome of this urban conjuncture) in so far as it is perceived not as a failure (impotence) nor even as an open bracket (temporary halt) waiting to be closed, but as a stop imposed by force on the bourgeoisie by the popular movement. This stop clearly marks a threshold which will require the development of the urban struggle to a higher political level before it can be crossed. This will require, among other things:

(1) the progressive development of base organizations linking individualized urban demands, not only at the level of a particular district but at the level of the Paris region as a whole;

(2) the development of other organizations linking these demands to the new urban practices currently emerging (especially in the transport field).

(3) the possibility of linking all these urban demands, by means of a political organization following a correct line, to political practices outside the urban field.

Hic rhodus, hic salta!

Location	Stake	Social base	Organizational characteristics	Social force	Opponent
1. Rue d'Argolide	Developer's profits and renewal programme Housing of residents	Algerian workers	Welfare-protest organization concerned with immigrants (local branch)	Workers + students + militants from area and from outside area	Owner Semi-public renewal agency Prefecture Town Hall
			Political and trade-union organizations: economic and political-electoralist demands (local branches)		⟶
			Political organizations from outside area, with local support: political and ideological contestation		⟶
			Local political organizations: political-ideological contestation		⟶

Specific demands	Global demands	Action	Repression	Urban effect	Political effect
	Renewal programme (highly schematic): national political organization with strong local support		Evictions Damage to building by owner Eviction of 17 workers		
Compliance with basic sanitary conditions prior to evacuation and demolition of building, and gradual rehousing	Renewal programme: organization serving 'bourgeois policies to working class'	Unauthorized rehousing of 14 workers Tracts Posters			Sensitization of local population
		Setting up of guard for hostel	Riot police with dogs Identity checks Tearing down of posters		Ending of police intervention
Rehousing in new buildings in same area at reasonable rents. In the meantime, continued residence in present accommodation		Written questions to Prefect of Paris Deputation to Health Dept of Prefecture Unauthorized restoration of electricity and water supplies Meetings Leaflets		Restoration of electricity supply Letters delivered again	Sabotage and slander by political organization serving 'bourgeois policies to working class'
Rehousing in same area and restoration of sanitary conditions		Speeches Door-to-door visits Petitions Mass deputation to Town Hall Information meeting on evictions Squatting	Prohibition by Town Hall. Police sent		
		Occupation, mass march to see local councillor presiding over renewal agency Volunteer repairs to building by militants		Repair of all installations at expense of semi-public renewal agency *Tenants continue to live in same accommodation*	Ending of police intervention Setting up of local political organization on basis of spontaneous struggle triggered off by action no. 2

Location	Stake	Social base	Organizational characteristics	Social force	Opponent
2. Rue d'Argolide	Capitalist profit Extended reproduction of labour power	–	Local political organization: political-ideological contestation	Students from local *lycée* Local militants Young French and immigrant workers	Semi-public urban renewal agency
3. H.L.M. de Ténédos	Construction of H.L.M. by City of Paris Housing conditions and provision of facilities	Residents of H.L.M.	Local protest organization of residents of H.L.M. de Ténédos	Multiclass, excepting management and immigrant workers	Town Hall and local council O.P.H.L.M. Prefect of Paris

Specific demand	Global demand	Action	Repression	Urban effects	Political effects
Halt to demolition in area Cultural and leisure facilities Medical advice Resistance to renewal	Internal imperialism & colonialism Critique of bourgeoisie & 'metro-work-bed' everyday life General meetings Festivals Legal and medical advice services Literacy Medical information meetings Women's liberation group	Take-over of unoccupied café and creation of 'Maison des Danaens'	Deliberate damage to Maison des Danaens to make it uninhabitable Police support (3 buses of security police, 1 bus of ordinary policemen, plain-clothes men, etc.) Arrests Wall slogans painted over One worker killed during demolition work	–	–
Better housing and sanitary conditions Fire safety equipment Welfare facilities (in buildings provided) esp. provision of crèche	–	Approaches to local councillors Petitions Letters with hundreds of signatures Street demonstration Display of banner Slowing down of traffic, emptying rubbish on street	Appearance and disappearance of police	Deputation received by O.P.H.L.M. sub-office Rubbish cleared away Footpaths ordered and built after visit to site by O.P.H.L.M. official Starting of works and exemption of tenants from rent increases until works completed	–

Location	Stake	Social base	Organizational characteristics	Social force	Opponent
4. Rue de Pylor	Same as in No. 1	Mainly immigrant workers (40 tenants)	National political organization with local support Welfare-protest organization concerned with immigrants (local branch)	Local workers and militants	Owner Private developer
5. Rue d'Aulis	Same as in No. 1	Senegalese and Malian workers	Tenants' committees Political organization from outside area, with local support	Immigrant workers + school students + militants	Private developers

Specific demand	Global demand	Action	Repression	Urban effects	Political effects
Continued residence in hotel, opposition to illegal eviction	Renewal programme of national political organisation with strong local support	Rent strike lasting one year	Attempted eviction		Support by local workers
		Continued residence in hotel until adequate rehousing provided	Attempted eviction / Threat of eviction	Promise of rehousing	Retreat of police and speculators
Rehousing in new dwellings in same area at reasonable rents		Workers organize to resist damage	Deliberate damage to premises		
Meanwhile: rehousing in unoccupied buildings, or else improvement of existing accommodation		Petition to authorities with support of lawyers		Damage stopped	Sensitization of local population
		Developer is almost lynched, after visiting premises		Bailiff called to visit premises, observes irregular damage	
		Workers and militants undertake repair of damage voluntarily		Order to rebuild and repair damage	
		Information meeting		Evictions remain in 'hands of law'	Political organization acting in area merges with a locally-based group (ideological and political contestation
		Showing of films	Prohibited by Prefecture	*Tenants continue to live in same accommodation*	
Resistance to eviction until rehousing secured	Creation of a tenants' committee	Legal action	Attempted eviction		—
Rehousing in the near future		Mobilization of social base for resistance		*Tenants continue to live in same accommodation*	

Location	Stake	Social base	Organizational characteristics	Social force	Opponent
6. Rue d'Hyria	Same as in No. 1	Immigrant and French workers (71 and 2, respectively)	National political organization combining economic and political demands Local political organization combining political and ideological contestation	Workers + militants from outside area + school students	Developer
7. Rue d'Eléone	Same as in No. 1	Immigrant workers	Tenants' committee Welfare-protest organization concerned with immigrants Local political organization: ideological and political demands	Same as in No. 6	Owners Semi-public renewal agency
8. Rue de Thespie	Same as in No. 1	Algerian immigrant workers	Welfare-protest organization concerned with immigrants	Workers and militants without local connexions	Semi-public renewal agency
9. Rue de Graïa	Same as in No. 1	Immigrant workers	Same as in No. 8	Same as in No. 8	Owner Private property development company Prefect of Paris Local police

Specific demand	Global demand	Action	Repression	Urban effects	Political effects
Rehousing in adequate conditions (sanitation, location, rent)	Same as in No. 4	General meeting of local residents Tracts Meetings	–	*Continued residence in accommodation*	Small shop-keepers supported by organization serving bourgeois policies to working class, attempt to divert the action carried out by other organizations
Restoration of housing conditions Rehousing in same area, if possible	–	Petitions to police headquarters and to local councillor Meetings	Threat of eviction Deliberate damage to premises	*'Adequate' rehousing*	–
Rehousing in same area, if possible, and at same rent	–	Petitions	Threat of eviction	*'Adequate' rehousing*	–
Same as in No. 8	–	Petitions to Prefect of Paris and local police Authorized petition presented by lawyer	Deliberate damage to premises Prohibition by authorities Attempt at legal eviction leading to demand for rehousing Threat of eviction by Technical Assistance Dept → Intervention of Technical Assistance Dept.	Evictions halted *Eviction and deportation*	–

Location	Stake	Social base	Organizational characteristics	Social force	Opponent
10. Rue d'Oponte	Owner's profit Workers' housing	Algerian workers	Political organization involved in contestation of a mainly ideological type	Immigrants + militants from outside area + school students	Owner Manager
11. Bessa *métro* station	Profits of transport undertaking Reproduction of labour power (real income)	–	Political-ideological protest organization from outside area	Militants from outside area	Transport undertaking (R.A.T.P.) City of Paris
12. Cité d'Aliarte	Urban land speculation Extended reproduction of labour power	–	Tenants' protest organization	Multiclass	Town Hall
13. Cité d'Aliarte	Same as in No. 11	–	Trade-union organization	Militants from outside area	Transport undertaking (*R.A.T.P.*)
14. 14 Boulevard d'Eubée	Hostel accommodation for immigrant workers Housing conditions	Immigrant workers	Welfare-protest organization Political-ideological organization	Catholic instructors from local literacy centre Local militants Immigrant workers	Owners of hostel Prefecture of Seine area
15. Rue d'Ilèse	Same as in No. 1	French and immigrant workers	National political organization with local support	Workers and militants from outside area	Semi-public renewal agency
16. 77 Rue d'Aulis	Same as in No. 1	Algerian and Tunisian workers	Welfare-protest organization Local political ideological organization	Immigrant workers + local militants	Owner Private property development company Prefecture

Specific demand	Global demand	Action	Repression	Urban effects	Political effects
Rent reductions An end to corrupt administration of hostel manager	–	Rent strike ⟶ Posters displayed in street General meeting of tenants Proceedings against manager	Arrival of police Electricity supply cut Refuse collection stopped New manager stops strike, supported by police *Rent increases*	Manager dismissed Basic sanitary conditions restored	–
Free travel	Free travel	*Métro* tickets given away free Red flag Singing of 'Internationale'	–	–	–
School facilities	School facilities	Speeches Meetings Petition Councillor (deposit of file on need for school facilities in Cité d'Aliarte)	–	–	
Against increased fares	–	Distribution of leaflets	Arrests	–	–
Sanitary conditions Overcrowding (new dwellings) End to police control	–	Literacy Legal protests concerning housing Violent small group action	Police repression	–	–
Rehousing	–	Posters	*Evictions carried out*	–	–
Rehousing	–	Action delayed	*Evictions carried out*	–	–

C. G. Pickvance

8

On the study of urban social movements[†]

The aim of this article is to initiate a discussion of the recent series of studies of 'urban social movements'. These studies share a common conceptual framework which is derived from a 'structuralist'[1] reading of Marx and is set out in a preliminary form by Castells in *La Question Urbaine*.[2] This framework marks a break with the Anglo-Saxon tradition of 'participation' studies, which are characterized by a focus on the individual and his membership of, or participation in, a smaller or greater variety of 'voluntary associations' and other groupings.[3] Within this tradition large-scale survey studies are carried out to establish the degree of 'participation', as opposed to the extent of 'anomie', of the population. The social implications of organizational membership are *inferred*, not studied explicitly. Thus membership may be seen as entailing participation in decision-making, in so far as the organization has an informal or formal position in the local social structure, or, on the other hand as facilitating the acquisition of skills and democratic values which encourage political activity in other contexts. What has been lacking within the

[†]This is a slightly modified version of a paper read at an international urban sociology symposium at the Universidad Autonoma de Barcelona in January 1974.

[1] The term 'structuralist' requires clarification since it is the subject of considerable debate (especially among those wishing to disown its applicability to their own work). It is used here to refer to the broad approach according to which, ' "Structure" refers not to observed social relations but to a more abstract level of reality, and is the syntax of transformations which is present only in its manifestations but can never be observed as such in itself' (M. Glucksmann, *Structuralist Analysis in Contemporary Social Thought, a Comparison of the Theories of C. Lévi-Strauss and L. Althusser* (Routledge and Kegan Paul, London, 1974) 45). For an argument that the reading of Marx referred to here can be described as 'structuralist', see Glucksmann, *op. cit.*, 163, 167–73. For a contrary view, see 169–73 in the excellent (though largely uncritical) exposition of the Althusserian reading of Marx by S. Karsz, *Théorie et Politique: Louis Althusser* (Fayard, Paris, 1974).

[2] M. Castells, *La Question Urbaine* (Maspero, Paris, 1972).

[3] For a discussion of this tradition, see C. G. Pickvance, Voluntary associations, in E. Gittus (ed.), *Key Variables in Social Research*, II, *Politics, Voluntary Associations and Demographic Variables* (Heinemann, London, 1975).

'participation' tradition is any intensive study of voluntary
associations and other groupings to establish empirically (rather than
by inference) what functions membership has.

Conversely, studies within the 'urban social movements' approach,
first, de-emphasize the *form* of the organization in which 'participation'
takes place[4] and view organization primarily as a means by which
contradictions are linked, and, secondly, stress the *effects* or otherwise
of the movement. These points will be discussed briefly, in turn.

Organizations, according to Castells,[5] are precisely the wrong
starting-point for studies of urban social movements. This does not
mean that concrete organizations, or as Ash[6] would call them,
'movement organizations', can be ignored. On the contrary, as the
studies to be discussed will indicate, concrete movement organizations
are the locus of *observation*. The point is that they are not the frame
of *analysis*. The focus is rather on the 'problems', 'issues' or 'stakes'
the organization pursues and their structural determination. It is the
structural contradictions which are the crucial level of analysis, and
organizations are seen as means for their expression and articulation.
Thus the point is that organizations cannot be analyzed without
reference to these functions, not that organizations are unimportant.
In this respect the 'urban social movements' approach is opposed to
the 'participation' approach, for which the analysis of organizations and
their resources is an important focus of analysis, to which we will
return in section (4).

The emphasis on 'effects' is part of the definition of urban social
movements, which must now be briefly examined since it is the source
of some ambiguity. An *urban social movement* is defined as:

> a system of practices resulting from the articulation of a
> conjuncture of the system of urban agents with other social
> practices, such that its development tends objectively towards the
> structural transformation of the urban system, or towards a
> substantial change in the balance of forces in the class struggle, that
> is to say, in the power of the State.[7]

---

[4] This is evident from a perusal of any of the studies to be discussed. 'The
genesis of organization is not the concern of an analysis of social movements,
for only its effects are of importance' (Castells, *op. cit.*, 339. N.B. All
translations are my own, and therefore approximate.) In section (4) I shall argue
that the resources available to an organization affect both its survival and
success.
[5] Castells, *op. cit.*, 341.
[6] R. Ash, *Social Movements in America* (Markham, Chicago, 1972) 2.
[7] Castells, *op. cit.*, 329.

The important point about this definition is that it defines urban social movements by a specific type of *effect*. It follows that when these effects are not obtained (or, to be precise, when the 'objective development' of the organization would not lead to such effects), then the description 'urban social movement' is not applicable. For this reason Castells identifies two lower levels of effect, namely, *'reform'*, that is, change in an element of the urban system without any change in its relations with other elements; and *'control'*, that is, the reproduction of the urban system. When these levels of effect result, the corresponding types of organization are described as *'protest'* and *'participation'* respectively. Thus, according to the effects achieved, an organization can be placed on the scale: 'participation' — 'protest' — 'urban social movement'. Castells argues that an organization where the contradictions involved are purely 'urban' (i.e., concerned with the spatial unit of the process of reproduction of labour power[8] — e.g. issues such as housing, education and collective facilities) and not linked to the 'political' or 'economic' aspects of class struggle, can at most be an 'instrument of *reform*'.[9] It is only when an urban social movement unites economic or political contradictions with urban contradictions, that the term in its strict sense can be said to apply.

In the studies to be discussed, urban social movements are generally not linked to trade unions or political parties. However, we shall follow the practice they adopt and use the term urban social movement irrespective of the level of effects.

There is also an ambiguity in the use of the term 'effect'. We shall follow Olives[10] and refer to urban effects as those urban objectives which have been successfully achieved, rather than Lentin[11] who includes both failures and successes. (A similar difference can be seen in the treatment of 'political effects'.)

We can now proceed to analyze a number of features of recent 'structuralist' studies of urban social movements in France. Our discussion will be in four parts:

---

[8] *Ibid.*, 295–304.
[9] *Ibid.*, 340.
[10] J. Olives, La lutte contre la rénovation urbaine dans le quartier de la 'Cité d'Aliarte' (Paris), *Espaces et Sociétés*, 6–7 (1972) 9–27, (chapter 7 in this book).
[11] F. Lentin, Le quartier de La Mouffe en rébellion (une lutte urbaine tenace dans la ville de Paris), *Espaces et Sociétés* 9 (1973) 99–113.

(1) the identification of urban effects;
(2) local authorities and urban effects;
(3) institutional action and urban effects;
(4) organizational resources and urban effects.

My aim is not to question the usefulness of the structuralist Marxist
approach, nor to attempt a full-scale critique of the studies so far
carried out, but simply to indicate several fields which deserve further
cultivation.

1 The identification of urban effects

To talk about the effects of a movement organization (or 'system of
practices') is to imply that an antecedent event causes a subsequent
event, for example, that a petition against eviction causes a decision to
rehouse the tenants concerned, by an authority.

In order to make a causal inference of this sort it is necessary but
not sufficient that the two events occur in a given temporal order. To
establish the existence of a causal relation we need additional
evidence. Strictly speaking, if we follow Blalock's analysis of causality,
it is never possible to observe causality, since it is a notion belonging
to a theoretical rather than an observational language.[12] In other
words, we can never have entirely satisfactory evidence of causality,
But *causal inference* requires two types of evidence: evidence about
temporal order, and evidence about the perceptions of the relevant
actors. (These correspond to Weber's requirements of causal
adequacy, and adequacy at the level of meaning for sociological
understanding.)[13]

The argument I wish to advance is that the structuralist studies of
urban social movements frequently fail to offer both types of
evidence. In particular *they emphasize the actions of the movement
organization at the expense of the actions of the 'authority'*. There
would appear to be two reasons for this bias. The first is practical; the
second is theoretical.

The practical reason derives from the differing accessibility of
movement organizations and 'authorities' to the research-worker.
Movement organizations are more easily penetrated by the research-

[12] H. M. Blalock, *Causal Inferences in Non-Experimental Research* (University
of North Carolina Press, Chapel Hill, 1964), chapters 1 and 2.
[13] M. Weber, *The Theory of Social and Economic Organization* (1922) (Free
Press, New York, 1947) 98–100.

worker and it is natural that the information gathered on them will be correspondingly richer.[14] This greater accessibility facilitates the understanding of the subjective meaning of action to the actors, and enables it to be correctly characterized as a particular type of 'action' rather than as 'behaviour', to follow Weber's distinction.[15] Participant observation in movement organizations also enables action to be observed as it takes place and thereby avoids reliance on *accounts* by participants given after the event in response to interviewing.

The accessibility of movement organizations carries with it a risk for the research-worker. Namely, that he comes to identify with the organization and its aims, and thus loses his ability to present a more complete analysis. In particular, I suggest, *there is a danger that the research-worker tends to attribute too much causal influence to the actions of the movement organization and insufficient influence to the actions of the authority. His inferences about cause and effect thus become 'movement-centred' because of his involvement in the movement organization.*

For example, Lentin describes the attempts by local residents to prevent the construction of a new building in an old quarter of Paris, and the 'institutional approaches' they made (e.g. a written question to the Prefect of Paris, sent via municipal councillors, and an interview with the M.P./Mayor). She then continues:

> The retort was not long in coming: a new building permit was issued, this time accompanied by an agreement from the Ministry of Cultural Affairs.[16]

The fact that the word 'retort' is used indicates the way in which (negative) causal influence is attributed to the movement organization. The fact that the permit was issued after the 'institutional approaches' may, rather, have been a coincidence. For example, the pressure by the developers, to which Lentin alludes, may have been continuing for some time.

This leads us to a second and theoretical reason which could account for the emphasis placed on the actions of the movement organization at the expense of the actions of the authority. Namely, the theoretical assumptions made about 'authorities' within the structuralist Marxist approach. As will be indicated in more detail in

[14] It has been pointed out to me that this is not necessarily true: movement organizations may be difficult to penetrate.
[15] Weber, *op. cit.*, 88–90.
[16] Lentin, *op. cit.*, 97.

the next section, it is taken as axiomatic within this approach that authorities will not grant changes which threaten the stability of the mode of production. But, as we saw earlier, purely urban social movements are not considered to be capable of provoking changes of this scale and the empirical studies bear this out. It appears to me that a different theoretical assumption is also being made, namely, that 'authorities' will not grant concessions *of any scale* without the intervention of social movements. This assumption, if indeed it is being made, is highly debatable, and, in any case, does not follow from the axiom just mentioned. Thus, I suggest, *acceptance of the assumption that 'authorities' will grant no concessions at all unless forced to by social movements is a second possible explanation of the movement-centred influences about cause and effect.*[17]

In order to identify the causes of urban effects more accurately it would seem necessary:

> to be aware of the risks of over-involvement in movement organizations, and
> to examine the assumptions being made about the role of authorities as causes of change. This requires empirical study of the authorities. It is to this subject that we now turn.

2 Local authorities and urban effects
The relative roles of the State and urban social movements in producing urban effects are spelled out by Castells as follows:

> If it is true that the State expresses, *in the last instance and through the necessary mediations*, the overall interests of the dominant classes, then urban planning cannot be an instrument of social change, but only one of domination, integration and *regulation of contradictions.*[18]
> A process of social change starting from this new field of urban contradictions occurs when, on the basis of these themes, popular mobilization takes place, social needs are given political expression and alternative forms of organization of collective consumption, in contradiction with the dominant social logic, are set up. *Thus it is urban social movements and not planning institutions which are the true sources of change and innovation in the city.*[19]

[17] Castells has suggested to me that it is this rather than the first explanation ('over-involvement') which is relevant.
[18] M. Castells, *Luttes Urbaines* (Maspero, Paris, 1973) 18.
[19] *Ibid.*, 19.

These two quotations identify urban planning on the one hand, and urban social movements on the other, with the functions of control and innovation respectively. They derive from a specifically Marxist view of the State, and it is this view which requires examination. The two quotations contain a slight ambiguity, namely, as to whether the 'social change' which authorities seek to control refers only to major changes, or whether it also refers to minor changes. We shall assume that the latter interpretation is correct, and therefore that even small changes can only be brought about by social movements. This certainly seems to be the assumption of the empirical studies of urban social movements.

In this section our aim is to argue that governmental institutions cannot be dismissed as sources of minor changes, and to this extent must be treated as sources of urban effects in the same way as social movements. In other words, that the role of authorities in initiating change is an empirical question, requiring analysis of policy-formation within governmental institutions.

In the previous section we argued that the inaccessibility of authorities to the research-worker was one practical reason for their neglect as sources of urban effect. It is only by studying processes of policy-formation within authorities (i.e. establishing their degree of autonomy) that one can correctly estimate the relative importance of social movements, on the one hand, and factors internal to the State, on the other.

One study which does attempt to consider policy-making is that by Dearlove,[20] which concerns the London Borough of Kensington and Chelsea. He shows that pressure groups are evaluated by the local authority in terms of three factors: their image ('helpful' or 'unhelpful'), the demands they advance (conforming or conflicting with existing policy and resource allocation) and their style of action (communication via local councillors, petitions, use of local press, demonstrations, etc.).[21] He suggests that the most successful pressure groups are those which are perceived as 'helpful', those whose demands conform to council policy, and those which adopt 'acceptable' modes of action. Unfortunately his conclusions are based on interviews with councillors on policy-making in general rather than

[20] J. Dearlove, *The Politics of Policy in Local Government* (Cambridge University Press, London, 1973).
[21] *Ibid.*, chapter 8. The criterion of extent of support was not among those explicitly mentioned.

on a detailed analysis of the formation of specific policies which
would enable his arguments about the relative success of different
pressure groups to be tested. Thus he does not succeed in
demonstrating the authority's autonomy in dealing with pressure
groups. However, the councillors' perceptions he reports are
consistent with the existence of such autonomy.

A second study concerning an urban social movement whose
success is explicitly related by the author to pressures *internal* to the
local authority is that by Ferris,[22] carried out in the London
Borough of Islington. The study shows, *inter alia*, how the Barnsbury
Association, an organization of newly-arrived middle-class
owner-occupiers concerned over the threat to the amenity value of the
area posed by council redevelopment plans, proposes and is successful
in getting approved a 'traffic management scheme' by which traffic is
routed around the area. (The majority of the population,
long-established tenants, opposed the traffic scheme which they saw
as irrelevant to their needs, and through another organization, the
Barnsbury Action Group, sought to improve their own housing
conditions, if necessary through council redevelopment.) The traffic
scheme was not accepted without considerable effort by the
Association. This included getting Association members elected as
local councillors and putting pressure on the local authority in this
way. However, the important point for present purposes is that the
Barnsbury Association's traffic proposals fitted in with *central
government policy* which was 'to change local authority attitudes
towards large redevelopment projects', since the latter were very
costly in terms of public funds, and to encourage 'ways of upgrading
existing environments . . . [by applying] Buchanan's ideas on traffic,
and improving older housing were possible'.[23] It seems unlikely that
the Association would have been successful without the favourable
'policy environment' of central government. Thus the 'urban effect'
obtained was the result of the movement organization *and factors
internal to the authority.*[24]

A third study in which internal as well as external pressures are

[22] J. Ferris, *Participation in Urban Planning: The Barnsbury Case; a Study of
Environmental Improvement in London*, Occasional Papers in Social
Administration 48, (Bell, London, 1972).
[23] *Ibid.*, 66.
[24] Admittedly the 'effect' posed no threat to the urban system: it was favoured
by property developers since it raised property values, but opposed by the *local*
authority for financial reasons.

seen as leading to governmental action is Lipsky's study of rent strikes
in Harlem in the 1960s.[25] He explicitly rejects a 'simple pressure
model' of change in which city government responds to outside
pressure.[26] In place of this essentially 'passive' model he argues that
there were internal pressures for action on housing maintenance which
pre-existed the strikes, and that the effect of the latter was to change
the relative power positions of officials in different departments, and
alter the priority given to different programmes. Thus, 'the rent
strikes were welcomed by city officials whose bargaining positions
were enhanced by the attention called to slum housing'.[27] Finally,
Lipsky draws attention to the power of officials to present a
particular interpretation of their actions: sometimes they would
attribute innovations to their own continuing efforts, at other times
they would seek to reward (presumably 'helpful') pressure groups by
admitting that they too had a role in bringing about a change.

A similar model of local government is advanced by Muchnik in
his discussion of the role of community councils in urban renewal in
Liverpool. He describes the conflicts between the different
departments of the local authority, and suggests that community
councils were encouraged by the Planning Department in its struggle
with the Housing Department, since they would put forward pressure
(and hence provide legitimacy for) the comprehensive redevelopment
policy sought by the Planning Department.[28]

The importance of pressure other than by social movements is
hinted at in two other studies. Pingeot and Robert, in their study of a
movement against a proposal to expand an airport, write that the
major part of the struggle in the second (and decisive) phase 'no
longer took place in public (in the street and in the press) but in the
corridors of Prefectorates and Ministries',[29] where 'the pressure
brought to bear is a direct reflection of the place of each of the
protagonists in the social structure'.[30] Similarly, Lentin argues that
the decision to issue a building permit 'invites us to suppose the

[25] M. Lipsky, *Protest in City Politics* (Rand McNally, Chicago, 1970) esp.
chapter 4.
[26] *Ibid.*, 116.
[27] *Ibid.*, 91.
[28] D. M. Muchnik, *Urban Renewal in Liverpool: A Study in the Politics of
Redevelopment*, Occasional Papers in Social Administration 33 (Bell, London,
1970) 76—9.
[29] F. Pingeot and M. Robert, Environment, lutte urbaine et interêts de classe,
Espaces et Sociétés 9, 133—42 at p. 137.
[30] *Ibid.*, 141.

supremacy of one ministry over another, reflecting the strength of the pressure group constituted by the property developers over the bearers of urban ideology, represented by the Ministry of Cultural Affairs'.[31]

While one can agree with the Marxist studies that local authorities should not be seen as immune to external pressure, there seems no justification for going to the extreme of saying that urban social movements are the exclusive sources of (small) changes. On the one hand such a view ignores the pressures exerted by other urban actors (e.g. land-owners, financial institutions) and on the other hand it fails to recognize that local authorities have their own policy preferences which result fron the clash between departments (and groups of professionals), local-central conflicts, the goals of the controlling political party, etc. *It is only when particular local authorities are made the subject of study, admittedly a difficult requirement to meet, that it will be possible to attribute the 'urban effects' in particular cases to the actions of urban social movements, authority policy and other urban actors.*[32]

3 Institutional action and urban effects

A reading of the structuralist studies of urban social movements in France makes clear the emphasis on the role of 'popular mobilization' and 'non-institutional' means in achieving urban effects. By contrast, 'institutional' action is de-emphasized. Thus, for example, Lentin writes that the issuing of a building permit despite the approaches of local residents 'shows the limits of institutional action'.[33] But, as mentioned before, Lentin herself refers to the pressure of the property developers, which would appear to be an alternative explanation of the residents' 'failure'. In other words, her characterization of the 'failure' indicates a certain attitude to 'institutional action'.

It is worth noting here that the term 'institutional action' is somewhat ambiguous, since the concept 'institution' is itself open to various interpretations. It will be assumed here that 'institutional action' is action which takes place within existing political institutions

---

[31] Lentin, *op. cit.*, 97.
[32] The distinction between urban social movements, authority policy and other urban actors is unsatisfactory, since, for example, authority policy itself will be partly a response to pressure from previous social movements (e.g. for public housing) and other urban actors.
[33] Lentin, *op. cit.*, 97.

(e.g. voting, petitions to local councillors, deputations, legal demonstrations, or the formation of legal political parties) or within the framework of the law. 'Non-institutional' action thus includes illegal action (violent demonstrations, 'direct action') and the formation of illegal political parties. Mobilization cannot itself be said to be institutional or otherwise; this depends on the forms which it takes.

The question we need to ask is whether 'popular mobilization' is in fact the only successful mode of political action. The study by Olives[34] is particularly helpful in answering this question. Olives discusses sixteen urban social movements in the 'Cité d'Aliarte', in Paris. In nine cases (Nos 1, 3–10) the objectives sought were at least partly attained.[35] The remaining seven cases (Nos 2, 11–16) resulted in failure.

In all but two of the nine cases, the elements of organization, mobilization, social base and 'large' stakes were present. In other words these seven cases corresponded to the idea of political action through mobilization. It will be instructive to examine the two exceptions to this rule. They are cases 7 and 8.

In case 8 an immigrant welfare association used petitions to secure adequate rehousing for immigrants threatened with eviction. This apparent success does not fit in with the idea of change through mobilization. (It corresponds to the *political* effect described as 'social integration (paternalism)' by Castells.)[36] In case 7 the same welfare association again succeeded in obtaining 'adequate rehousing' for immigrants threatened with eviction; a 'local political organization' was also involved. (The corresponding political effect here is described as 'political disintegration (institutional political integration)'.)

Olives's comments on cases 7 and 8 are interesting:

In [these] cases — even if the fact of securing [adequate] rehousing might lead one to believe that his type of action was more successful, we are inclined to believe the contrary to be true, in that either no mobilization of the social force took place (No. 8) or else it was too weak (No. 7) to impose as a precondition of 'adequate' rehousing, that residents should be able to remain in the hostel.[37]

[34] Olives, *op. cit.*
[35] These figures are based on the tables in the article (pp. 18–27 [pp. 188–97 in this book]. On p. 13 [p. 180] Olives refers to the 'seven actions which had an urban effect'. He appears to have excluded cases 7 and 8 from the nine cases so described in the tables.
[36] Olives, *op. cit.*, 16 [185].
[37] *Ibid.*, 15–16 [184].

For this reason, Olives considers that the only 'solidly-based urban effect' is the right of residents to remain in their homes after attempts at eviction 'in so far as it is the very evidence of a victory imposed by force, and hence capable of being capitalized on by political struggles'.[38] In other words he makes a distinction between 'solidly-based' urban effects obtained by force, and those obtained by the immigrant welfare association (viz. adequate rehousing) without mobilization. A distinction is made among the ends because of the differing means used. This is regrettable since it obscures the fact that *urban effects may be obtained by institutional as well as by non-institutional means.*[39]

Thus Olives's study demonstrates that urban effects may result (to an unknown extent) from both institutional and non-institutional modes of action. Admittedly, the types of effect concerned can, at most, be described as 'reform'. A different conclusion might be reached if the stakes were larger.

Bonnier, in a study of neighbourhood associations, also indicates the success of institutional means, as opposed to popular mobilization. He writes that:

> It can be seen that most of the neighbourhood associations' successes were in fact obtained by winning the attention of municipal leaders, less by any real mobilization of local residents than by the secret dealings or personal approaches by neighbourhood leaders to municipal figures.[40]

Bonnier describes these two models as 'new' (mobilization) and 'old' (personal relations). The justification for these descriptions is not entirely clear, but the important point is that they are analytically distinct modes of action for an urban social movement.[41]

[38] *Ibid.*, 16 [184].

[39] Of course, there may be political reasons for making such a distinction, namely, to deny the effectiveness of a type of action (institutional action) which does not correspond to the type regarded as basic, but this seems beside the point. (Certainly the fact that mobilization was not involved in obtaining adequate rehousing in cases 7 and 8 affects the potential of this 'effect' for future political action. But at the level of the urban system there seems no justification for a distinction between types of urban effect according to the means used.)

[40] F. Bonnier, Les pratiques des associations de quartier et les processus de 'récupération', *Espaces et Sociétés* 6–7 (1972) 29–35 at p. 32.

[41] The term 'institutional' is inappropriate to describe the personal relations model of political change since it is not institutionally provided for. Although it would result in confusion to introduce it here, Mitchell's distinction between 'structural' and 'personal' levels of analysis is relevant (J. C. Mitchell, The concept and use of social networks, in J. C. Mitchell (ed.), *Social Networks in Urban Situations* (Manchester University Press, Manchester, 1969) 9–10).

Finally, we will refer briefly to three urban social movements in Britain in which institutional means played an important part.

Dennis[42] describes the efforts by residents in an area designated for clearance in Sunderland to 'participate' in planning the future of the area. A residents' association was constituted, Dennis being the secretary. The association decided to communicate with the Planning Committee (of elected representatives) rather than with the Planning Department.[43] This decision resulted in a one-way communication, since the Planning Department refused to answer letters unless its competence was recognized. This the association refused to do: hence 'participation' terminated. This was not the end of the story, for the association then turned to local councillors and the press[44] and, according to Dennis, the result was the withdrawal of the plans to clear the area, and the provision of grants for house improvement, mortages for house purchase — that is, the 'revitalization' of the area. Unfortunately Dennis falls into the error identified above, of underestimating factors other than the actions of the association in producing this urban effect. For example, the growing central government disenchantment with large-scale redevelopment, mentioned by Ferris, may have been a factor. The point about Dennis's study is that in addition to the mobilization of public opinion in general (and not merely that of local residents) which may or may not be described as institutional, he attributes success to the intervention of local councillors, who clearly represent an institutional means of action.

A second study, by Davies[45] in Newcastle, may also be mentioned. Like Dennis, Davies acted as secretary of a residents' association in an area threatened by redevelopment. He writes that the association's demands, for example for the work to be phased over five years so that existing residents could benefit, and for council 'direct labour' to carry out the clearance/redevelopment operations, were only met when control of the local council changed from Labour to Conservative.[46] Again it is possible that the change in central government thinking on redevelopment played its part. This study reinforces our argument in section (2) that local authority policy must

---

[42] N. Dennis, *Public Participation and Planners' Blight* (Faber and Faber, London, 1972).
[43] *Ibid.*, chapters 13—16.
[44] *Ibid.*, 213.
[45] J. G. Davies, *The Evangelistic Bureaucrat* (Tavistock, London, 1972).
[46] *Ibid.*, 170.

be regarded as a factor capable of producing change, at least in
conjunction with urban social movements.

A third study in which institutional means were effective is that by
Ferris of the Barnsbury Association, already mentioned. The
interesting point for present purposes is that the local authority was
very much aware that the Barnsbury Association represented only a
minority (albeit a highly vocal one) of residents in Barnsbury (let
alone of residents in Islington as a whole). Nevertheless, due to the
favourable 'policy environment' at central government level, the
'personal approaches' (described further below) of the Association's
members and the election of three of them to the local council, the
Association succeeded in getting the traffic scheme plan adopted.
Thus it would appear that institutional means (associated with
mobilization of a small minority) were successful in Barnsbury.

In this section I hope to have demonstrated that 'mobilization of
the social base' is only one way in which urban effects are produced.
In two of Olives's cases, in most of Bonnier's, and in the three British
studies described, institutional approaches were also shown to be
effective. My aim is not to deny that mobilization is an important
source of social change, indeed I would suspect that the larger the
change the more important it would be, but simply to argue that both
types of action are empirically important, and that the neglect of
either is unjustified.

4 Organizational resources and urban effects

In this section we develop the point made briefly in the introduction,
that studies of urban social movements within the structuralist
Marxist tradition view organizations as means of linking
contradictions rather than as being of importance in themselves.

According to Olives,[47] the two primary factors influencing the
success of an urban social movement are the importance of the issue
or stake and the degree to which a 'social base' becomes organized
into a 'social force'. The latter transformation takes place through the
implantation of one or more organizations. The underlying
assumption here is clearly that change is produced through the
mobilization of the social base.[48] In other words, the larger the stake,

[47] Olives, op. cit.
[48] For a discussion of structuralist Marxist analyses of this process in studies of
'urban social movements', see my paper, From 'social base' to 'social force':
some analytical issues in the study of urban protest, prepared for the Eighth
World Congress of Sociology, Toronto, August 1974, to appear in Michael
Harloe (ed.), Captive Cities (Wiley, London and New York, 1976).

and the stronger the social force, the greater the degree of mobilization and hence the more likely an urban effect.

Thus the role of organization in the process of mobilization is important within the structuralist approach. Organizations are the means by which social forces develop and contradictions are expressed, and linked.

I wish to argue that by focussing on *organizational resources* we are able to see a feature of organizations (additional to their structural role) which affects the survival and success (i.e. urban effects) of an urban social movement. And this is true, I suggest, irrespective of whether political action is seen as occurring through mobilization, institutional means, or personal relations. The discussion will draw largely on studies of voluntary associations, in the absence of relevant data on urban social movements.

It has been argued by Ross that 'the dependence of voluntary associations on the resources of other organizations . . . makes co-operation and support a vital matter'.[49] In order to achieve this support, voluntary associations have two pairs of choices, neither of which is exclusive. They may be integrated *horizontally*, that is with other social systems in the community; and/or *vertically*, that is with systems outside the community. For example, a local branch of a national political party is, by definition, vertically integrated, and may also establish links with, say, an anti-apartheid organization in its locality (horizontal integration). Secondly, associations may be integrated with an *organization*, for example, a school or work-place, or with the *community* at large.

The purpose of these distinctions is not merely classificatory. It may be hypothesized that associations which are integrated horizontally (and not vertically), and with the community rather than with any organization within it, will encounter greater problems of survival and be less likely to produce urban effects. The underlying assumption here is that integration with an organization is likely to provide access to premises, secretarial facilities, personnel, funds and even members, whereas dependence on the community at large means that these resources have to be bargained for, and this may be difficult if the association is perceived as 'unhelpful' and 'unacceptable'. Similarly, vertical integration into a national hierarchy, in so far as the

---

[49] J. C. Ross, Toward a reconstruction of voluntary association theory, *British Journal of Sociology* 23 (1972) 20–32 at p. 22.

latter does not take the form of a federation of semi-autonomous affiliated units, but of a unified organization with local branches subject to central decisions (as in some trade unions) is likely to imply a more constant flow of resources of various kinds to sustain local activity. (This depends too on the financial structure of the organization. A common feature is that local branches have to raise funds, in addition to forwarding part of membership subscriptions, for the regional and national levels of the organization. On balance local branches may contribute more than they receive in terms of services in which case vertical integration would not be more conducive to survival.)

A priori it seems reasonable to assume that the degree of community and horizontal integration of urban social movements would be important both to their survival and to their success. Unfortunately the data which would allow us to apply this type of analysis to urban social movements[50] does not exist, although all manner of organizations are referred to in the empirical studies, ranging from the 'association' of friends of a businessman-intellectual[51] to tenants' associations, trade unions, immigrant welfare associations and local political organizations.[52] The participant account of squatting[53] shows the difficulties encountered by a militant outside political group in obtaining support for squatters. Similarly, in his discussion of squatting, Cherki refers to the 'squatters' committee' (of squatters themselves) and the 'support committee'[54] (of militants and local residents). Obviously these organizations play crucial roles in the establishment, sustenance and success of urban social movements, although we cannot yet say precisely how.

In addition to the resources a voluntary association derives from external sources, there are its considerable internal resources. The following remarks are based on my current study of a local branch of

[50] The study by Curtis and Zurcher of anti-pornography movements is suggestive of the type of data required (R. L. Curtis and L. A. Zurcher, Stable resources of protest movements. The multi-organizational field, Social Forces 52 (1973) 53—61).

[51] Lentin, op. cit., 96.

[52] Olives, op. cit., 18—27 [188—97].

[53] Anonymous, Logement et lutte de classes: compte-rendu d'une pratique militante de quartier, Espaces et Sociétés 6—7 (1972) 59—88.

[54] E. Cherki, Le mouvement d'occupation des maisons vides en France, Espaces et Sociétés 9 (1973) 63—91 at p. 72.

the United Nations Association, whose aim is to promote the work of, and support for, the United Nations. Although this is not of course an *urban* social movement, the way in which it secures resources probably holds true for such movements.

Every member of the U.N.A. can be seen as embedded in a social network. The term social network refers to the unbounded web of relationships of all kinds which is unanchored on any single individual. In order to use the term social network in an *analytical* rather than a *metaphorical* sense, we need to consider the networks of particular individuals, that is 'personal networks'.[55] The members of a given persons' network will be known in a variety of institutional contexts: work, church, political party, etc. Some will be known in only one context in which case the relation is 'uniplex', or single-stranded, while others will be known in several, in which case the relation is 'multiplex'.

Every relationship in a U.N.A. member's personal network, whether uniplex or multiplex is a potential resource for use within U.N.A. In particular I have been able to show that committee members use relationships initiated in a wide variety of contexts (work, church, association, etc.) to secure persons as speakers and chairmen for the branch's meetings. Their ability to do this is a function of the size of their personal networks, which in turn partly depends on the length of the time they have been resident in the area. Since meetings are the branch's main activity, it can be said that the 'social capital' represented by these personal networks is crucial to the association's ability to survive and succeed in its present form. (Conversely, an organization whose members lacked extensive personal networks could be expected to encounter difficulties in obtaining resources.)

Similarly, *the fact that committee members each hold positions in several institutional structures* (i.e. have 'multiple positions' due to the overlapping membership of these structures) *gives rise to further potential resources*. The branch has succeeded in obtaining duplicating facilities, noticeboard space, premises, and has circulated information in many contexts through the multiple positions of committee members. Indeed, the branch's connexions with one local church (initially limited, but now extensive due to the recruitment of church members into the U.N.A.) are so great, and the flow of resources so large, that one could almost say that the branch was (informally) integrated with the church, to use Ross's phrase.

[55] Mitchell, *op. cit.*, 13.

The way in which committee members use network contacts and multiple positions which pre-exist their membership of U.N.A. in order to pursue the ends of the association can be seen as a sort of 'social *bricolage*', to adapt Lévi-Strauss's use of the term. In other words, the network contacts and multiple positions of members can be seen as a stock of social tools, *available to the association*, which 'represent a set of actual and possible relations'.[56]

The underlying social process may be *social exchange*, that is, 'actions that are contingent on rewarding reactions from others and that cease when these expected reactions are not forthcoming.[57] In other words, for example, the persons a member knows at work are willing to provide services to him in a different context (the association) in expectation of future services which may be returned either in the work-place or in some new context to which only they belong. In this way existing relationships can be '*extended*'.

Alternatively, the social process may *not* involve social exchange but simply access to knowledge and even services which are 'free' and do not have to be repaid. The existence of 'free' services seems to be often neglected.' In my current study, the local libraries and local press provide free services to the association, viz. publicity for the branch meetings. The existence of such 'free resources' in an area obviously eases the problem of survival and facilitates success for those associations which know of their existence, and are allowed access to them. (Access was found to be restricted to 'acceptable' associations whose encouragement is consistent with library or newspaper policy.)

It might be objected that reliance on personal networks and mutiple positions is a response dictated by the branch's lack of money. On the one hand, one could answer that since this is the condition of many voluntary associations, such reliance will be extensive elsewhere. But, in my view, reliance on this type of resource is *not* due to limited funds, but is likely to be a feature of all organizations, since the occupation of positions in several structures and the possession of personal networks is quite general (though variable in degree). For this reason I would not agree with Bonnier that the use of personal relations in political action is in any way an 'old' pattern.

In order to illustrate the importance of the resources available to voluntary associations and urban social movements through the multiple positions and personal networks of their members, we will

[56] C. Lévi-Strauss, *The Savage Mind* (1962) (Weidenfeld and Nicolson, London, 1966) 56.
[57] P. M. Blau, *Exchange and Power in Social Life* (Wiley, New York, 1964) 6.

refer briefly again to Ferris's study of Barnsbury. First, the Barnsbury Association included professional planners and architects who used their professional skills and knowledge in drawing up the traffic scheme. (For example, 'they formulated their objectives in such a way as to make them acceptable to the Ministry of Housing and Local Government'[58] and took advantage of their knowledge of the favourable climate for traffic schemes). The (Labour) local councillors suspected that they were using 'information gained in their professional capacities within local authorities and had also exploited professional contacts in the Ministry of Housing and elsewhere'.[59] Secondly, Barnsbury Association members were elected to the local council in 1968 as 'independents'. They used their positions as councillors, assisted by the favourable attitude of the new Conservative majority, to advance the ends of the Association. One final example of organizational resources described by Ferris refers to the rival Barnsbury Action Group whose Secretary was 'a publishing executive who was able to contribute from his business office facilities such as typing and filing. He was also able to use his knowledge of the media to get press statements published.'[60] Thus we see how knowledge and services derived from multiple positions and personal networks are important resources for urban social movements.

So far we have been discussing what Ross calls the *association problem*, namely, the problems encountered and resources used by organizations in their efforts to reach goals. To conclude, we shall refer briefly to what he calls the *voluntarism problem*, that is how members are recruited and kept. (The term 'voluntarism' would perhaps be better replaced by the term 'volunteer', since it is the unpaid nature of participation in voluntary associations and not any idea that participation is uncaused that is important.)[61]

One of the most fruitful ways of tackling the 'voluntarism problem' would appear to be via the social exchange approach, in so far as potential members of a social movement balance the rewards of participation against the costs incurred. So far, to my knowledge, only one writer has attempted to apply the social exchange model in this

[58] Ferris, *op. cit.*, 35.
[59] *Ibid.*, 64.
[60] *Ibid.*, 56.
[61] See B. J. Palisi, A critical analysis of the voluntary association concept, *Sociology and Social Research* 52 (1968) 392–405; Pickvance, *op. cit.* and Ross, *op. cit.*, 27–8.

field. This is a study by Weissman[62] of a community council in an American city which seems to have been relatively successful in obtaining better 'urban' facilities for the area, at least in its earlier phase.

Weissman distinguishes four types of rewards available to individuals who participate in the council:[63]

emotional rewards: friendship, praise, self-esteem;
service rewards: engendered by services the council produces, e.g., a new school;
ideological rewards: those that satisfy ideological commitments such as 'being a good American';
negotiable rewards: those which have a negotiable value in structures other than the council, for example, getting oneself in the public eye.

(A similar analysis is applied to the council's success in recruiting different ethnic groups in the community. This fills out the notion of integration with the community, discussed earlier. The council was in fact integrated horizontally and vertically, with organizations and the community at large.)

The category 'negotiable rewards' relates to our earlier emphasis on multiple positions. Whereas previously we showed that personal networks and multiple positions could be used to '*import*' resources into an association, by the 'extension' of social relationships, the idea of 'negotiable rewards' indicates how participation in an association can result in resources which can be '*exported*' to the person's positions and relations in other structures. 'Negotiable rewards' may be difficult to assess since people are reluctant to admit to them.[64] In the U.N.A. branch they certainly exist: for example, for the political candidate or insurance broker who makes known these identities in the course of a talk.

Weissman argues that the absence of working-class participants in the community council he studied was due to the need for social skills, free time, money and willingness to engage in slow formal procedures which imposed higher costs on them.[65] Conversely, the

[62] H. H. Weissman, *Community Councils and Community Control: The Workings of Democratic Mythology* (University of Pittsburgh Press, Pittsburgh, 1970).
[63] *Ibid.*, 20–1.
[64] *Ibid.*, 98.
[65] *Ibid.*, chapter 8.

council's sports committee, where verbal skills and formal procedures were not necessary, was largely working-class in composition. The absence of Italians from the council is explained in terms of its connexion with a Protestant settlement and clergy; only through the sports committee did the Italians participate, and this was because of the (negotiable) rewards the baseball league furnished them in their positions as churchgoers at the various Catholic churches whose teams made up the league.

This study indicates the potential of a social exchange approach to the 'voluntarism problem'. However, it depends on the research-worker being able to establish empirically which type of reward, and what costs, are associated with participation. If the exchange model is to be preserved from tautology, it is not sufficient simply to *infer* the existence of costs and rewards to explain participation.

In this section we have argued that organization plays a greater role in social movements than simply permitting the linking of contradictions. It is suggested that the survival and success of such movements depends on the resources they are able to obtain, free or through social exchange, from organizations in the community, from higher levels of hierarchies, and from the personal networks and multiple position of their members. This is true irrespective of whether the underlying theory of political action stresses mobilization of the base, institutional means, or personal relations, though in the latter case it is more patent.

Index

Name Index

Subject Index